THE
ECONOMIC THEORY
OF
GROWTH AND DEVELOPMENT

THE
ECONOMIC THEORY
OF
GROWTH AND DEVELOPMENT

David Z. Rich

Westport, Connecticut
London

Library of Congress Cataloging-in-Publication Data

Rich, David Z.
    The economic theory of growth and development / by David Z. Rich.
      p. cm.
    Includes bibliographical references and index.
    ISBN 0-275-94687-8 (alk. paper)
    1. Economic development. I. Title.
  HD75.R53   1994
  338.9 – dc20   93-23474

British Library Cataloguing in Publication Data is available.

Library of Congress Catalog Card Number: 93-23474
ISBN: 0-275-94687-8

First published in 1994

Praeger Publishers, 88 Post Road West, Westport, CT 06881
An imprint of Greenwood Publishing Group, Inc.

Printed in the United States of America

The paper used in this book complies with the
Permanent Paper Standard issued by the National
Information Standards Organization (Z39.48-1984).

10 9 8 7 6 5 4 3 2 1

This work is dedicated to the memory of my beloved parents, my mother Vanessa, and my father Joseph, to my sisters, family and friends, to Desi Beckford for her wonderfulness, and especially to Diana Lerner, for chaos out of order and for order out of chaos.

CONTENTS

ACKNOWLEDGEMENTS

I would like to express my thanks and appreciation to my editor, Dr. James R. Ice, and especially to my project editor, Ms. Sasha Kintzler and my copy editor, Charles Eberline, for making this work presentable. Their editorial expertise has been of great value to me.

Also, my sincerest thanks and appreciation goes to Reuven Sheffer and his staff at Ein Nun Ein in Tel Aviv, Israel, for their expertise and dedication in the camera-ready preparation of this work. My special thanks to Eran Sheffer and to Ruthie Chazanovich for their dedication and hard work on my behalf.

These ideas have been developed since the publication of my first two books, *Contemporary Economics*: *A Unifying Approach* (Praeger, 1986), and *The Dynamics of Knowledge: A Contemporary View* (Greenwood Press, 1988). While I owe a debt to the thinkers from whom I learned, the ideas expressed in this work are my own and I bear the responsibility for their clarity and effectiveness.

Part I

THE PROBLEM SITUATION

Chapter 1

THE CONTEMPORARY SITUATION OF ECONOMIC DEVELOPMENT

> If we ask why a people has made a certain choice, the answer lies usually in history; but if we ask why it has had that particular history, we are back among the mysteries of the universe. Fortunately, not all the answers depend on history. It is possible for a nation to take a new turn if it is fortunate enough to have the right leadership at the right time. In the last analysis history is only the record of how individuals respond to the challenge of their times. All nations have opportunities which they may grasp if only they can summon the courage and the will.
>
> W. Arthur Lewis,
> *Theory of Economic Growth* [1]

The events of our recent history — the overthrowing of dictatorships in Eastern Europe, the dissolution of the Soviet empire, the reunification of Germany, the finalization of the European Common Market, and the beginning of the first real peace talks involving the combatants in the troubled Middle East — are certainly of the greatest historical significance. They pose problems and opportunities unique to our historical era.

In previous historical eras situations of such importance usually required that great leaders come to the fore to provide viable solutions for their peoples. The Congress of Vienna of 1815, which brought about relative peace in Europe for a hundred years, resulted in the Industrial Revolution taking hold on the Continent and provided sufficient stability for industry to develop and for each country to establish its own working patterns in industry according to its national characteristics. Competition in trade regulated quality in production, and internal competition provided the basis for new products to be developed to capture both the domestic and foreign markets. This stability ended with the military posturing that resulted in World War I.

After World War I the League of Nations, formed to arbitrate disputes among nations, proved unable to hold world conflict in check, partly because its charter was not ratified by the United States due to that country's isolationist position brought about by its geographical remoteness from the centers of conflict, but mainly because the bellicose countries still held old scores that they wanted to settle. Disregard for the League of Nations led Germany and Japan to rearm with impunity. This rearmament also provided economic growth in their depressed economies. These dynamics set in motion World War II, and from the ashes of that war's destruction rose the United Nations and its economic organizations, established to prevent further world conflict and to police local conflicts.

There are two noteworthy historical exceptions in which the great leaders did not establish on their own viable solutions for their peoples. These are the American Revolution against the British and the French Revolution against the monarchy, both of which were primarily grass-roots movements guided by the chosen leadership.

The disfranchisement and oppression felt by the peoples of these lands resulted in great political leadership rising to the occasions. These revolutions set the patterns for the situation in our historical era, in which the revolutions in the Soviet empire and in East Germany and Eastern Europe were the responses of leaders who emerged to realize the desires and political aspirations of the people from where they came. Thus, while the historical revolutions of our era differ from the American and French revolutions, they were undertaken in their predecessors' spirit that a people oppressed will not merely speak, but will do so in a voice and with actions that must be heeded.

It is important to note that during the events of our era several myths have been exposed. One such myth is that in the Communist state there is no poverty because all able-bodied workers are employed and those people unable to work are supported adequately by the state. This was exposed by the long food lines and the deficiencies in supplies. The central marketing board replaced the capitalist market allocation, so that planning, logistics, and quality control were determined by planners' concepts and visions according to their understanding of their countries' needs and requirements. Monies that would have been used to provide efficient production infrastructure and the moving of goods and produce were directed to projects such as defense and regulated education. The poverty that was exposed is due not to the lack of employment, but to restrictions on labor mobility and the low real value of money earned because of the lack of goods and services and inefficient uses of time by people who waited in line for foodstuffs, only to find the shelves empty or severely limited in supplies.[2]

The myth of capitalism, that because it is contrary to communism, only pockets of poverty exist in the industrialized Western-oriented countries, has been exposed by the increasing reliance on the welfare systems for unemployment subsidies, education, and medical services and the levying of higher taxes to finance these benefits.³ Greater reliance on such welfare programs is an important indicator that more than pockets of poverty exist in these countries. As social costs are increased through the demand for these services, taxation reduces production because manufacturers have to increase their prices to offset the cost of the taxes. Increased social costs result in reduced consumption and a consequent reduction in employment, thereby increasing the reliance on the welfare system. This is the paradox of contemporary industrialization and will be discussed further in part II of this volume, pages 92 and following, and part III, Chapter 9. It must be stated here, however, that this paradox results from both domestic and international competition and is not affected by changes in product nuances or styles. Competition among producers and retailers results in product cycles with a recessive phase of increased costs and consequent decreased revenues. It is during this phase that employment is affected, as cost-decreasing techniques are often introduced to increase profits, but again discussion of the effect that this has on the economies and a solution to this paradox must wait until part II.

The third myth, that underdevelopment pertains to those newly formed Third World countries that are seeking political stability and a sound economic basis for production and growth, most certainly has been exposed. Granted that underdevelopment is a condition of these Third World countries, and that their problems often result from political and military conflicts in the seizure of power — the Sudan and Ethiopia are only two countries that are in this predicament — underdevelopment is now being shared by the Third World countries with those countries that were once considered industrialized and are now being confronted by the necessity of reorganizing their economies in order to enter into competition with the developed countries. Moreover, the countries of the former Soviet Union are proclaiming their political and economic independence; this can only be done if they base their economies on those of the developed marketing countries. While their economic infrastructures are far more sound than those of the Sudan and Ethiopia, they are still far removed from the industrial capabilities of the European Common Market countries, Japan, and the United States. These countries are Third World only in the sense that they are part of a developing world in which each economy is struggling for greater production in light of competition; they simply have not incorporated sufficient economic infrastructure due to the diversion of resources to the political and military struggles for the establishment of power. But with the dissolution of the Soviet Union, the forming of the European Economic Community, and the advance of the Asian countries into positions of economic strength, the external circumstances of these countries compel them to resolve their problems swiftly and efficiently so that they can rise from the ashes of their destruction, remember their pasts as great historical struggles, and seek to realize the potential of their futures.

While the contemporary situation of economic development is pressing, the problems of economic development are certainly not unique to our era. The Industrial Revolution generated difficulties due to the migration of labor from the rural settlements to the cities, bringing about overcrowding, slums, disease, and a burden on the city officials in raising funds to cope with these difficulties while making the cities centers of intellectual and cultural activities. Moreover, as industries became more sophisticated, they relocated from city centers to unpopulated areas, bringing with them their labor forces and thereby establishing city infrastructures. The silicon chip industry that manufactures the integral parts of sophisticated computers is one example; the aircraft industry is another.

Indeed, the problems of economic development are probably as ancient as the organization of mankind into societies. Even in these societies the division of labor into farmers, hunters, and manufacturers of finished products was necessary to sustain the social organization. The military branch of these societies was formed for defense and for keeping the internal peace, and the legislative branch established the laws and norms of behavior in order to maintain the society in a functioning manner.[4] With increasing population expansion societies became more complex, and as a consequence the legislative, the military, and the overall governing branches to which both the military and legislative branches were expected to be subservient had to adopt policies and procedures to deal with these complexities in each society according to the temperaments of its people.

However, without commerce societies cannot survive, and if their military, legislative, and overall governing bodies lack the means for their support, they will be destroyed by the internal social pressures. St. Thomas Aquinas, in his book *On the Governance of Rulers* (written around 1260), related that when Alexander the Great of Macedonia was listening to Xenocrates, a brilliant architect, explain how a beautifully laid-out city could be built on a certain mountain, Alexander is said to have asked whether there were fields that could supply such a city with sufficient grain. Finding out that there were not, Alexander is said to have responded that a man who would build a city on such a site would be blameworthy; for just as a newborn infant cannot be fed or made to grow as it should except on its nurse's milk, so a city cannot have a large population, no matter how beautiful it is, without a large supply of foodstuffs. A ruler who built Xenocrates' beautiful city and provided foodstuffs sufficient to feed the population would have certainly built himself a monument for all of history to admire.

The notion of blameworthiness, important as it was in Alexander's time, is a part of the greater ethical concept of responsibility. The notion of responsibility and the other ethical issues related to economics during the Industrial Revolution were relegated to a minor position in the discussion of economic theory and the problems of development. The political economists, from J.B. Say to J.S. Mill and Alfred Marshall, treated economics as a science, using logic and mathematics to reason through their arguments. Even T.R. Malthus, who was a Cambridge economist as well as a preacher, let his economic training overcome his human feelings when he wrote about poverty, starvation, and the difficulties of population growth with respect to food.[5] The exceptions to this were the works of Karl Marx, who in his *Capital* used the tools of economic reasoning as they had then been developed and merged them with a materialistic quasi-Hegelian dialectic to argue that the capitalist system would eventually evolve into a humane communist system in which poverty and starvation would be eliminated and the rational allocation of goods and services would be carried out. Another exception was the development of welfare economics, especially during the Great Depression when the capitalist system gave evidence of undergoing serious problems. The works of A.C. Pigou, a neoclassical economist who argued that the business cycle would eventually move upward, and J.M. Keynes's work *The General Theory of Employment Interest and Money* shed new light on the capitalist system and provided it with a greater humanity.[6] Ethical considerations of responsibility and the abolition of unemployment and poverty have since been incorporated to some extent into economic reasoning, even though economists as scientists must remain as scientifically objective as possible in the treatment of the various aspects of their discipline.

At the end of World War II, with the establishment of the United Nations, the International Monetary Fund, and the General Agreement on Tariffs and Trade, the problems of economic development came to the fore as matters of serious study for economists. Not only were there difficulties involved in the reconstruction of Europe, laid waste by war, and of Japan, ravaged and demoralized by the nuclear devastation of Hiroshima and Nagasaki, but as the economic situations of Latin and South America became known, and especially as countries sought to shed their colonial status and gain independence, economic development economists turned their attention to these regions. The European countries and to some extent Japan had undergone the dynamics of the Industrial Revolution and therefore had a work ethic appropriate to their cultures and histories. The political considerations of the Cold War had to be dealt with during reconstruction, and the victorious Soviet Union — itself undergoing reconstruction, but under the dictatorship of Josef Stalin — and the United States provided the means for development within the terms of their own political systems and geopolitical dynamics as they were evolving.

The concern of economists over developing and underdeveloped countries was justified also on the grounds that while Europe, Japan, and the

Soviet Union were undergoing reconstruction, the emerging and developing countries provided challenges because of their positions relative to the countries that were developed and physically unscathed by the war. The establishment of viable economic infrastructure and the formation of those factions competing for political control were of interest as these countries were observed in their processes for forming viable countries capable of competing in the world markets.

Moreover, there was a basis for this interest in the literature of economic theory, for these were the topics that concerned Adam Smith, J.B. Say, David Ricardo, and the other classical economists up to, and to some extent beyond, Karl Marx.[7] One postwar economic thinker, W.W. Rostow, wrote of undergraduate studies in the mid-1930s, when he decided to work professionally on applying modern economic theory to the problems of modern economic history and the broader problem of relating economics to social and political forces in the workings of whole societies.[8] That was the period of the Great Depression, and the problem of relating economics to the political and social forces of societies was considered by many macroeconomic thinkers. This was also a Marxist problem, as *Capital* was the watershed between classical economics, in which political and social forces were rendered subservient to the new science of economics, and the theories of social economics — especially Darwinian economic and social theory that followed Marx.

During the Great Depression attention was focused mainly on the industrialized economies, those that had undergone the Industrial Revolution. The argument then was that economic and social forces are inseparable, even though much of the neoclassical economic theory was focused on the firm and its dynamics. In his *General Theory* Keynes, in the spirit of Pigou and J.A. Schumpeter, reoriented the focus onto the macro economy and its relation to the state as the representation of society. For example, concerning expenditures, Keynes wrote:

> Thus it is natural — at any rate on the average of the community — that current consumption should be expanded when employment increases, but by less than full increment of real income. Moreover, what is true of the average of individuals is likely to be also true of governments, especially in an age when a progressive increase of unemployment will usually force the State to provide relief out of borrowed funds.[9]

After World War II the question was then considered of relating the theory of economics of the firm, and of the macro economy and international trade to the problems of the developing and emerging countries. In light of this, Sir John Maud stated in the Stamp Memorial Lecture of 1963 that the rich industrialized countries produce and consume more than two-thirds of the world's goods and earn four-fifths of the whole world's income. That the industrialized countries' output increases more rapidly than their population is a strong indicator of the tremendous gap between the rich and poor countries and results in an average rise in their populations' average incomes.

> The gap between the rich and poor thus widens, the rich becoming richer at a much faster rate than that at which the poor become less poor. And it can plausibly be said that this gap would still continue to grow even if the under-developed countries succeeded in increasing the average income of their peoples ten times faster than the developed countries did.[10]

These underdeveloped countries were little touched by the dynamics of industrialization that the developed countries had undergone. Aid to the underdeveloped countries, targeted for the construction of infrastructure, for improving medical facilities and treatment, and for raising the levels of education with the goal of making these countries competitive, was of some help. Those leaders of underdeveloped countries who possessed wisdom and concern for their peoples applied foreign aid in ways that brought their countries into various stages of development. Other leaders preferred self-aggrandizement and used portions of the funds for their own purposes, relying in part on the initiative of their peoples to make their own way, and in part on directing the funds that remained into the targeted projects.

Aid was also used as a strategy in the Cold War as the Soviet Union and its allies sought to gain supporters in its ideological and sometimes military adventures. Conflicts between countries that diplomacy failed to resolve to the satisfaction of the antagonists often led to military action; these countries then turned to the great powers, which, in turn, had to choose sides and support their beneficiaries with military as well as diplomatic and financial aid.

The problems of development often resulted in rebellion on the grass-roots level of peoples against regimes supported by one or the other superpower. The rebellion against the Vietnam regime, for example, brought the French into military conflict with the northern region. The French armies suffered in battle and withdrew, leaving a political vacuum that was filled by the United States. The Vietnam War was fought by the United States and its allies against the popular uprising and the North Vietnamese armies, supported by China and the Soviet Union. The withdrawal of the U.S. and allied forces left still another vacuum that China tried unsuccessfully to fill, but the region sought aid in reconstruction and rearming from the Soviet Union. The rebellion against the Soviet-sponsored leadership in Afghanistan was exploited by the Western superpowers and brought about the withdrawal of Soviet forces from that country.

Both the Western and the Soviet superpowers learned great lessons from the Vietnam and Afghanistan adventures. One such lesson was that an unpopular war could be won only at terrible costs to life and property and that if such a commitment to this destruction is not made and implemented, then the war against popular uprisings has little chance of succeeding, and the resources involved can be better employed elsewhere. On the fields of battle it was learned that a World War II type of military operation can no longer be fought because the weapons of war have become so fierce that the consequences of deploying and using them are unacceptable, no matter who comes out ahead. Also learned was that military action taken by a superpower had to have well-defined objectives; the action had to be swift and decisive, with withdrawal undertaken as soon as possible after these objectives had been achieved.[11] Finally, military action could be undertaken against a U.N. member country if the majority of the other members considered that country's actions illegal and reprehensible, and that country was unmoved by the U.N. members' requests to alter its ways, as in the case of Iraq's invasion of Kuwait and the U.S.-led action to force Iraq to cease its invasion and withdraw to its own borders.

From the end of World War II to our present situation, then, the subject of economic development has been related to the emerging and developing countries of the non-Western areas. The question as to why these countries were not influenced by the Industrial Revolution must be approached from the point of view that in many instances they were not countries but colonial territories to be exploited, with internal investment made to ease this exploitation. For this reason these regions, when they gained independence as countries, had to rely on what was best understood by their leaders and citizens, their cultures as they had evolved under the yoke of colonialism. Also, these ancient cultures did not allow any great economic initiative on the part of the individual. Hence in many of the emerging and developing countries today the political systems are political or religious dictatorships or a combination of both, unreceptive to rational argument and thought and ignoring empirical demonstration. The combination of religious and political influences in these countries restricts individual enterprise, allowing, in the old spirit of colonialism, initiative only to the extent that the monies generated will maintain the system and its religious and political leadership.

The significance of an enduring question lies in the different ways in which its answers have been given and interpreted in different historical eras. Adam Smith's question of the origins and causes of the wealth of nations is such an enduring question, and its given answers differ for the Industrial Revolution for which Smith provided the theoretical basis and for our historical era of knowledge with its emerging and developing economies. In spite of the great changes that the Westernized countries have undergone, religion in the emerging and developing countries holds people under the command of powers outside their control and comprehension, rendering many of their activities and thoughts subject to forces that they cannot understand. Their thoughts and consciences are oriented to spheres unfamiliar through experience. The entrepreneurial activity necessary for real economic growth and development stands in direct conflict to this orientation, for such activity requires the rational exertion of control over resources and their applications in market development. The entrepreneur qua entrepreneur is answerable only to his or her clients and himself or herself, as these are forces that he or she understands and with which he or she works.

Dictatorship hinders deviations from the accepted behavioral models that have evolved over time-deviations that are necessary for entrepreneurial activity. These behavioral models are always deeply rooted in the national conceptualizations of the people, as can be evidenced by the reactions in the former Soviet Union to the newly acquired freedoms and the complaints that the new liberalization offers no real benefits and that a dictatorship may certainly handle the socioeconomic problems decisively. Dictatorships are modern expressions of authoritarianism and rely on the imposition of dictatorial ideas and methods by enforcement, tolerating deviation to the extent of the dictator's attitudes and the degree of deviation in question. However, while authoritarianism is an evolved form of rule, usually accepted by the people as part of the national heritage, dictatorships are imposed by force, with social evolution having little or no role in their establishment. Dictatorships have no real root in past national history nor in ideas of the collective social psyche justifying their power. They are an alien type of rule, liable to be overthrown by the very forces that placed them in power when the conditions are right. Dictatorships rely on the personality cult necessary for establishing an authoritarian figure who might have come to political prominence through social evolution and might have been a different sort of ruler. The personality cult of dictatorships, however, is as unstable as human passion, and heroes of the state and the people, as dictators tend to portray themselves, can become public enemies once they are deposed.

This does not mean that the nations at the time of the Industrial Revolution were free from authoritarianism and dogmatism. The Catholic and Protestant churches had great influence over their followers, but that historical situation differs greatly from the historical era and the social time of the emerging and developing countries today. The Protestant Reformation and the reaction within the Catholic church to its own behavior during the Inquisition, as well as the scientific progress made during and after the Renaissance, led to the evolution of a work ethos that separated work from religion by leading the churches to deal with the needs of the spirit and the subsequent industrialization with the material satisfactions. Although there was most certainy controversy, after the Inquisition there were never serious social conflicts between material and spiritual needs. The consequence was that industrialization and religion accommodated each other very well.

Authoritarianism and religion posed no serious problems for industrialization for two reasons. One reason was the impact on society made by industrialization due to the radical changes that were occurring in manufacturing (from manus, "hand," and facere, "to make"). Industrialization began when science merged with the processes of production, resulting in productive technology. This merger brought about the replacement of tedious processes of hand work by the implementation of more efficient machinery. The freedom of production gained from this merger was enhanced by individual initiative for accumulating the means of output in industry and by the development of new markets through innovation in products and their applications. This emphasis on individualism was soon recognized as industrialization continued and authoritarianism as a dominant sociopolitical force shifted from that of the ruler to the authority of the parents in the family. The religious leaders in society consented to share their dominant positions with material forces, making possible a social justification for further inquiry into the sciences and endeavors in the fields of the arts and commerce.

The second reason why authoritarianism and industrialization had no serious problems with mutual accommodation is that industrialization was not the result of forces held in check that had gathered momentum and burst on society in the form of a social revolution or rebellion, but gradually occurred as the sciences were applied to production.[12] The fertile ground for industrialization was prepared by the changing attitudes toward the arts and sciences, so that when industrialization began and Adam Smith's writing appeared, a new era of political and social development had begun that would not clash with religion and that was greeted with great interest as industries were formed that were operated with new production processes and that opened new markets.

Hence part of the difficulty the emerging and developing countries face in their striving for economic development lies in their not being fully incorporated into our contemporary historical era. This era will be discussed in detail in chapter 2, but it suffices to say here that these countries lack political stability because of this lack of incorporation that is necessary for establishing the inner dynamism required to unleash the forces of individualism on which industrialization effectively relies. These countries' histories of tribalism and/or religious sects sharing common territory and often at war were altered somewhat during the period of colonialization, when the Christian-oriented countries sought to expand their trade and domination over their neighbors as they searched for raw materials in distant lands to improve their wealth and trading power.

The religious beliefs of these countries were certainly strange to the colonizers, and the differences in beliefs and customs among these tribal peoples provided an advantage to those who conquered and controlled them. Missionaries were brought in to unite these peoples in a common belief, and this led to exploitation through religion when the force of arms was met with resistance. This provided an effective method of colonial domination and also allowed for intrigue among the colonizing powers as they sought to dominate peoples colonized by other powers.

In a very real sense this situation changed with the development of our era. During World War II many battles were fought in several of these colonialized countries, and their peoples who served in the armed forces for the most part distinguished themselves in battle, gaining for themselves a new respect. It was put forth to them that when they were able to adopt the forms of government of their colonizers, they would be granted independence. Political independence does not mean economic independence, and while these countries had achieved a high degree of political sophistication, their economies lacked the necessary integration and infrastructure to be viable. Their internal markets were not well established, their natural resources, transferred to their control, were not well exploited, and their main commercial forces were still controlled by their previous colonial rulers. As long as real economic independence was not achieved, political independence remained a sophisticated form of colonialization and, to some degree, oppression.

This situation was complicated further when the great powers waged their political and economic wars in these very countries. This became another form of colonialization, under which these countries puppet governments, controlled by their sponsors, ruled their peoples. The imposition of this control and its acceptance were justified on the grounds of political and economic strategy as the superpowers sought to outmaneuver each other in these sensitive areas of the world. This situation has often led to political corruption, instability, bloody and bloodless coups, and internal oppression using the techniques of spying on neighbors and the implements of torture — all without any guarantee of economic improvement.

Such has been the fate of many of the emerging and developing countries. In those few countries where democracy has taken root, the political soil in which it has been planted is still very unstable. Ruling parties have suffered coups, and their leaders have been deported, jailed, or even executed. Corruption is often rampant, with the nonpolitical populace suffering. Instability is certainly found in the developed countries, but it is a form of instability allowed and nurtured by their respective systems. This instability is a dynamic form that from its early beginnings allowed for industrialization and the social development necessary to enhance greater production and market expansion. The instability of the emerging and developing countries, in contrast, often leads to bloodshed, revolution, and coups.

The cultures of these emerging and developing countries, ancient and important, have not been able to prepare them for our contemporary era, so that for the most part their political and economic systems do not enable them to produce the goods and services taken for granted in the developed Westernized countries. Hence they are unable to compete internationally, except in those cases and with those products manufactured by multinational corporations resident on their respective soils. The presence of these multinationals is an indication that amid all the turmoil is the recognition by both the developed powers and the former colonialized countries that a common will and understanding are necessary to rid the emerging and developing countries of the ignorance and poverty that are the main causes of instability. Responsible leaders (as opposed to the barbarian dictators who care only to maintain their personality cults) have therefore sought the guidance of the politicians and industrial leaders of the developed countries on how to bring their economies into our era. To the extent that the advice is received and transformed to suit the conditions of their respective countries, it can justly be said that many of these countries are emerging from economic systems totally irrelevant to our historical era and are developing toward managerially based economic systems, although the road to development is long and uncertain indeed. Herman Kahn has written that "There are many roads up each mountain and many mountains up to heaven. Modernization seems increasingly likely to take different paths in different countries."[13]

But the paths up the mountain of growth are determined by the internal conditions of the countries and the wisdom of the political and economic leaders.

NOTES

1. W. Arthur Lewis, *Theory of Economic Growth* (London: George Allen and Unwin, 1955), p. 418.

2. In the Soviet Union, for example, less-than-efficient techniques for harvesting crops and transporting them to marketing centers resulted in long queues at the stores, and people who waited long hours often found the shelves bare when their turn arrived for being served. Since the dissolution of the Soviet Union, the situation in its former countries has worsened. Revolution in Georgia and the attempted take-over by the rebels in Russia in October, 1993, for example, have increased the need for financial assistance by the major capitalist countries. It is anticipated that the changeover to capitalism, for all its growing pains, will bring Russia and its previous republics into the great world centers of economic growth.

3. The subject of welfare economics and possible solutions to the problems of welfare have been discussed in David Z. Rich, *The Economics of Welfare: A Contemporary Analysis* (New York: Praeger, 1989).

4. This situation is as ancient as the Bible and is the source of Jethro's criticism of Moses about the latter's failure to delegate power to subordinates to handle the social problems of the wandering tribes of Israel. See Exodus 18: 13-27.

5. For example, see T.R. Malthus, *On Population*, (New York: Modern Library, Random House 1960). This is the definitive Gertrude Himmelfarb edition that includes the first edition (1798) and the revised editions (1805 and following).

6. See Arthur C. Pigou, *Economics of Welfare* (London: Macmillan, 1920), and J.M. Keynes's critique of Pigou's theory in *The General Theory of Employment Interest and Money* (London: Macmillan, 1947), pp. 272-279.

7. See Adam Smith, *An Inquiry into the Nature and Causes of the Wealth of Nations,* ed. Edwin Cannan (London: Methuen, 1950); J.B. Say, *Principles of Political Economy,* ed. W.J. Ashley (London: Longmans, Green, 1909); David Ricardo, *On the Principles of Political Economy and Taxation,* ed. P. Sraffa (Cambridge: Cambridge University Press, 1951); Karl Marx, *Capital* (Moscow: Foreign Languages Publishing House, 1961).

8. W.W. Rostow, *The Stages of Economic Growth: A Non-Communist Manifesto* (New York: Cambridge University Press, 1961), p. ix.

9. J.M. Keynes, *General Theory,* p. 251.

10. Sir John Maud, *Aid for the Developing Countries,* Stamp Memorial Lecture, 1963 (London: Athlone Press, 1964), p. 6.

11. Examples are the U.S. invasions of Grenada and Panama and the British invasion of the Falklands (Malvinas) Islands. Even the United Nations' actions, as in Cyprus, are well defined, and because of the lesson learned at the outset of the 1967 Six-Day War, before which Egypt asked the U.N. troops to withdraw and had its request granted, both sides to a conflict must not only request the U.N. peacekeeping forces, but must also agree to their withdrawal.

12. See, for example, Immanuel Wallerstein, *The Capitalist World-Economy* (New York: Cambridge University Press, 1987), chap. 1, "The Inequality of Core and Periphery", pp. 1-64. This is a somewhat socialist view, but is relevant nevertheless.

13. Herman Kahn and the Hudson Institute, *World Economic Development: 1979 and Beyond* (New York: Morrow Quill Paperbacks, 1979), p. 117.

Chapter 2

THE PROBLEMS OF ECONOMIC DEVELOPMENT

A STATEMENT OF THE PROBLEMS

For both theoretical and practical economic considerations, the problems of economic development are those raised by Adam Smith and the classical economists who followed, including Karl Marx. The neoclassical economists, such as Alfred Marshall, for the most part focused on the firm in the Smithian sense to analyze production with respect to profit maximization in light of the business cycle that had set in as a result of industrialization. Because the firm is the generator of economic activity, efficient production throughout the economy would maintain economic development and growth, regardless of the cycle's phase.

During the period of classical economic thinking there were no emerging on underdeveloped countries as they are considered today. There were colonies, territories controlled by countries, but without political or economic independence. The problems that Smith (and his contemporary and friend David Hume) contended with were those of the abolition of British mercantilism and French physiocracy as the policies of development and growth, and the focusing of the new economic force of industrialization due to the merger of science with the possibilities and means of production.

Industrialization did not abolish the mercantilist idea, but altered it to the extent that the exploitation of these territories was for the raw materials for manufacturing.It was a blight on mankind since the usurpation of peoples as slaves in foreign lands and as servants and lowly workers in the occupied territories was a manifestation of physiocracy, in which land is the source of all wealth.[1] To some extent this usurpation was mitigated as industrialization increased; the union of science with production required raw materials and a work force, but as technology increased, a tendency was introduced to render a fully employed work force somewhat redundant. Machines could do more work than the amount of labor hired previously, so unemployment became a part of the industrialized scene.

The solution to unemployment was for the work force to undergo training to operate the machines and to be prepared for the new technologies that the merger of science with the processes of production raised. The guilds of the preindustrial period still maintained their existence and their exclusiveness, but with the demand for skilled labor they expanded their membership as more people sought their skills. Moreover, with industrialization, cities arose that served as residences for labor. Schooling became increasingly important for gainful employment, so the cities provided general education, while specialized education had to be paid for by those receiving it. General education enabled the work force to gain greater sophistication, and technical education provided the specific tools for those with the interest and abilities to go into industry and find employment suitable to their education. As cities grew, cultural amenities were established that provided diversion from work. These activities, together with sports, enabled people to live and work in the cities as contributors to industrial output and economic development and growth. Hence from Smith through Marx the answers to the origins and causes of the wealth of nations rested not in the mercantilistic and physiocratic philosophies that were necessary for the earlier establishment of trade and the accumulation of raw materials and a work force, but in industrialization and the efficient merger of science with the means of production.

The business cycle is a consequence of industrialization.[2] Industrialization allowed the innovative individual to begin business with unique products and to sell them for a profit until close competitors entered the markets and reduced revenues. Market saturation resulted in lower prices to allow the merchandise to move, and those close competitors who could not withstand the competition phased out the product. With industrialization this situation became greatly expanded, employing the nation's industrial work force and affecting the agricultural sector through purchases. When markets in the macro economy became too saturated with production and with close competitors, prices were lowered and employment was reduced accordingly. This unemployment affected purchasing patterns through reduced consumption that required other businesses to cut back on employment; the consequence was a downward cyclical movement into depression, with the economy being revived by businesses allocating their remaining liquidity to restocking of goods and services. This required the hiring of labor to work the manufacturing and wholesale plants, and their wages were brought into the economy as consumption, further generating reemployment and consumption, moving the cycle back upward again. Moreover, with greater liquidity available, the financial institutions that developed along with business and industry had greater funds available to loan to promising innovative entrepreneurs. Innovative production and marketing resulted in profits, close competitors, and eventually market saturation. The long-term consequences of this process were a skilled labor force, relocation of industries from established areas to new areas, thereby reducing the pressures of population, and a further involvement in the merger of science with production through the research and development of increasingly sophisticated technologies.

This form of the business cycle was certainly inherent in the processes of industrialization from the beginning of the Industrial Revolution to the Great Depression, but in 1929, when the Great Depression had begun, a different set of circumstances existed. First, the depression was not one of industrialization alone, in which business cycles were generated by market development and market saturation. This was also a depression in which financial institutions were severely affected because the trade in commercial paper had become a market in its own right, but its profits and losses were not due to the production of goods and services of industrialization, which was the very foundation of the Industrial Revolution. The two markets were intertwined by the use of money, and the monies available for investment in production were also those gained from the profits of buying and selling of commercial paper. When this commercial paper had become overinflated in value, people began selling, and the selling fever took hold. Because there were sellers and no serious buyers, the financial markets fell, and personal fortunes were wiped out almost overnight. The decline of personal liquidity and the run on the banks that ensued from the falling markets reduced the degree of consumption to the extent that businesses closed and well-established industries began reducing their empoyment levels due to the sharp decline in demand.

Second, unlike all previous depressions, the interinvolvement between industry and the financial institutions that had developed to support industry had become so strong that even though different types of markets were involved, the sharp decline in the stock exchanges and the lack of confidence that ensued and persisted could not allow new entrepreneurs or even established industrialists to borrow sufficiently to open new markets. Both plants and labor were idle, and the cyclical upswing that had become so much a part of the business cycle was nonexistent.

The third set of circumstances was due to the first two sets, and these led to the awareness that this depression was unlike all others that had occurred since the Industrial Revolution. While financial institutions had been involved to some extent in all other depressions, this depression had brought the entire financial sector of the industrialized countries to crises and closures. The dynamics of industrialization and the resilience of the processes of economic development were of no avail because of the extent of the involvement between the financial and business sectors and because of the rapidity and extent of the cyclical downswing. There was an awareness that the cycle could not move upward on its own but needed governmental assistance.

Throughout the Industrial Revolution the government was instrumental in providing support for business and finance. This support was passive, consisting of the granting of land rights, the opening of new territories, and, where appropriate, providing defense against piracy and invaders. Direct intervention in the economies of the industrializing countries was considered unnecessary and unwanted, for such involvement, according to the liberal thinking of the economists, would eventually result in government control, with all the bureaucratic implications involved. According to the Jeffersonian dictum, the government that governs best governs least, and because industrialists, financial consultants, and entrepreneurs reap the profits, they alone must bear the risks.

With the drastic decline in business activity and the high and persistent unemployment levels accompanied by the fall of financial institutions, the understanding grew that this depression was unlike all others and required governmental activity to revive the ailing economies. Two different approaches to this activity were undertaken. In the United States, Great Britain, and France, for example, governments did intervene in their respective economies with public works projects and welfare programs. These were public in the sense that they did not bear directly on the industrial sectors, and their object was to provide work and by so doing to inject money into the economy in the form of wages so that demand could be stimulated and industry and the financial institutions could be revived as a consequence.

Other approaches, however, were taken by Germany and Japan each with its own reasons for rejecting the public projects and welfare programs being undertaken by the other countries. Germany had been defeated in World War I, but had also been humiliated in the peace treaties it had signed with its former enemies. Because of the great losses it had suffered in manpower and because of the restrictions on rearming imposed on it, its industries never reached the stage of development that its potential allowed. Inflation set in that further hindered industrial activity, and its democratically elected government proved unable to cope with the situation. The Industrial Revolution in Germany came to an end with World War I, and the consequence was the eventual preindustrial activities of mercantilism and physiocracy — two philosophies that had long endured and had been effective for national wealth prior to industrialization. A dictatorship resulted that was effective in mobilizing the majority of the German people and that provided work in the arms industries, the incomes derived from which were used to stimulate demand and bring about economic revival. Working on the assumptions that for real economic revival the arms industries had to continue to produce, the Germans invaded Czechoslovakia, to the chagrin of a stunned but silent world, and then Poland, an act that provoked the declaration of war. The League of Nations had collapsed, and with the Japanese employing the mercantilist and physiocratic philosophies in China and expanding toward Hawaii, the

United States, which had previously embarked on an isolationist policy, especially in light of its problems in the Great Depression, entered the war. World War II had begun, with all its fury and consequences.

In the aftermath of World War II the problems of economic development were raised. The industrialized countries that were victorious sought guarantees that another war on this scale would never occur again. The United States could no longer revert to its isolationist policy and ratified the charter of the United Nations. Great Britain and France, devastated economically and with tremendous losses of manpower and wealth as a result of the two world wars, could no longer hold on to their colonial territories. With their sanctions and that of the United Nations, these territories began to proclaim their independence and to form countries with their own governments and economic systems. With economic viability comes political stability, and the issue was how these new countries could become economically viable. They could not undergo the dynamics of the Industrial Revolution, as these were inappropriate. Industrialization existed, and these countries sought the aid and knowledge of the industrialized countries and the ability to adapt this aid and knowledge to suit the conditions of their peoples and geographic conditions.

It was soon realized that the knowledge of the developed countries is not easily transferable to these emerging countries, and that not only is the development of economic infrastructure necessary, but the education of the people is required to understand the sophisticated manufacturing methods of the industrialized countries and the products they turn out. Associated with this is marketing, bringing the products to potential consumers and instilling awareness of these products and their close competitive substitutes.

One method used for the development of infrastructure and industrial awareness, that of aid, has been demonstrated to be a double-edged factor in the process of constructing countries and preparing them for development. Corrupt rulers often siphon off large amounts of money for their own uses, taking advantage of their positions of power and of the benefits of nontaxable Swiss bank and offshore accounts. Moreover, the power of these rulers keeps their peoples in line and therefore maintains their own positions, allowing this usurpation of aid to continue until the givers cease their generosity. These rulers, although they are untouchable among their own peoples, are targets for those close to them who want their power and the benefits it brings. Hence revolutions are not uncommon in these countries, but these revolutions are not grass-roots oriented but palace instigated, often with the military and financial support of the aid givers, who seek possible alternative leaders to provide direction in economic emergence.

Aid, however, has been beneficial in many of the emerging countries not expoited by corrupt rulers, but led by patriots who understand their countries' past histories and the meaning of the yoke of colonialism. In these cases aid has demonstrated utility and has gone a long way in providing the resources and training for setting patterns of economic growth. Sir John Maud has written that the ultimate goal of all this aid is that each country may achieve a state of self-sustaining growth; "that is, that its own resources of men and materials may be so developed as to sustain, with imports and exports, a tolerable and rising standard of living for all its people."[3] Maud then stated, however, that the condition for such self-sustaining growth for any country is its ability to export what it has to sell and to do this on a scale sufficient to pay for what it must import, as well as paying interest on loans made to it from other countries.

> Sooner or later, therefore, *trade* is what developing countries need most of all. A fall in the prices paid for their products may ruin the chances of development offered them by 'aid.' Aid, in fact, is always marginal. But it remains quite essential while we take time to find a solution to world trading problems.[4]

Because developing and emerging countries are weaker than their developed sponsors, aid is not merely a benevolent cause, to bring these countries up to trading par with the developed countries, but is also an instrument of political leverage and influence in the internal policies of these countries, even though this is often denied by the developed aid-giving countries. Because of the temptations aid provides to those in power to misuse it for their personal gain, it is viewed by both the donor and receiving countries as a second-best alternative to stimulating economic development. The question that remains to be considered, and indeed is one of the great economic questions of our time, is what the best approach can be. This is certainly one of the problems of contemporary economic development.

What of Sir John Maud's contention that sooner or later it is trade that the developing and emerging countries need most of all? The slogan Trade, Not Aid, emphasized in the 1960s, is still heard today. The rationale for this slogan is that through trade the emerging and developing countries could stimulate industrial activity, thereby providing employment and acquiring enough sophistication to approach the stage of growth of becoming economic partners and competitors instead of recipients of aid. Also, through trade much of the corruption that occurs through the receiving of aid would end, and industry, supported by both domestic and foreign demand, would provide empoyment and hence internal financial liquidity, leading to increased consumer awareness and sophistication. Trade would be the generator of internal development and the means of bringing the economies of the emerging and developing countries into the contemporary age of industrialization.

The condition that Sir John Maud stated for self-sustaining growth, that of a country being able to export what it has to sell, is questionable.

Certainly, trade is of great importance for economic growth, and for this reason the Bretton Woods Conference was held and the General Agreement on Tariffs and Trade was established. The impact of the beggar-thy-neighbor policies that countries implemented during the Great Depression to protect their own industries, and the rebounding consequences of these policies, are understood.[5] But there is a prior condition for self- sustaining growth, one that results in trade. This condition is that a country must be able to produce goods and services attractive to its own citizens and to those of other countries. Hence the idealistic slogan Trade, Not Aid raises the question of what to trade. Those goods and services, apart from tourism, produced by the emerging and developing countries are no match for those of the postindustrial countries, with the consequence that any terms of trade that include the products of the emerging and developing countries apart from those produced by multinational firms that take advantage of geography and working conditions tend to be charity in disguise. Under such trade conditions the emerging and developing countries would remain client states and thus be hindered from achieving their economic and to some extent political independence. The problem of economic development for the emerging and deveoping economies, pressing as it was during the period after World War II and through the decades that followed, remains very much with us today.

There is, however, another serious problem of economic development that has been recently recognized. With the dissolution of the Soviet Union and the formation of the Commonwealth of Independent States that has risen instead, those states within the commonwealth no longer have the planning and centralized support of Moscow. Where previously their economies were geared toward fulfilling the programs of the centralized planning board, their newly gained independence has placed the burden of economic development on themselves and their political leaders.

Related to this is the problem, raised earlier, of those Communist oriented countries that were not strictly part of the Soviet Union. Poland, Hungary, Czechoslovakia, and to a lesser extent Yugoslavia, Albania, and Romania are just a few examples of these countries.[6] While their industries were developed to some extent, they were oriented toward trade with their sponsor countries. The Warsaw Pact, formed to counter the North Atlantic Treaty Organization, was a military union, but the Comecon was its economic counterpart, organized along the principles of a customs union, but dominated by the Soviet Union. This provided a degree of economic security for those Eastern European countries that had suffered during the war and enabled reconstruction of industry to the degree that some economic independence was achieved. But the main policies were dictated from Moscow. Since the breakup of the Soviet Union, with Moscow the capital of Russia only, these countries also have had the status of developing countries. They differ, of course, from the developing countries that were formed after World War II and have achieved some degree of economic and political independence. These countries and their peoples have long histories and were at one time or another in the center stage of European development, but their positions of influence and power were disrupted by the two world wars.

These countries do not have the difficulties of emerging before becoming self-sufficient industrially to reach the stage of developing countries. Their cultures are intact and their work ethic established. Because their individual liberties were restrained for so long while they were forched to perform according to the dictates of their benefactor, their drive is for full economic development, but their understanding of the techniques, the policies, and the approaches to production for achieving this are inadequate in comparison to postindustrial societies. These countries cannot undergo the social changes that the postindustrial societies experienced any more than the newly formed emerging and developing countries can undergo the Industrial Revolution of the past era. Here, as in the case of the emerging and developing countries, the issue of trade arises, but also that of aid for investment to replace obsolete manufacturing procedures, to reeducate the working public to deal with new production and marketing techniques, and to exploit the natural resources of their countries for economic development. For these purposes there is no either-trade-or-aid situation; aid is provided with the explicit purpose of developing the economies internally so that they can compete internationally.

Hence in our era the concept of economic development has been expanded from referring to the emerging and developing countries that were formed after World War II to include those countries that have achieved independence from the once-dominant Soviet Union. The types of economies these countries will eventually construct is still uncertain. The impact that central planning has had on them is great, but their peoples have seen that such a system has its difficulties, which is why, when General Secretary Mikhail Gorbachev of the Soviet Union introduced internal reforms to make the economy more efficient, the influence of the central planning board was weakened and a form of market economy took its place.

Moreover, the ideology of communism is embedded in these countries, although the distinctions between ideology and the practices of communism have been very much exposed. There was no withering away of the state apparatus, indeed no sign of it, for this apparatus was strengthened for reasons of internal security and to maintain the system. For example, with the destruction of the Berlin Wall and the unification of East and West Germany, the extent of internal spying of neighbors on one another is just coming out into the open. Such was the situation in varying degrees throughout the Soviet-controlled countries. The situation of needs being satisfied regardless of one's abilities was, of course, never realized. The long and often futile queues for food and clothing testified to this, while goods and services of the capitalist countries were extremely scarce to the majority of the population and hence were highly valued, to the extent that American chewing gum, cigarettes, and dungarees were status symbols, and jazz gained respect as an art form with the performances of such musicians as Louis Armstrong, Benny Goodman, and other great musicians.

Two more types of economic development still need to be mentioned. The developing countries of South America that are established and have long histories have never achieved the standards of production and living of the United States, Great Britain, France, and Germany. These are developing countries that have been beset with varying degrees of political instability, being governed alternately by democratically elected rulers and military leaders. Countries such as Venezuela tend to exploit a single resource such as oil and have their economies subject to world supply and demand. Other natural resources remain relatively unexploited, with the consequence that these economies remain in the developing stage and never achieve full industrialization or postindustrialization.[7]

Finally, there is the problem of economic development for the postindustrialized countries. While the emerging and developing countries have the examples of the postindustrialized countries set for their potential achievements, the postindustrialized economies have not reached a mature economy condition in which the patterns of supply and demand are in equilibrium. On the contrary, these economies are expanding even though they experience sharply rising and declining business cycles. The difficulty here is to determine where they can go still further and what greater sophistication in manufacturing and marketing can be accomplished to maintain their development.

The postindustrialized economies therefore have no examples to follow, but must cope with their own realities to ensure their continuing development. These realities include the developing European Economic Community (EEC), the competition between Japan and the EEC and the United States, the rise of the Asian countries such as South Korea and Taiwan, and international competition with similar products, which tends to reduce markets and hence affect employment. This, again, is the paradox of industrialization and is influencing the progress of the postindustrial economies in their economic development. Market saturation tends to set in internationally as well as domestically, with close competitors offering similar products. When the significant differences among these competing products are reflected in their prices and terms of payment, profits are reduced due to competition, lower inventories are held, and the employment effect is generated in reverse, bringing about the decline in the business cycle.[8] Stagnation sets in, and a well-trained and educated work force is maintained only at the level necessary for competitive production, while the remainder of the work force is placed on the unemployment and welfare rolls. Under a different approach to industrialization and to international competition this need not be the case.

The concept of economic development has thus evolved from one pertaining to the emerging and developing countries to one that involves those countries that have found independence in Eastern Europe and the postindustrialized countries themselves. Each set of countries has its own unique problems, and each country within each set has specific social and economic problems that distinguish it from the others. While these differences are important, more significant are their similarities. Tribal, political, and caste tensions may exist in many of these countries, but they all share the desire for better living standards, better health and education, and more secure economies. Each country has natural resources and the abilities of the various populations to be productive. The problems of economic development are, therefore, twofold. One problem is how to apply postindustrial conceptualizations of industrialization to the developing and emerging countries, including the newly independent countries in Eastern Europe; the other problem is the maintaining of economic dynamics in the postindustrial countries in light of both domestic and foreign competition. These are the problems that economists and politicians must treat, and that will be discussed in detail in this work.

COMMENTS ON OUR CONTEMPORARY ERA
Further comments on economic development must be made with respect to our contemporary era and our specific social time. While economic deveopment in the beginning of our era encompassed the problems of the emerging and developing countries because of the Cold War strategies of the superpowers that emerged from World War II and because of the altruistic desire to help these countries get established and to bring them into industrialization, as our era progressed to our present social time, the issues of economic development became far more complex. The concept of economic development now includes not only the emerging and developing countries, some of which have made great strides into industrialization such as South Korea and Singapore but also those newly formed independent countries that broke from the defunct Soviet Union and the postindustrial countries that, as a result of their strength, are confronted with the paradox of industrialization and tend to be at a standstill with respect to growth. Our era must be clarified in this context, and our specific social time must be discussed for the concept of economic development as it now stands to be understood. Each era is both historically unique and represents the continuum of human history. No era begins in isolation from the past and ends its uniqueness regardless of the future; therefore, each era contains the dynamics of the past that are relevant as well as the contributions of the present era and its values and difficulties. Hence two questions must be raised. First, what are the factors that bring about the demise of

an era and the beginning of another? Second, what is the uniqueness of our era and how do these factors work for us?[9]

Until the Industrial Revolution the dynamics that generated the delineation of an era were those brought to the fore by the gentry and the artists, musicians, and people of letters who associated with them, and by the military leaders who shaped national boundaries and allowed for people and materials to be empoyed and worked and converted into economic prosperity. Since the earliest human history the strongest have ruled, and to these rulers artists and musicians have turned for employment and protection. Leaders needed artists and musicians to uplift them from the mundane and often nasty chores of ruling. This situation arose in the prehistoric age when the human psyche came into its own with the enlargement and development of the brain and its complex nervous system. The Bronze Age did not differ in these respects; societies became more complex as tribes were replaced by nations, and artists and musicians occupied special places in the royal courts, with their professions being the glorification of their peoples' gods and the praise and at times the deification of the rulers.

The period of the ancient Israelites also illustrates the roles of the artists, musicians, and scribes. The building of the Tabernacle in the wilderness was certainly an endeavor requiring great thought and employing the abilities of artisans whose program was later to be recognized in the Temple of Solomon in the holy city of Jerusalem. Moreover, the Psalms written in part by Moses, attributed in part to the first man Adam, and added to by David, his son Solomon, and the Levites who served the priests in the Temple attest to the abilities of this ancient people. However, these abilities were directed primarily to religious and political matters and related primarily to the Temple and its services.

The period of the Roman Empire was similar in the respect that the artists and musicians were at the service of the emperors and the ruling class, and the scribes came mainly from that class. After the decline and fall of Rome and the establishment of the Holy Roman Empire, music and painting took on an extremely religious aura, portraying the story of Christ, with variations on this theme due to personal interpretations of the story and its events. The only exception was the folk arts, which permitted self-expression on themes not accepted by the authorities, and which may have been the first rumblings of social (as contrasted to political) rebellion. Indeed, social rebellion was manifested in the thawing of the Dark Ages, and the Renaissance man entered the world picture. This all-around person, knowledgeable about the academic literature of the time and extremely curious about the applications of ideas to the artistic and scientific issues of the day, brought about an open intellectual rebellion that is still prevalent today. The patterns of established forms and concepts and fixed and reliable methods of thought and procedure certainly are important, but their results are predictable and therefore remain valid only for those problems and procedures for which they were formulated. Other issues that arise cannot be resolved using the established methods, so that other approaches must be formulated that will have new validity, in spite of the vested political, artistic, and scientific interests that maintain the established methods and approaches. Rebellion as expressed in the arts and intellectual activity became partly defused as a cause of social unrest when the experimentations of writers, musicians, painters and sculptors, and scientists became acceptable to the current vested interest groups, who, in turn, had their concepts and attitudes influenced by the artistic and scientific intellectuals.

Each historical era carries in it the past and its own unique present. In the earliest of historical times when people were engaged in commerce, most of the participants who developed existing markets and explored new ones were literate. The development of writing aided commerce, and only after the period of the Israelite Exodus from Egypt did literature expand and diversify to its several forms. Hence in imperial Rome the writers were historians, lawgivers, and, to some extent, philosophers. In the time of the ancient Greeks they were philosophers, lawgivers such as Solon, conjecturalists, and, to some extent, historians who were storytellers in their own right, basing their history on past events mingled with the prevailing mythology. The people of letters during the Dark Ages were Scholastic philosophers, and except for such thinkers as John Duns Scotus and Jean Buridan, who lived during the decline of the Dark Ages and on the threshold of the rebirth of knowledge, men of letters were concerned primarily with heaven and its hierarchies.

At the time of the demise of the Renaissance and the beginning of the Industrial Revolution, the merger of science with the means of production that brought industrialization was confronted by certain forces that echoed the Dark Ages of economic and spiritual control. While the changes in production methods led to changes in clothing styles due to the textile factories of Rochdale in England and the centers of manufacturing that were being formed in the United States and other countries influenced by the new industrialization, religion still exerted a very strong influence on the newly formed industrial wealthy classes that controlled banking and business. This situation was due to the fact that in the early stages of industrialization entrepreneurs did not understand the dynamics that were developing, nor had they the knowledge to fully comprehend their newly acquired means of production and economic activity. It was, therefore, somewhat natural that the patterns of history of widening control and power over people through religion prevailed to some extent. People sought solace for their activities in religion, but the religious institutions of all faiths also sought the newly formed wealth for their own maintenance; this relationship loosened the hold that religion held over society.

Very early in the development of industrialization a paradox was brought to the fore. For the first time in history both entrepreneurs and workers alike became aware that workers with low pay will purchase only subsistence goods and services, while industrialists vie with each other to gain the consumers' money. The social conditions that developed during industrialization had thus to be treated in a manner unique to that era. The techniques of production that were employed resulted in new markets being opened and new demand being generated, which led to competition. Low wages and the consequent subsistence consumption were certainly not conducive to industrial expansion. Hence as part of the Industrial Revolution there was another revolution taking place, that of labor speaking out for its rights for the first time in history within a mass workers' movement.

While this was one of the many unique contributions of the Industrial Revolution, it too had its roots in history, although it gained its fullest expression only in the later period of industrialization. In the Dark Ages, for example, people engaged in subsistence living, primarily working the land, consuming what they could of their products and seeking to trade off the rest.[10] Specialization of labor did exist, of course. Tailors, blacksmiths, and members of all the other professions traded their skills for food and the produce of the land. All real control of the economies was conducted by the religious authorities together with the political rulers. This system continued throughout the Middle Ages, but it was broken during the Renaissance when both secular and religious learning had spread, especially with the aid of the printing press, resulting in the expansion of education that helped the laborers to cope with the changing world.

When entrepreneurs began applying scientific techniques to production, local and national economies developed the means of commerce to handle the marketing and sales of the products and brought international trade into the era of industrialization, even though elements of mercantilism and physiocracy still lingered on in the terms of trade and procedures. Machinery was exported, and ideas on production and sales crossed the oceans. Labor was elevated from Dark Ages subsistence to productive employees in the new era. Previously specialization had been concerned only with expertise, but through Adam Smith's concept of the division and specialization of labor within the plant, both production techniques and the competition that resulted from industrialization brought about efficiency in industry and generated the ability to expand into new markets and stimulate further competition.

The era of the Industrial Revolution came to an end with the Great Depression. Productive capital and a skilled working force remained idle and unproductive, while the financial markets were very slow to respond to the uncertain treatment that bewildered government leaders sought to apply. By means of its greatness in the productive sector the Industrial Revolution brought about cities, culture, and great works in the arts and sciences because of the greater availabilities that industrialization offered. After its demise the cities still existed and the great centers for the arts and sciences still remained. The finances on which these are based were not forthcoming, however, and governments sought to retain the writers and artists in government service because of their awareness of the importance that the arts and sciences have for humanity. By the beginning of World War II the process of industrialization had been completed within the conceptual framework of the era; in the aftermath of the war a new era began, founded on the contributions of the previous historical eras but more specifically on the contributions made in the Industrial Revolution.

Thus, while every historical era is unique, delineated by the circumstances that bring it about and defined by the activities that occur in it, our historical era of knowledge is perhaps the most dynamic in the chronological-historical existence of humanity. This is because the opportunities that are available to us for our own personal exploitation, as well as the possibilities provided by society in its various stages of economic development, can, if properly used, lift humanity out of the difficult conditions that exist, bringing us into another dimension of living in which knowledge is exploited for the betterment of humankind. This era holds for us both a promise of a better future and a choice of the way we make our future, both collectively and personally. It also holds for us a warning that our basic humanism should not be lost in the wonderment of knowledge, that the ancient Greek philosophers who sought wisdom by argument and the probing of nature should not be ignored but should serve as an example while the dazzle of the search for knowledge and the development of knowledge tantalizes us in its pursuit.

In our contemporary period there are consistencies that have remained more or less throughout history. Rich and prosperous nations, nations plagued with poverty, and the situations in which nations confront each other in battle and in which internal rebellion results in the taking up of arms to defend principles and positions of power are constants. So are economic crises, diseases that debilitate, poor education, and those who are socially exploited by those who exploit. Despite the progress made in science and production during the Industrial Revolution, there were still two world wars fought, with untold losses for the past, present, and future of humanity.

How does our contemporary historical era differ from those past? The world has been plunged into major recessions, the emerging and developing countries have suffered setbacks in their advancements due to the oil power game, regions that held promise for flourishing life have become deserts due to battles, people turn to the wealthy nations to save them from perishing in their time of starvation, and countries that have newly declared their independence are struggling to find their economic basis for development and growth. Where, then, are the benefits of our era of knowledge?

These arguments are certainly valid, but the philosophical assumption on which they are based can be questioned. These are events that have occurred and are occurring in our social time, but our era is in its early stage and should be understood for its benefits to be realized. Because an era is not isolated from its past, it cannot easily make previous conditions irrelevant. The grip of darkness was very strong in the early stages of the Renaissance, so much so that a backlash occurred in Spain and other countries in the form of the Inquisition. The influences of physiocracy in the form of feudalism were so ingrained in the United States that during its early stages of political and industrial development the Civil War was fought, in which the industrialized North was victorious. The outstanding contributions of historical eras are often found in the eras that follow, cultivated by the receiving eras and altered accordingly as the new eras advance within their own historical contexts.

When eras changes there is a clash of concepts of the past, many of whose promises are fulfilled in the new era's development, with the present, whose promises are yet to be realized. In our present era we now posses the means to remove poverty from our midst, to eliminate many of the diseases that have afflicted us and to confront those that are new, and to raise the levels of education throughout the world to enable people to participate in our era.

Our era has been called the computer age and the atomic age, but these terms are inaccurate, or they refer to differing aspects of the greater historical era, that of knowledge. While these developments, conducted mostly in the postwar period, have had great influences on our lives, they are due to the accumulation of sophisticated knowledge and the application of this knowledge to the fields of energy and physical research and to the fields of computation, calculation, and projection into future scenarios. There is no doubt that over the next few years, given intensive research and the uncertainty over oil supplies, atomic energy plants could be developed, thereby ridding the world of the threat of politicization over decreasing supplies of fossil fuels; they would also provide cheap and endless supplies of energy and expand technologies for industrial production and domestic and foreign consumption.

Computers provide great efficiency in calculation and also serve as instruments of entertainment. They are still being developed, and their applications in science, the arts, and industry are still being explored. The field of artificial intelligence, for example, is not only providing more efficient production methods at lower costs than had existed previously; it also supplies models for living organisms and establishes alternative methods for understanding biological operations.[11] Moreover, while computers are necessary for controlling energy in our complex systems of energy distribution, this very energy is applied, in part, to power the computers.

These ages however, are incorporated into a greater and more encompassing historical era of knowledge. The expansion and control of atomic energy requires ever-increasing sophisticated knowledge, obtained by great amounts of money and research. The development and expansion of computers, from computer toys to the instruments that control high-level industrial production and assist in scientific research, are subject to increasing investigation into the language possibilities and the manufacture of computers. The silicon chip, once considered the highest degree of microproduction, it itself becoming more complex and sophisticated, especially as competition among the various firms in competing countries such as Japan and the United States drives intensive research and greater understanding of the possibilities for theoretical and practical expansion in the near future.

Hence the computer age and the atomic age rely on the accumulation of comprehension and the utility of information pertinent to the problems at hand, that is, on knowledge. However, knowledge is far from stable, for what we comprehend and accept as valid now will most likely be shown to be inadequate at a future date as problems shift and the means for dealing with the problems are revised. The growth and development of knowledge depend on human ingenuity, as the development of atomic physics and its expansion into both cosmology and microbiology, the rapid turnover of the generations of computers, and the formulation of new computer languages as well as the opening of new fields to which computers are made applicable have shown.

Our era of knowledge is one of change at a pace more rapid than in any other historical era, but it is still in its infancy. The great advancements in medicine, such as organ transplants and research into cancer, the growth of the number of countries seeking economic and political independence, the breakup of the Soviet empire, and explorations in space and walking on the moon attest to our era's dynamics. The developments in these fields depend on research, but what of the development of the world's economies? How are they affected by the dynamics of our era?

COMMENTS ON SOCIAL TIME
Each historical era is broken down into its periods of social time, with social time in each era delineated by the specific universal contributions made in that era. For example, the development of the steel industry during the Industrial Revolution can be understood as occurring during the social time span that existed from the time the Bessemer process was developed to convert iron ore into steel for industrial use to the spread of competing steel companies throughout the industrializing countries, with consequent improvements made in the iron-ore-processing techniques due to the competition.

An era is, therefore, defined by the many social times within it, the events of each time having a common property uniting them with the events of each era. The Bessemer process was developed during a historical era when the uses of iron were expanding and a stronger form of iron was required to allow for this expansion. Without industrialization there would have been no need for steel, and the process of converting iron ore into steel would not have been developed. We would certainly not treat history seriously if we considered the social time for the development of electricity as occurring in the Renaissance, although electricity (from *elektron*, Greek for "amber," which was magnetized and used for games and by fortune tellers) was certainly known in its very primitive form. While the nature of the atom was considered by the Greek Democritus (c. 460 c.-370 B.C.) and by the Roman Lucretius (c. 96 c.-55 B.C.), we would say that although the atomic social time began in the last years of the nineteenth century and continued prior to the Great Depression, the great practical and theoretical advancements were made in our era, when atomic energy came on line in power plants and the uses of the atom in medicine were developed. We would be treating history respectfully, however, if we considered the relationship between the Renaissance and electricity, because the rebirth of knowledge opened a period of contemplation and exploration never before undertaken by humanity, with magnets and electric current one of the areas being explored.[12]

The question that must now be considered is this: How can we determine which ages or social times are part of our unique era? Indeed, does the movement of historical and economic events indicate a cyclical periodicity in which circumstances are similar, so that eras can be delineated by the similarity of events, as in Kondratieff and Beckman cycles?[13] For example, the intellectual inquiry of the ancient Greeks resulted in many questions being raised that are relevant today, among them being the problems of mathematical infinity and the basic structural material of the universe. The combined contributions of the Greek and Roman civilizations should have enabled us to flourish, and our cultures should have developed at an enormous rate. Political instability and conflict resulted in the destruction of these great civilizations, but their contributions remained in the library of Alexandria. There the intellectuals worked and wrote, but had little contact with the rest of the population; this brought about great resentment because the benefits of the intellectual activity remained within the library's walls. The library at Alexandria was sacked and destroyed, plunging the world into darkness. During the Renaissance the world reawoke to the traditions of the ancient civilizations and began to expand on their artistic and intellectual contributions, bringing them into new areas and conceptualizations. Then followed a period of relative intellectual calm, one that differed from darkness, for the civilized world was no longer prepared to destroy or abandon what had already been accomplished. But lacking was the historical legacy for the applications of the ideas of the ancient civilizations, and this resulted in a pattern of searching. With this search came experimentation and such social and political incongruities as the aftermath of the French Revolution, the struggle for democracy in America during the growth of the country and the Industrial Revolution, the paradox of great wealth generated by production and the actual poverty that existed in the newly formed slums, and the inability to distribute wealth according to the economic forces that were evolving during industrialization.

The consequences of this searching were situations in society in which intellectual processes were still developing and the arts and sciences were still being explored and brought into new areas, while the greater social inabilities to cope with the intellectual progress and artistic contributions resulted in social conflicts and finally, as countries sought to reclaim the illusory glory of the great past, ignoring the progress in intellectual activity and artistic endeavors, in two world wars of such destruction as had never been witnessed in history. Can these events be interpreted validly in a cyclical framework? In our era, are we not engaging in a period of intellectual activity never experienced since the ancient library in Alexandria flourished, or since the other historical peak, the Renaissance, broke loose on the world?

Of course, there are great differences among these periods. The period of the shift from Rome to Alexandria and the glory of its library represented an era in which knowledge and wisdom were being codified and expanded, but without applying this knowledge and wisdom to the social, political, and economic conditions at the time. The Renaissance was the era in which knowledge and wisdom of an earlier era were being viewed for the first time, and with a degree of trepidation because the chill of the age of darkness was still felt. The Renaissance man was not only well rounded educationally, but was aware of the social, political, and economic difficulties and often participated in the social dynamics of the time. Our era of knowledge is one in which knowledge and society are so well integrated that knowledge is incorporated into society through technology, medicine, and the academies of learning to which more people have access than at any other historical time. Our knowledge cannot be dissociated from society, nor is it being formulated in an era that bases itself on earlier and ancient eras. It is an era in which knowledge does not remain special to a society, but moves across national and linguistic barriers, becoming universal and to be used by all countries. The difficulty with the development of societies in our era is their ability to use the new knowledge. Emerging or underdeveloped economies lack the technical skills for applying sophisticated knowledge and must rely on the developed economies for assistance. This will be discussed in chapter II of this work. Developed economies compete with one another in the advancement of knowledge and its applications, and because of their similar economic structures this often results in the paradox of industrialization.

Social time is thus delineated by the events, processes, and circumstances that impress their utilities on the eras in which they occur. Individual social times may be occurring in the era, or several such times may be occurring more or less simultaneously, depending on the specific contributions they make and the influences they exert. There may also be contributions that are of such significance that they dominate their specific fields, perhaps to the extent of depriving rival contributions of the opportunity to be exploited for their benefits. Charles Darwin's theory of evolution is one such example; its influence was so great that even the social sciences could not be released from its grip. All of biology came into its sphere, and despite the significance of Lamarckian evolution, Darwin's theory greatly overshadowed it and reduced it to insignificance, perhaps wrongly. Contributing to its near demise was its misadoption by T.D. Lysenko in the Soviet Union as official policy on sociobiological evolution.[14]

Social time is dependent on the era in which it occurs because the events in that era have value in the specific social time. This may seem tautological, but it is not and on closer inspection reveals itself as a historical truth. Just as an era is delineated by the demise of its predecessor, being formed by the events in the past and crystallized into a set of unique circumstances, these circumstances are the manifestations of events, of social times, that impart to the era its uniqueness. For example, while wars have been fought throughout history, with the coming together of nations because of the ideology of unity (a concept advocated by Immanuel Kant and given expression in the League of Nations and later the United Nations) and the improvements in transportation (specific to the Industrial Revolution in the areas of rail transportation, seagoing transportation, and air transportation in its early stages), the methods of war became so complex that combatants of many countries were brought to face each other in destruction. World War I was such a war, and the attempt made by the formation of the League of Nations to establish world unity failed because of the misapplications of the fruits of industrialization to alleviate the difficulties that resulted from the outcome of the armistice. The conditions imposed on Germany became intolerable, especially when the Great Depression set in and hindered the production of weapons and other types of warlike materials that could have relieved the unemployment situation. The failure to understand the difficulties of neoclassical economics, such as the assumption of full employment presented by A.C. Pigou, also hindered economic revitalization in the defeated countries and the industrialized countries as well.[15]

Because of the tremendous potential demand in the post-World War II period when our era of knowledge began, industry was ready and able to absorb the newly demobilized soldiers. The questions confronting both government authorities and industrialists, as well as the civilian population expanded by the demobilization, were what should be produced, how to underwrite the economy to prevent another serious depression, and how the people could best prepare themselves for the new era after the Great Depression and the war.

The answers to these questions were provided by the new social dynamic then being formed and developed. Because industrialization had already been established and unions had been formed during the depression to protect workers' rights, and because social legislation had been enacted to protect consumers and producers alike, the potential of both industry and the labor force lay open for exploitation. This exploitation took the form of product research, the development of new products to stimulate demand, and the entering of new markets that hitherto had not existed. The standard products, such as refrigerators and automobiles and the like, were, of course, continued, but were also improved in performance. But with computers and television coming into their own, and with the new electronics (and the uses of atomic power for peaceful research, as well as the new medicines to fight diseases) our era of knowledge had come into existence by exploiting research and development and basing consumer production on their findings.

As the complexities of international relations increased, and especially as the previously isolationist United States became the dominant world power and competed for markets and spheres of influence with its former ally in arms, the Soviet Union, the problems of the emerging and developing economies became critical. Those countries in need of financial assistance and markets for their own products began to play the big-power game, setting one power against the other to get the best deals for themselves. This game was not without dangerous consequences, as the example of Castro's Cuba shows, and often economies suffered and people sought refuge in other countries that could provide them with better economic opportunities. In light of the Cold War, another form of knowledge industry was developed, that of the think tanks, which were formed to prepare scenarios of possible Cold War situations and to provide viable actions and reactions that could then be analyzed and acted upon when necessary. With the benefits of our era, therefore, came the burden of bringing the newly formed and developing countries to the standards of development and industrialization. The Cold War served as one way of achieving this, but it was based on the ideologies of mercantilism, physiocracy, and the ancient attitudes of imperialist conquest and control. Only in our social time have these obsolete ideologies been discarded with the demise of the Soviet Union, and the politicization that was prevalent has been reduced in importance. The problems are still pressing, and new approaches are required.

Chronologically, our time is a progression, the accumulation of years calculated according to the various traditions based on religious considerations and astronomical computations. In the known history of humanity humankind has changed little in personality and behavior. The great ancient civilizations have yielded impressive humanistic contributions in the arts, sciences, and philosophy; they have also been breeding grounds for poverty, ignorance, jealousy, and civil strife. But history is past, open for understanding and speculation, interpretation, and debate. History allows us to reflect on our past in order to understand the present and to project into the future. Chronological time is the time of the past, present, and future; as such, this time is without content. Historical time is chronological time with content, that is, with the events of human history; historical time, therefore, contains the great historical eras. It is both historical time and social time, with respect to our present era, that are of interest to us now, for these times represent the various stages our era has undergone, from the applications of wartime techniques to peacetime production in the immediate postwar period, to the reactions of those who sought to maintain the status quo, thereby threatening those in every society who sought knowledge and who were exploring the first new grounds of our era, to our present social time with its emphasis on knowledge forms and the new economic situation in our world. Our era of knowledge provides us a chance to be different from our historical ancestors and to place our era on the continuum of chronological time as a milestone in the historical time evolution. We are now confronted with the opportunities provided by the end of the Cold War for economic growth and development, ending the poverty that still remains as a blight to mankind. The struggles for political power that are resulting in the shedding of blood and the loss of life are vestiges of bygone eras; the real struggle is for economic opportunity, for growth and independence, and for the distribution of the knowledge of the postindustrial countries to those that are still emerging and developing. For this to be achieved, the developed economies must maintain their inner dynamism in light of the strenuous competition for wealth among the world's economies.

Old theories of economic growth, relevant for other eras and social times, are of little significance for us in our era and social time. A new theory of economic development must be formulated, one that encompasses both the postindustrial societies and those that are emerging and developing. Such a theory will provide unification among the different economies in their stages of development, bringing them into a working economic relationship. Such a theory will be developed in the second part of this work and applied in the third part.

NOTES

1. While mercantilism and physiocracy in the United States during the Industrial Revolution were relegated to minor positions, their influences were felt nevertheless. In the South, where industrialization progressed more slowly than in the North, the physiocratic influence was hesitant to yield to the new historical era, and the Civil War was required to place it in its proper perspective of agricultural development. Mercantilism retained its influence with respect to trade, because currencies were calculated in terms of gold, and the holding of foreign currencies strengthened a country's trading position. But what was more important was the selling of goods and services, because this maintained industrial output and hence empoyment. The mystique of mercantilism had vanished, but its vestiges were found in the terms of trade. This ended with the dynamics of the Great Depression, when beggar-thy-neighbor tactics dismally failed to maintain the trading countries' positions.

2. For a discussion of business cycles as long-wave in orientation, see Joshua S. Goldstein, *Long Cycles* (New Haven: Yale University Press, 1988), and Brian J.L. Berry, *Long-Wave Rhythms in Economic Development and Political Behavior* (Baltimore: Johns Hopkins University Press, 1991).

3. Sir John Maud, *Aid for the Developing Countries* (London: Athlone Press, University of London, 1964), p. 7. This was the Stamp Memorial Lecture, delivered before the University of London on November 12, 1963.

4. Maud, *Aid for the Developing Countries,* p. 8. Italics in the original.

5. See David Z. Rich, *The Economics of International Trade: An Independent View* (New York: Quorum Books, 1992), pt. 1, for a discussion of beggar-thy-neighbor policies during the Great Depression and their consequences for trade and economic stability.

6. Albania's position was somewhat ambiguous because it tended to both the Chinese and Soviet camps, but it has now established a democratically elected government.

7. However, development of natural resources is not always a clear-cut issue, as the controversy over the exploitation of the vast resources of the Brazilian rain forest illustrates. Brazil's economic growth could be greatly increased by using the timber and other resources that this vast area holds, but the consequences to the environment that would ensue from the destruction of this lush area are perhaps incalculable. In this situation the real choice is how to utilize different resources for growth, resources such as labor, tourism, and the development of unique industries that will provide that country and others in similar situations with an exploitable advantage. This requires great acumen on the parts of the government, industrial leaders, and the unions.

8. The employment effect is the generation of more employment with increasing demans and the impact this has on the business cycle. This will be discussed in part II, Chapter 8 section 2 especially in the context of the paradox of industrialization.

9. In a slightly different context the present writer expressed the following sentiment:

> It must be considered that there are universalities concerning social dynamics, regardless of the era under discussion. This is because all

humans have common traits that unite them in humanity for all the good and bad this entails. But it must be understood that the differences among people — partly due to genetic make-up and partly due to the environment — are the generators of social specifics that determine (the term is used here loosely) the dynamics of social interactions, the duration of these dynamics, and, most important, the directions they take.

David Z. Rich, *The Dynamics of Knowledge: A Contemporary View* (Westport, Conn.: Greenwood Press, 1988), p. 22,23.

10. This was the foundation of physiocracy, for then the land and its yield and the skills of those who worked it provided the main source of wealth. Trade routes were developed mainly to exploit the various spices and food products, as well as to provide the most efficient method for transporting and trading these products. Mercantilism, then, is an offshoot of physiocracy, and its own sophistication was developed as trading among the nations gained in significance.

11. See, for example, Richard Dawkins, *The Blind Watchmaker* (New York: W.W. Norton, 1987). In the appendix of this work Dawkins constructed a program for the Macintosh computer for the evolutionary development of biomorphological forms. This is a fascinating project.

12. Luigi Galvani (1737-1798), Count Alessandro Volta (1745-1827), and James Watt (1736-1819) learned and worked in the latter stages of the Renaissance and in the early stages of the Industrial Revolution. Andre-Marie Ampere (1885-1836) had the hindsight and wisdom of the Renaissance and the dynamics of the Industrial Revolution when he worked. Hans Christian Oersted (1777-1851) lived to see industrialization developing, and his work contributed to this development. With respect to Oersted, consider Arthur Koestler's remarks:

Lodestones magnets were known in antiquity as a curiosity of Nature. In the Middle Ages they were used for two purposes: as navigators' compasses and as a means to attract an estranged wife back to her husband. Equally well known were the curious properties of amber which, when rubbed, acquired the virtue of attracting flimsy objects. The Greek word for amber is *elektron,* but the Greeks were not much interested in electricity; nor were the Middle Ages. For nearly two thousand years, electricity and magnetism were considered as separate phenomena, in no way related to each other. In 1820 Hans Christian Oersted discovered that an electric current flowing through a wire deflected a magnetic compass which happened to be lying on his table. At that moment the two concepts began to fuse into one: electro-magnetism, creating a kind of chain which is still continuing and gaining in momentum.

Arthur Koestler, *The Ghost in the Machine* (London: Pan Books, 1967), p. 214. For further comments on Koestler's discussion of Oersted and Koestler's approach to creativity, and a different approach to the same topic, see Rich, *Dynamics of Knowledge,* pt. 2, pp. 41-128.

13. See Nikolai D. Kondratieff, *The World Economy and Its Conditions during and after the War* English Translation (Moscow: Volgada Press, 1922), and Robert Beckman's two works, *The Downwave* (Portsmouth, England: Milestone Publications, 1983), and *Into the Upwave* (Portsmouth, England: Milestone

Publications, 1988). Kondratieff's cycle is economic, while Beckman's wave is psychological in nature.

14. Lamarck was certainly a great biologist and perhaps the first influential evolutionist. His work was published in 1808 and paved the way for Charles Darwin's great contribution. See J. B. P. A. de Monet de Lamarck, *Zoological Philosophy,* trans. Hugh Elliot, Jr. (Chicago: University of Chicago Press, 1984). For a Lamarckian argument, see Arthur Koestler, *The Case of the Midwife Toad* (London: Hutchinson, 1971).

15. See Arthur C. Pigou, *Economics of Welfare* (London: Macmillan, 1920), and Keynes's argument against Pigou in *The General Theory of Employment Interest and Money* (London: Macmillan, 1947), pp. 272- 279. Keynes was referring to the fourth edition of Pigou's work, which appeared in 1932 during the depths of the Great Depression.

Chapter 3

BUSINESS CYCLES: COMMENTS ON
METHOD

Without invoking a misplaced methodological analogy, the task of securing a massive flow of primary economic data can be compared to that of providing the high-energy physicists with a gigantic accelerator. The scientists have their machines while the economists are still waiting for their data. In our case not only must the society be willing to provide year after year the millions of dollars required for maintenance of a vast statistical machine, but a large number of citizens must be prepared to play, at least, a passive and occasionally even an active part in actual fact-finding operations. It is as if the electrons and protons had to be persuaded to cooperate with the physicist.[1]

Wassily Leontief
"Theoretical Assumptions and Nonobserved Facts" [1]

THE ECONOMIST AS SCIENTIST IN THE CONTEMPORARY WORLD

For those not trained in the discipline of economics, this field of social inquiry and policy-making is certainly baffling. Economics deals with the generation of wealth and the allocation of scarce resources among competing factors. The purpose of this allocation is to establish a strong industrial base that provides employment and promotes the general well-being of the populace. However, in light of the business cycle's fluctuations, in which wealth is seemingly generated as the cycle moves upward to prosperity and taken away as the cycle declines into recession, to the untrained person economics may appear to be a discipline in which discussions held among its practitioners have no effect on conditions as they are, so that the processes of business activity continue regardless of what the professional economists say or do.

For example, government leaders state proposals for generating growth, yet business cycles come and go as if they are immune to these proposals. Economists, employing extremely sophisticated econometric models, attempt to determine the frequencies and intensities of these cycles, and Nikolai Kondratieff and several other economists have sought long-wave dynamics for specific business cycles. Economists are often kept off guard by the intensities and influences of the cycles. A speech by a leader of a big corporation, or the falling ill of a national leader while visiting a foreign and competing country, can send shock waves through the economy and influence activity in ways not previously considered. The activities and policies of a foreign country can influence the home economy's markets in ways that the economist can understand only after they have taken effect; moreover, the extent of their secondary influences can often be evaluated only after they have made their impacts on the economy.

It is equally puzzling for the layperson that economists prefer to relate to their discipline as a science, as seen in the example of Leontief's sentiment, even though he did not intend to invoke a misplaced methodological analogy, as by its very nature economics lacks the precision in prediction and analysis that exists in the physical sciences. The layperson may open an academic text on economics and find advanced mathematics therein that seems to endow economics with the semblance of being scientific, but then the person reads about poverty, unemployment, the struggling emerging and developing economies, the breaking apart of a once-mighty empire, and the homeless walking the streets of the world's great cities — the daily material in the newspapers and magazines. These events certainly raise questions about the validity of economics as a scientific discipline.

In spite of this baffling situation, however, the layperson should understand the economist's position. Economics is not unlike the study of medicine, a discipline in which a degree of uncertainty exists in both diagnosis and prognosis. Indeed, in medicine the well-being of a patient often depends on the physician's abilities, sensitivity, and understanding in prescribing treatment geared to that patient's particular needs. A person who is ill may affect other people nearby, including loved ones, but this certainly does not determine the well-being of the entire society. Nevertheless, economic activity is a general social condition, and the isolation of an economic malaise cannot be conducted on a single economic sector, but must be done on a large scale, embracing several sectors. The understanding of the causes and consequences of the malaise depends on the economist's training and skill and on sensitivity in dealing with a given problem.

Since the end of the Great Depression economists have become increasingly aware of the difficulties of their discipline, especially the business cycle and its causes. Indeed, during the economic upheaval that signaled the termination of the Industrial Revolution, economists argued among themselves over the issues of full employment and economic growth and development. Perhaps only Keynes pointed to the real problem: The neoclassical assumption as the basis of economic theory and policy-making — a position eloquently stated earlier by Pigou — was inadequate and indeed invalid. While it is correct to maintain that the lessons of the Great Depression have been learned well, that taxation and social security payments have been established to alleviate economic distress, that governments have assumed the role of economic protectors of the banking systems, and that unemployment insurance is a form of buffer against personal poverty, nevertheless, as the layperson will readily point out, poverty in the world's economies still exists and is debilitating, both personally and socially. In the postindustrial societies and in the emerging and developing economies taxation is a burden, the social security and national insurance systems provide little assistance in ensuring a living standard reasonable in our time, and unemployment insurance and welfare payments are far from adequate as a means of combatting the ravages of personal poverty. Granted, these measures are better than being without them, as was the situation during the Great Depression, but they are insufficiant in our contemporary economic reality in the postindustrial, emerging, and developing economies.

The evaluation of these measures requires the amassing of empirical data on labor, employment, housing, health, and education, and specific economic information in the economies' various sectors. These data gathered by economists and statisticians are supposed to clarify the current situation in every economy and provide material for the economist to treat in projections and in theory form. While this information differs both qualitatively and quantitatively from that of the physicist, the economist is nevertheless a scientist in the sense that he or she seeks to make sense of the amassed information about economies in general and their various sectors in particular. The economist must consider the overall operations of business and the government's activity as regulator; as a scientist the economist must construct theories for his or her specific branch of concern and seek to apply them, either in competition with other theories or as paradigmatic constructions that dominate the defined and delineated areas of concern. Unlike physics, however, economics cannot be restricted to a laboratory because it deals with the social dynamics of the allocation of scarce resources among competing ends, the alternative uses of resources in the manufacturing processes, the investment of profits in sales, and, in the macro realm, the efficient uses of national resources, including production, for the betterment of the general economy. Indeed, the problem with testing economic theory in the sense of testing physical theory is that for economics there is a marked absence of laboratory conditions. This results in theories being tested for their internal logic and their contributions in comparison to other theories to the body of economic knowledge.

Economics does share with physics and the other natural sciences the situation that these disciplines are somewhat esoteric, understood in depth mainly by their practitioners. While laypeople may study these disciplines as hobbies or with passing interest, the consequence is that for the most part the practitioners of these disciplines converse professionally mainly among themselves; with respect to economists, however, the conversation has to extend to business representatives who have some orientation in the discipline's language and theories, but excludes most laypeople. However, as Leontief has stated:

> We, I mean the academic economists, are ready to expound, to anyone ready to lend an ear, our views on public policy, give advice on the best ways to maintain full employment, to fight inflation, to foster economic growth. We should be equally prepared to share with the wider public the hopes and disappointments which accompany the advance of our own desperately difficult, but always exciting intellectual enterprise. The public has amply demonstrated its readiness to back the pursuit of knowledge. It will lend its generous support to our venture too, if we take the trouble to explain what it is all about.[2]

Leontief's sentiment is difficult to put into practice even in the best of circumstances, because of all the academic disciplines, economics most directly touches people's lives, but the way economics works is widely misunderstood if not utterly confusing. Moreover, people are most reluctant to discuss economics with academic economists when they realize that the debates among economists seem not to lead to resolutions and that the economy continues with its cyclic movements regardless of what the economists say or do.

Our contemporary situation provides material for much heated debate among economists. Not only is the geopolitical world undergoing great and dramatic changes, but during all these changes the basic economic needs remain to be fulfilled. The role of the government, traditionally that of backing the economy after Keynes's contributions, is certainly not being carried out. There is an argument for economic efficiency, for those firms and businesses that cannot compete to go under. But this is not the case, because the amount of consumer liquidity has been reduced considerably due to the prevailing economic recession. Moreover, our current recession is unlike all others for several reasons. One is the effects felt from international competition that are manifested in the paradox of industrialization and are given expression in the unemployment effect; another is the breaking up of the Soviet empire and the reliance on aid by these newly independent countries, so that monies that could be reinvested in the postindustrial economies' infrastructures are being directed to these independent countries, with uncertain utility concerning their uses, as discussed in chapter II. There is still another reason for the current recession's uniqueness, that the tools governments are using to combat it and bring the cycle to moving upward are out-of-date, given our present circumstances. With the European Community coming together, the Eastern European states pulling apart, the decline of the Soviet Union and the slow rising of Communist China, the forging of common bonds in Indochina together with the assertion of dominance by the competing countries there, the changing situation in South Africa and its position of power with respect to the rest of the African continent, the struggle of the South American countries to improve their industry and combat severe unemployment, and the Middle East still being the center of troubles, a theory of economic development is required that will relate to these variegated and changing dynamic situations.

The current deficit spending will no longer serve to bolster these economies, for as has been learned, money printed to cover these deficits comes back to the source, the government, in terms of inflation. Moreover, the Keynesian emphasis on production and output alone is insufficient, because competition reduces the profits of competing businesses to the point that employment is reduced and the unemployed are eventually placed on welfare, while the government, businesses, and labor wait for the cycle to move up again. Certainly, then, there is a need to coordinate the levels of money in circulation with the amount of products on the market, but this is extremely difficult because of the diversity of products, the consuming patterns of countries' regions, and the value of money with respect to its purchasing power in these various regions. While there are prevailing uniting and dividing tendencies among the nations of the world, the business cycle is becoming a factor common to all countries. This is manifested in the amount of aid available during periods of prosperity and of recession, aid that the newly independent countries as well as the emerging and developing countries urgently need. As the amount of available funds declines, the economic activity recesses. These countries experience their own minicycles, but they are in effect epicycles, moving around the big economic cycle that moves in turn throughout the postindustrialized world.

Hence the economist as scientist does not have the luxury of a laboratory with techniques for constructing experiments and subjecting them to various controls. The economist's laboratory as such is the world's economies, and these are subject to political, economic, and in some cases natural influences, such as major earthquakes or volcanic eruptions and their effects on the countries in which they occur. Moreover, the policies of one country very often affect those of others, as in the case of the Iraqi invasion of Kuwait and the Gulf War that followed. The economist as scientist does have econometric models of the various economies based on the available statistical inputs and subject to built-in variables. But as Leontief pointed out, a large number of citizens must be prepared to play a part in supplying these statistics, and very often governments are reluctant to share them with economists from other countries. The control here is the squaring away of a model with economic behavior according to the statistical evidence as well as with econometric predictions according to these statistics and without them, analysis in the latter case being based on the economy's performances as correlated with the model's dynamics.

The difficulties that economists have in practicing their discipline in its many forms can thus be understood. The point is not whether economics is a science, for in the sense of the natural sciences this is the issue that is debated. The lack of a laboratory prevents the theoretical and experimental precision that exists in the natural sciences. But as a study of the allocation of scarce resources among competing ends for the purpose of generating wealth and economic growth and development, economics is most definitely a science. It has theories that are confirmed or refuted by the experience of economic activity; it has models that can be tested against this reality; it relies on the gathering of statistical data for its information. Where it differs from the natural sciences is in its inability to control economic conditions for testing. But this is a statement for the human spirit that rebels against controls, and after all it was the great economist Adam Smith and the political theorist Thomas Jefferson who argued against controls, for to control the economy, to impose on it laboratory conditions, is to control the people who are the actors and performers in the economic world. While such control may be possible for a while, as the demise of the Soviet Union and the declaration of independence among the former Soviet states has illustrated, it cannot endure, and its imposition results in great suffering and economic loss.

BUSINESS CYCLES: METHODOLOGICAL APPROACHES
With the Russian Revolution during World War I and the forming of the Soviet Union thereafter, two economic camps were established, the industrializing capitalist camp and the newly socializing camp. Within the industrializing nations business cycles occurred. Depressions were experienced with the social loss of labor and output, but recovery also occurred, bringing the capitalist economies to a new level of production. The socialist camp of the Soviet Union also had a degree of industrialization, but after the breakdown of the system there during World War I and the overthrow of the czarist regime, the establishment of the Soviet Union placed that great country in somewhat of a dilemma. Traidtionally, the industrializing countries relied on the agricultural sectors to supply the foods necessary to maintain economic activity, while a sector of industry serviced the agricultural sector with farming equipment and in the marketing of the produce through its distribution in stores. The leaders of the new

country saw the capitalist system as a threat to its existence and considered capitalism anathema to the values of humanity. The system sought to remove the blight of unemployment from the face of the earth, to rid the world of poverty, and to provide for the welfare of each person not according to that person's abilities, as in the capitalist system, but, in the spirit of Karl Marx and Friedrich Engels, to each according to the individual's specific needs.

The leaders of the Soviet Union accepted Marx's scientific socialist economics and recognized that the country had to undergo a stage of semicapitalist development, one that did not operate through the free markets with their business cycles and the unemployment and poverty that result from the cycle's depressions. To achieve this stage of development, both the agricultural and industrial sectors had to be built up rapidly if competition with the capitalist countries was to be viable and ultimately successful by bringing the capitalist countries down.

Under the influence of scientific socialism planning boards were established to regulate agricultural and industrial output and to set production quotas for the betterment of the economy. The problems of overproduction and underemployment were thus approached within an equilibrium method with the intention of keeping the economy on an even growth pattern. People had to be moved to the sectors that the planning boards considered most in need of skills and basic manpower, but the people, in whose name the revolution was undertaken, often did not understand this. Great diseconomies resulted, and much poverty and starvation brought tremendous suffering to a people that had not yet recovered from the war and the impact of the revolution. A dictator was required to establish the new Soviet Union and place it in a position of viable competition with the capitalist system. Josef Stalin became that dictator, and many good people were executed under his regime. One such person was Nikolai D. Kondratieff, an economist, who sought to understand the resilience of the capitalist system — a program that the Stalinists approved. But his findings were that within capitalism the cycle takes over for long periods, with minicycles occurring within the greater cycle. The capitalist system will hence always recover from its depressions in the long run, while short-run distortions will always exist. Capitalism, for Kondratieff, will always survive because of its inner cyclic dynamics. For his conclusions he was executed.

Brian J.L. Berry discussed three empirical patterns that Kondratieff discerned in the cycle and suggested that they may aid in understanding long waves. One pattern is that prior to and during the beginning of the rising wave of the long cycle, a society's economic life undergoes considerable changes. These changes are usually seen in production and exchange techniques preceded by significant technological discoveries and inventions, gold-production and money-circulation conditions, and/or involvement of new countries in worldwide economic relations.

The second pattern concerns the period of the rising long-wave cycle and is characterized by a far greater number of social upheavals and radical changes to society than the period of the downward wave. But the downward waves of the long cycles are characterized, in Kondratieff's view, by prolonged and serious depressions in agriculture. Concluding that the historical material relating to the development of economic and social life as a whole conforms to the hypothesis of long cyclical economic waves, Kondratieff argued that the strength of the capitalist system lies in its ability to exploit the long wave, to develop new technologies, to cope with the social upheavals and radical social changes, and to bring the depressions in agriculture to an end by the new technologies and social changes. These points were iterated by Berry in the following manner:

> 1. Prosperity and depression, with all their profound social implications, are tied to the upswings and downswings of the long waves.
> 2. During long-wave downswings agriculture suffers an especially pronounced depression.
> 3. During long-wave downswings a large number of important discoveries and inventions in production techniques and communications are made, but these must wait for the upswing to be fully implemented.
> 4. Worldwide gold production increases on the wave's upswing, and the global market for commodities and manufactured goods is enlarged by the assimilation of new national territories and colonies.
> 5. It is during the rise of the long waves that the most disastrous and extensive wars and revolutions occur, as a rule, because of the period of high tension caused by expanding economic forces. Also, the rising long wave is associated with the replacement and expansion of basic capital goods and the radical regrouping and changing of productive forces and the allocation of resources in society.[3]

But as Leontief indicated, statistical information about countries, unlike data in the laboratories of scientists, is obtained with difficulty. Moreover, as Joshua S. Goldstein has demonstrated, statistical interpretations differ, yielding differing theoretical conclusions among economists concerned with this issue.[4]

There is another element in the long-wave-cycle approach that was considered in part by Kondratieff, but has since become of great importance in the method of long-cycle research. This is the consideration of noneconomic forces and their influences on the economy.

One such force is war, which, according to Kondratieff, comes on the long-wave rise and is due to the high tension among the expanding economic forces. War, political efforts toward world hegemony, regional domination and the conflict for global domination, and the tendencies for world unification and for its fracture into socioeconomic units that stand in economic competition and perhaps verge on military confrontation are factors that have now become included in the long-wave cycle. The justification for these inclusions is that while economists have to isolate their specific branches of inquiry with the ceteris paribus clause, in the real world economics cannot be separated from politics and ultimately from global cooperation and conflict.

To a certain extent this is indeed the case. But little impact is made on the microeconomics of the firm in domestic competition by the political events in another faraway country. The difficulty with the long-wave theorists is that they are macroeconomic when they discuss their subject, but they are not macroeconomic in the traditional Keynesian sense of the word. Their problem area is not that of the national economy in isolation from other countries' economies — although the Keynesian economists that worked with trade theory first broke with this macroeconomic tradition. Their area of concern is the study of the long wave with its elements of economic growth and the economic, political, and social changes that result from the wave's motion. The consequences for the single competitive firm in the long wave's motion are like the personal history of a family circle during the period of a great epoch. The family is certainly influenced by the events that occur, and indeed, some of its members may rise to the occasion to shape these events. The individual competitive firm may expand and grow, occupying a major role in its markets over the long run, and this may be significant for micro and macro economists for study and analysis, and for those hired to advise. But this, in a sense, is being inside the economy and looking out; the method of the long-wave economists is based on the general overview, with glimpses into the economies to obtain statistics and other information, such as the political shifts within countries, military alliances, and economic shifts that result from significant changes in production, distribution, and marketing techniques. Using the statistics and the other information, they formulate their theories of the long wave.

During the development of economics as a body of scientific knowledge the various theories from Smith through Keynes and Milton Friedman finally came together as working bodies of knowledge in the scientific sense. Just as in physics there are the Einsteinians and the Heisenbergian quantum physicists, after World War II the separate bodies of economic theory merged into scientific schools that were able to be exploited and expanded upon. Granted, there was some unification prior to the Great Depression, but this unification was partial, with the unifying point being the neoclassical assumption of full employment.

The search for the long-wave cycle is part of the scientific endeavor undertaken to place economics on a more solid basis so that both the understanding of the past and present can be achieved more clearly, and projections into the future can be made on a firmer basis. The modern long-wave-cycle theories differ from that of Kondratieff, because Kondratieff sought the long wave to understand and explain the viability of the capitalist system. In his investigations he found that the Marxist calling for workers in the capitalist countries to unite in conflict against the owners of the means of production is unrealistic on a grand scale. What he found was a system that, from the Industrial Revolution's inception to World War I, had an internal strength to overcome its difficulties, incorporating the necessary accommodations that will allow for its continuance and strength.

The modern long-wave theorists have another set of problems to consider. These include the unification of Europe in the Common Market, the decline of the Soviet Union as a force and the rise of the Commonwealth of Independent States, the struggles for markets among the great postindustrialized powers, and the struggles on the African and South American continents. Indochina, with its vast population and inner strengths, is awakening after the nightmare of the Vietnam War, and the region is beginning to embark on serious economic activity. The Middle East still smoulders from its many wars, but now that U.S. hegemony is established in that region and the peace talks are under way, there are chances for a taming of the passions that run high there and for the introduction of reason based on economic needs and requirements. Given the near-harmonious phases of the cycle among the postindustrialized economies, and the influences of these economies on the emerging and developing economies, the study of the long wave has taken on a significance other than that ascribed to it by Kondratieff.

While this is certainly a scientific pursuit within the context of economics, the question must be raised as to its real significance. While there may indeed be long-term economic trends, their relevance for a specific business cycle is somewhat questionable. Granted, even during the pre-Industrial Revolution era there were business cycles of sorts. These took the form of market surpluses that drove prices down and market shortages that resulted in high prices. Such cycles operated within the framework of classical economic theory in which high prices result in increased production and competition, so that surpluses of a product are achieved and prices are brought down to clear the markets. They differed from the industrial business cycle that relies to a large extent on innovation and imitation. However, while elements of this classical cycle still exist, it is posited here that it is not the dynamics of the classical cycle that prevail today but of another type of cycle that will be discussed in detail in chapter[8].

Nevertheless, the long-wave cycles in the preindustrial period are those considered by Kondratieff and his contemporary followers. Study of these cycles is based methodologically on such constants over time as agriculture, building, and, in the noneconomic realm, geopolitical shifts. Although cycles in agriculture, building and construction, and political shifts within the geopolitical forces do exist, for building and agriculture these cycles are primarily economic; political elements are involved when economics is used as a geopolitical weapon, as is the case with embargoes. The cycles in political shifts are not really cycles in themselves, but are due to the dynamics of economics, such as occurred when the Soviet leaders sought to liberalize their economy to make it competitive with the European Community, Japan, and the United States.

This liberalization resulted in the realization that the heavily bureaucratic Soviet monolith could not compete effectively as such and led to the declaration of the independence of the former Soviet states and their formation into a commonwealth of independent states that could readily merge into an Eastern European common market capable of viable competition with the great contemporary powers.

While this is not the place to trace these cycles as they are manifested in agriculture, building and construction, and geopolitical shifts, comments must be made on such methodological pursuits. Brian Berry, for example, showed similar cyclical patterns over time from 1790 to 1990. While such patterns may demonstrate great similarities, they differ in one important point: the industrial and general economic infrastructural changes that have occurred during this two-hundred-year period. Cycles are formed by patterns, such as depressions and prosperity, and while such events certainly occurred during the time period that Berry was considering, the economy of 1990 would certainly be unfamiliar to a person who lived in the 1800s. The cyclical patterns may be similar, but their economic contents are extremely different. This is true even from the period 1945-55 to 1980-90.[5]

ON THE METHOD OF THIS WORK: AN ALTERNATIVE APPROACH TO THE LONG-WAVE CYCLE

Whether long-wave cycles exist or not is not really significant for contemporary economics. To state that such cycles exist and then to attempt to plot them may be significant for a branch of economic thought that could perhaps be termed 'metaeconomics,' but it is certainly not relevant for economists and politicians concerned with the everyday life of the economies. The point of the existence of business cycles was recognized by the early classical economists. Both Smith and Ricardo, for example, discussed cycles in markets, Smith with respect to production and Ricardo with respect to the value of land. Malthus discussed the longer-trend cycle in food supplies and population, and Say's law of markets is itself a regulator of small cyclic fluctuations over the short run.[6] Moreover, to argue that there will be business cycles and political shifts among the world's countries contributes very little to the understanding of the economic and political dynamics of our world. The long-wave-cycle theorists may plot economic, political, and war cycles in the past — and among these theorists there are significant discrepancies concerning the cycles' durations and even their dates — and here they may have contributions to make to the bodies of economic, political, and military knowledge; but this is the study of history. To make viable assessments about the future as a result of the past studies of the long waves is futurology, an interesting discipline in itself, but also erratic and very often in serious error when the present and the future meet in the dates of the futuristic scenario.[7]

This does not mean that another approach to long-wave cycles cannot be considered without these difficulties, but to do so is to minimize the metaeconomics involved in such an endeavor. It is posited here, therefore, that cycles, as integral parts of economics, are long-wave in the sense that they are both era and social-time oriented. The business cycles that occurred during the Industrial Revolution were certainly different in dimension and in content from those of our contemporary historical era. Moreover, a cycle of such depth and extent as that of the Great Depression, brought about by the extreme rise in the stock markets and the decline of the Industrial Revolution, cannot exist again. The attitudes to international commerce now differ from those during the depression, so that worldwide economic relations are not worsened by obsolete and ineffective techniques such as tariffs and devaluations as beggar-thy-neighbor policies.

Another difference is that the world's economies have become so interrelated that a recession in the United States bears directly on the cyclic downturn in all other countries. The development stage of a particular country makes no difference here, because of the interrelationships among the countries and the effects that a major economy has on all the others.

Of course, a similar influence was exerted during the Great Depression, when the major industrial countries were experiencing a major downward cyclical turn. This curtailed their trading, their economic activities, and of course their financial support for their client states. The difference, however, lies in the extent to which such prosperous economies as those of Singapore and South Korea rely on the economies of Great Britain, France, the United States, and the other highly developed economies for their technologies and their markets. A slowdown in economic activity usually results in a decline in technological developments because of the unemployemnt and the lack of marketing that exist. When the developing economies exploit the same technologies, they enter into competition, both domestically and internationally, with the postindustrial economies; the latter's advantage in resources, infrastructure, and marketing ability, as well as the international prestige of their products, sets this competition entirely to the postindustrial economies' advantage, and even the logistical problems of markets are overcome by multinational corporations. Moreover, the isolationism that existed in U.S. policy prior to its involvement in World War II restricted its economic activity within the spirit of fair trading, allowing the focus of economic activity to be centered on protecting domestic industry in light of the Great Depression. In trade the policies were those of its trading partners, defensive and protective, and this lengthened the duration of the crisis. The insights gained after the war were then lacking. After the war's conclusion the realization that a stable world economy could contribute greatly to world peace brought the United States into the new era as the major economic force, building up both the victors and the vanquished and facing the Soviet Union and its newly acquired allies in the Cold War. The cycles associated with the Industrial Revolution ceased with the Great Depression, and those associated with our contemporary era, in which the former Soviet states have become independent and the economies in their various stages of development have become closely interrelated. Cycles exist, but they are long-wave only in the sense of their permanence as a phenomenon of economic activity. But for each cycle the dynamics are different and the circumstances are different, but usually the remedies for the recessions are those applied in the previous recessions. During the recession in the 1970s, for example, the Soviet Union was still a force to be contended with, and the thought of United Nations involvement in a war with Iraq was never considered. In the current economic situation the remnants of the Soviet Union are vieing for aid and for markets for trade, while the European Economic Community is coming together as an economic force for serious competition with the United States, Japan, and other industrial nonmembers. The dynamics of the business cycle are permanent, but the manner in which they are manifested depends on the particular social time, as expressed by the innovation, imitation, industrial composition, and subsequent market development in the historical era.

The treatment of economic development in this work will therefore pertain to contemporary conditions as they exist in our current social time. The analysis of the long economic waves will be left to those theorists concerned with metaeconomics, who can argue their individual opinions and formulate their differing long-wave cycles. Kondratieff had begun a project for which much work still remains to be done, but the problems of contemporary development and the role the business cycle has in this activity are too pressing in our changing world to be set aside, and the treatment of economic development and the business cycle within our present context is the material of the present volume.

NOTES

1. Wassily Leontief, "Theoretical Assumptions and Nonobserved Facts," in Leontief, *Essays in Economics* (New Brunswick, N.J.: Transaction Books, 1985), p. 280.

2. Leontief, "Theoretical Assumptions and Nonobserved Facts," p. 282.

3. See Brian J.L. Berry's interesting work, *Long-Wave Rhythms in Economic Development and Political Behavior* (Baltimore: Johns Hopkins University Press, 1991), pp. 39-40. Berry's points have been restated somewhat for brevity.

4. See, for example, Joshua S. Goldstein, *Long Cycles* (New Haven: Yale University Press, 1988), chapts. 1-7, pp. 1-172. In his part 3, "History", Goldstein looked at the political and economic cycles from 1485 into our present era and projected into the future.

5. See Berry, *Long-Wave Rhythms in Economic Development and Political Behavior,* app. A, "Price Dynamics: The Growth Rates of Prices Smoothed by Successively Longer Moving Averages," and app. B, "Growth Dynamics: The Growth Rates of Real Per Capita GNP Smoothed by Successively Longer Moving Averages," pp. 199-211. For both appendices the time span is from 1790 to 1990.

6. See Adam Smith, *An Inquiry into the Nature and Causes of the Wealth of Nations,* ed. Edwin Cannan (London: Methuen, 1950); T.R. Malthus, *An Essay on the Principle of Population* (New York: Random House, 1960); David Ricardo, *On the Principles of Political Economy and Taxation,* ed. P. Sraffa (Cambridge: Cambridge University Press, 1951); and J.B. Say, *Treatise on Political Economy* Trans. C.R. Prinsep. (London: Longman, Hurst, Rees, Orme, and Brown, 1821). With respect to Say's argument in modern economic thought, see David Z. Rich, *Contemporary Economics: A Unifying Approach* (New York: Praeger, 1986), pp. 8-25.

7. See, for example, Herman Kahn, with William Brown, Leon Martel, and the Hudson Institute, *The Next 200 Years* (New York: Wm. Morrow, 1976). The contemporary futurologists, unlike Nostradamus, are extremely sophisticated and far from vague.

Part II

THE THEORY OF ECONOMIC
DEVELOPMENT

Chapter 4

STAGES OF ECONOMIC GROWTH

In surveying now the broad contours of each step-of-growth we are
examining, then, not merely the sectorial structure of economies, as they
transformed themselves for growth and grew; we are also examining a
succession of strategic choices made by various societies concerning the
disposition of their resources, which include but transcend the income
— and price-elasticities of demand.

W.W. Rostow,
The Stages of Economic Growth [1]

"Social systems," wrote Jürgen Habermas, "regulate their exchanges with
their social and natural environments by way of coordinated interventions
into the external world."[2] The external world to which Habermas referred
is that of the other social systems, each different in its unique history and
social ethos, yet each similar because the people who compose each of them
have similar needs and wants. Rostow's sentiment referred to a society in
its process of growth from what he termed the "take-off" to maturity
from a primarily national macroeconomic position. Habermas's opinion
can be considered as social development within an international macro-
oriented social system. While Habermas's concern was not specifically with
economics, his view can be interpreted as being internationally economic
oriented because within the framework of international economics countries'
interventions into the external world by way of the international markets
provide coordinated economic relations among the exporting and importing
countries. Through the processes of international trade people become
acquainted with other cultures and societies; in our current economic
and political situation, in which the European Economic Community
is coming into its own as a viable trading bloc, and in which great
changes are taking place in Russia and Eastern Europe, as well as in

the developments of economies being opened throughout the world, the dynamics of international trade are very useful in breaking down hostilities among nations that have existed previously. Habermas's statement can be expanded by saying that the natural and social environments of societies are their internal and external ambiences. Their internal ambiences include their natural resources and economic infrastructures; their external ambiences include their geographical neighbors, with whom they carry on political and economic relations in the best of times and political conflict and war in the worst of times.

We are witnessing two distinct trends in our geopolitical economic world, trends that are neverless bound by the common factor of the business cycle: the dissolving of such unions as the Soviet Union, whose former member countries still maintain relations but seek their own destinies, and the formation of the Common Market, whose members have united even though they have histories of hatred, violence, and two world wars. We are also witnessing countries undergoing various phases of development, and this entails maintaining good relations with their geographical neighbors as well as with other countries outside their immediate geographical spheres. We are seeing nations looking into their own cultures and histories for their sources of strength in our changing and uncertain world, while at the same time they are looking outward, seeking to expand their political and economic influences. Those countries in the emerging and underdeveloped phases of their economic situations must rely heavily on their international macroeconomics for aid and trade, while the postindustrial economies have their problems with international competition, as manifested in the paradox of industrialization and the consequent employment effect. With respect to the emerging and developing countries, issue must be taken with Rostow's stages of economic growth. Even in such war-torn countries as the Sudan and Ethiopia, where hunger is rife because of the wars and climatic conditions, the validity of Rostow's points must be questioned. While he stated that the stages of growth are an arbitrary and limited way of looking at the sequence of modern history and are in fact in no absolute sense a correct way, he added: "They are designed, in fact, to dramatize not merely the uniformities in the sequence of modernization, but also — and equally — the uniqueness of each nation's experience."[3] To dramatize the uniqueness of each nation's experience would require an in-depth analysis of each nation's history and its development. This is certainly not within the scope of Rostow's work; nor indeed can a single work do justice to such a vast and tremendous undertaking. His stages of growth are legitimate in the sense that they provide a basis for analysis of general principles of economic development; as such, therefore, they are subject to critique.

Rostow's first stage refers to what he termed the "traditional society," in which its economic structure is developed within the framework of pre-

Newtonian that is, pre-Industrial Revolution attitudes toward the physical world. He stated that the traditional society is in no sense static, but that a ceiling exists on the level of attainable output per capita. These societies have to devote a very high proportion of their resources to agriculture and thus rely on the political systems that have emerged through the societies' evolution. Power generally lies in the hands of those who control the lands in which agriculture is extensive.

The second stage, that of the preconditions for the take-off, occurs when the insights of modern, that is, Newtonian, science begin to become absorbed in the economy and to be translated into new production techniques for industry and agriculture. There is a conflict during this stage as economic development occurs in societies still mainly characterized by traditional low-productivity methods, by the old social structures and values, and also by the politically based institutions that evolved with them. Indeed, Rostow maintained that a decisive factor in entering the pre take-off stage is often political, in which political changes are initiated to provide the basis of the take-off stage; he considers this as an almost universally necessary condition in this stage leading to the take-off.

The third stage, that of take-off, is the interval when the old blocs and resistance to steady growth are finally overcome. The forces of economic progress, which hitherto yielded limited modern activity, expand and begin to dominate the societies. Growth becomes the economic norm, and compound interest is built into the societies' habits and institutional structures. Effective savings may rise from 5 percent to 10 percent or more, and new industries expand rapidly, yielding profits, a large proportion of which is reinvested in new plants. Supporting industries are developed, resulting in the expansion of industries and businesses into urban areas and areas hitherto untouched. Agriculture undergoes revolutionary changes because of the applications of new techniques, so that modernization of societies requires an effective agricultural base to supply produce to feed the working population.

The fourth stage, the drive to maturity, follows a long period of sustained but fluctuating progress as the growing economies strive to extend modern technology over the entire economic front. Some 15 to 20 percent of the national income is steadily invested, allowing output to outstrip the growing population. The economies change as production techniques improve, allowing new and modern industries to accelerate in growth while older and less technologically advanced industries level off in production and sometimes close down. These economies become active internationally, with goods and services formerly imported being produced domestically and new products and services being exported. It is during this stage that the economies demonstrate their abilities to produce any goods and services they choose, given international competition.

The fifth stage that Rostow discussed is that of the age of high mass consumption, where the leading economic sectors shift to the manufacture of durable goods and services. Real per capita income rises to a point where a large number of persons gain a command over consumption that transcends basic food, clothing, and shelter. The structure of the working force has changed in ways that have increased both the proportion of urban to total population and the proportion of those working in offices and in skilled factory jobs. Rostow pointed out that these economies cease to accept further extensions of modern technology as an overriding objective.

In critique it can be said that no economy today is in a traditional-society stage as discussed by Rostow. The advances in communications, the dynamics of international politics, and influences of the postindustrial societies are predominant in the emerging and developing societies to the extent that while traditional values of these societies are important, they are not in severe conflict in the long run with the forces of economic change due to the introduction of new technologies. The conflicts with tradition come from the youth, who question the values of their elders as they seek to find their way and formulate their own values, ones — in their opinion — of greater importance and lasting significance.

With regard to the second stage of the preconditions for take-off, the fruits of modern technology exist even in those economies in their earliest stages of emergence. The automobile, the airplane and airports, and advanced communications systems exist in these countries, although they perhaps have not yet "trickled down" to the general population. Low-productivity methods of manufacture exist along with more technological methods, obtained through the pressures of international politics and through these countries playing the big-power game of using their strategic positions for economic and political favors. The political conflicts in these countries are not due to the repression of modern technologies, but to the struggle for power by those who consider themselves best able to lead their countries in the contemporary economic and political situation.

With respect to the third stage, in the emerging countries the old guard is struggling with the younger forces, and revolutions are certainly not infrequent. This type of struggle is not for changes in values, however, but for changes in regimes. Granted, during such struggles the economies are hurt by reallocation of resources from growth to revolutions, but economic take-off — to use Rostow's term — does not depend on the old versus the new regimes, as both seek economic growth. These revolutions take place for power and nothing else. As for industries expanding rapidly, this depends on the extent of both domestic and foreign demand, and this requires marketing and very often the support of postindustrialized countries. Agriculture expands according to the abilities of these countries to exploit their lands. This depends on the quality of the soil, the types of crops that will grow in the soil, and the uses of advanced agricultural technologies to adopt different crops within the countries. The availability of abundant nonsaline water is also significant; in the Sudan and Ethiopia the lack of water is a serious problem, albeit aggravated still further by the continuing struggles for power in these countries.

Concerning the drive to maturity, the world's countries today have not the luxury of such a drive in itself. After two world wars and the subsequent battles that have taken place throughout the world, as well as the disruptive and often indecisive revolutions, the leisure of a 10 to 20 percent steady investment of national income is difficult to attain. Moreover, some sectors of the emerging and developing economies are able to absorb high technologies — defense and communications are examples — while other sectors, such as construction and domestic public transportation, usually fall behind.

Finally, with regard to the fifth stage, the possession of such durable goods as refrigerators, washing machines, and automobiles is found in various secotrs of the emerging and developing economies. There is relatively high mass consumption of domestic and foreign products, but the control of demand beyond basic food, clothing, and shelter depends more on the largesse of the governments than on per capita purchasing power. There are shifts into urban areas because this is where industries and their supporting businesses reside, but agriculture still plays an important role. But neither the emerging, the developing, nor the postindustrial economies have ceased to accept the further extension of technology as an overriding objective; competition among the postindustrial economies, for example, encourages the further exploitation of technologies in all branches of production and consumer uses. Hence the stage of high mass consumption is oriented to the production and purchasing of increasingly sophisticated and improved products. Indeed, these are often the attractions for the emerging and developing economies, leading to situations unacceptable in the postindustrial societies such as televisions in homes without running water, as is sometimes the case in the emerging economies. Still another point to be made about this fifth stage concerns the existence of sectors in countries in which deprived peoples live near those priviledged by the legal system. Such is the case of the black townships in South Africa that are suburbs of the wealthier white areas. While the legal system maintaining apartheid in South Africa has been abolished, the change in public opinion that will renovate the black townships and bring them up to the standards of the wealthier sections, making interracial contacts that much easier on the social level, is still yet to come. Until this happens, South Africa, and also countries in South America and in Indochina, have the conditions not of the advanced postindustrial economies, but of the emerging economies. In this situation the advanced sectors seek the benefits of high mass consumption, while the emerging sectors seek the take-off stage, hoping to achieve this through the intermingling of the sectors. Apartheid has been officially abolished in South Africa, and it does not exist legally in any other country. The problem has therefore shifted from being racial in orientation to being economic in orientation, as it should be.

Just as Rostow's fifth stage of economies being in high mass consumption is questionable, so are his other stages. What Rostow has in fact provided is a five-stage plan for economic growth and development suitable for the Industrial Revolution, but certainly not for now. His discussion of the traditional society as being pre-Newtonian in its technological situation certainly does not exist in any country in our era. There are sectors that the Newtonian revolution seems to have bypassed, but the people in these sectors are familiar with automobiles and have seen airplanes flying. It is not the Newtonian revolution that has missed these sectors, but real economic development and growth, usually due to politics, wars, and resentment that keep these peoples isolated and lacking the benefits of economic progress. This resentment is perhaps due to religious beliefs in which cultural and physical separation may be practiced. But such cultural practices have existed throughout history without preventing the benefits of economic progress. Religion and politics can be used to keep peoples isolated in Rostow's traditional-society sense, but the dynamics of economic progress result in the loosening of the hold of tradition in those sectors in which it still dominates. This loosening is not in Rostow's sense that the Newtonian revolution is felt and economics wins over tradition, but is in the sense that the benefits of economic growth are felt, that tradition adapts to these new forces of economics, and that politics seeks the exploitation of these forces.

The take-off stage as such is absent in the contemporary economics of the emerging countries. These countries engage in international trade, selling their natural resources. Unfortunately, as these are often single products and several countries export these products, a surplus of supplies in the world markets reduces the prices for these products and affects adversely these countries' foreign currency holdings. As these countries' economies are not sufficiently self-sustaining, they have to rely on imports, and with depleted foreign currency holdings their ability to import is seriously limited. Moreover, the drastic rises in the price of oil and other energy sources over the years following the 1973 Yom Kippur War have forced the emerging and developing countries to rely increasingly on their abilities to maneuver among the big powers for economic aid and trade, and their client-state positions have restricted their own abilities to achieve economic growth. Because their economies are weakened by their dependence, these countries are more susceptible to palace revolutions in which the governments are overthrown resulting in the consequent changes in the domestic economy, but externally there is business as usual. The luxury of a 5 to 10 percent steady investment of the national product per annum is certainly lacking in these countries. Their budgets tend to be short-run, directed to supplying basic goods and services for their populations and to purchasing weapons to defend their borders from neighbors that appear to them to have expansionist policies. Their reliance on the industrialized countries for their weapons systems and political support also inhibits their independence, because the client-patron relations must be maintained.

This situation is even more critical now than at the time that Rostow described his five growth stages. The big-power game has undergone a reorganization and redirection. Because the Soviet Union is no longer a force, and the countries that once composed this union are themselves in various stages of economic development, the rules of the big-power game have changed. No longer is support offered to the once-contending powers in return for economic aid and military assistance. In the era of the establishment of the European Economic Community, the rise of Japan as an economic power, and U.S. military and economic dominance throughout the world, the emerging countries — and to some extent the developing countries — are seeking economic favors in the form of the moral suasion for aid and trade, without the previous bargaining card of providing political support in the international arena. The emerging and developing countries are achieving economic development and growth not as Rostow described them, but by receiving aid and engaging in trade, by opening their economies to multinational corporations that provide their citizens with education and training, and by seeking to maintain political stability and provide for the welfare of their citizens.

Those countries that Rostow placed within the stage of the drive to maturity are also engaged in mass consumption to the extent that it exists in their markets. Usually, the reference to those economies in their drive to maturity is to the developing countries, as they have already more than a basic infrastructure and their internal industries exhibit strong competition to the benefit of the consumers when governments abstain from levying taxes to increase revenues and reduce consumption in the attempt to encourage these industries to turn to international markets. Nevertheless, where such taxation is levied — in the form of value-added taxes, purchase taxes, or whatever the taxes may be — high cheating on taxes allows for mass consumption to continue to a certain extent, with industries seeking greater profits in the highly competitive international markets. In this respect governments achieve their objective of forcing their successful industries into international competition, but this success is only partial. Such industries are certainly not prepared to take on their competitors from the postindustrial countries. The governments of these developing countries therefore have to seek aid and other benefits such as free-trade zones and favored-nation status, so that tariffs against their products are either reduced significantly or eliminated altogether, while reciprocal tariffs are also eliminated in the case of the free-trade zones, or are maintained to give their own domestic industries the competitive edge in the domestic markets, while allowing these industries to continue development — this with the consent of their postindustrial trading partners.

However, the emerging economies are also mass-consumption oriented as far as their currencies will allow and as far as their markets are stocked. Of course, their economic infrastructures are just beginning to be developed, and their markets are primitive in the areas of advertising and the mobility of goods and services. But consumption is there, and it is mass consumption with respect to the economies' abilities to provide goods and services. Imports are high, and foreign currency holdings fluctuate with the export of these countries' chief products. In their processes of emergence these countries recognize the difficulties of relying on one or only a few natural resources, because international price fluctuations of these resources due to supply and demand have adverse dynamic effects on their economies. Through their foreign currency holdings and the strengths of their national currencies they seek to expand their economies. But because their infrastructures are lacking in this process, they turn to international organizations such as the World Bank and the International Monetary Fund for assistance. Also, they seek help from the postindustrial countries and often turn to commercial banks to finance national projects, for which the funding is backed by the guarantees of the emerging and developing countries' governments and central banks. Unfortunately, as in the case of Zaire, for example, many of these countries are unable to pay both the principal and the interest and have to call for debt rescheduling or threaten forfeiture. Prior to the decline of the Soviet Union these countries could employ the big-power game and threaten to move from one camp to the other if favorable terms for debt rescheduling were withheld. This game no longer exists, and governments are being more careful in their borrowing and in their negotiations for terms of payment and interest rates. The reasons why these countries had this difficulty was the lack of consideration of the utility of money when these projects were planned. The reluctance of a vocal opposition to make itself heard was also a factor when these projects went through, and the relative ease with which these emerging and developing countries could play one superpower off against the other for political favors and financial support was an almost-certain guarantee that they could receive the backing they sought.

The dissolution of the Soviet Union and the various stages of political and economic development of its composite countries mean that the bargaining position once enjoyed by the emerging and developing countries no longer exists, and their considerations for national undertakings must be the very same as those of the postindustrial countries. These are whether the project as proposed will achieve its objective, or other proposals can be more effective; the utility of money invested in the project, in the sense that the money might be better spent for other projects; and finally whether the funding can be provided by private sources or strictly public sources or a combination of both. Floating bonds for such projects may be proposed, and hence the public's response is a fairly good indicator of the project's utility.

Countries exploit their export potential, no matter at what stage they are in economic development. The difficulty for the developing and emerging countries in this respect is to determine just what goods and services they have that are exportable. Those countries with single products are subject to market-price fluctuations for the demand of these products, and as experience has shown with such products as coffee, copper, and, to some extent, petroleum, countries' fortunes are made and broken by the fickle markets. Often close substitutes are found for these products, either in untapped resources or as the result of industrial or scientific research. A valid indicator that a country is moving into emergence, therefore, is that country's attempt to seek export-market diversification and to obtain foreign currencies on the basis of its own merits as a producer. Otherwise, the country stagnates and remains at the mercy of the postindustrial countries for their largesse.

Developing countries, by this standard, are those that have already achieved a degree of export-market diversification. In their emergence stage they applied with utility the resources available to construct viable infrastructure in the form of roads, rail transport, airport facilities, and, where their geographies entitle them to waterways, efficient docks for shipping and receiving. Moreover, their governments encouraged private enterprise and competition while applying monetary and fiscal techniques to combat inflation in their small but growing domestic markets. Hence a criterion for a country to be entering the stage of emergence is the beginning of the formation of the business cycle within its economy. Another criterion is the concern for welfare, for coping with the unemployment that becomes an official statistic as soon as the business cycle sets in. With concerns over employment come the unions, and the demarcations between government, industry, and labor are established. Once government is firmly established not only to govern politically, but to exert its influence over the economy, once industry is sufficiently strong not only to provide domestic competition but also to place on the foreign markets diversified exports, including tourism, which has its own unique infrastructure, and once labor is sufficiently entrenched in industry to provide a viable voice for its own self-interest and an opposition to both governmental and industrial wage and welfare policies, this country has moved from the emerging to the developing stage of growth.

The move from being a developing country to being a postindustrial country is not as smooth. It requires the applications of advanced technologies to industry, communications, and educational methods. Developing countries can achieve this with the proper training for their talented peoples, but the transition requires more than this. People in developing countries study in the postindustrial countries and bring their education back to their own countries.[4] But this is a one-way street, because educational and technological leaders do not go to the developing countries unless they are invited or are on vacations or sabbaticals. However, such traffic is two-way among the postindustrial countries, and this is one important criterion for assessing whether a country has moved into the postindustrial stage. There is another criterion that is very important. This is the ability for people in the country to innovate new technologies and to apply them within their own national borders. This means that there is sufficient technological infrastructure for the various aspects of such innovations to be developed with the country's resources. Where such projects are undertaken in the developing countries, they are usually government financed or backed by foreign sources, such as grants. The postindustrial societies have the resources, private or in the form of grants, to finance these projects, and the economy is able to absorb the projects, providing they achieve the objectives attributed to them, while the developing countries tend to export the projects to the postindustrial countries because their own economies are not sufficiently technologically oriented to absorb the projects.

Hence the move from being a developing country to being a postindustrial society is not the smooth transition that exists between the emerging countries and the developing countries. The transition is not evolutionary in the sense that exists between the emerging and developing countries, where rational planning, the development of viable infrastructure, the exploitation of natural and competitive resources among entrepreneurs, the establishment of serious competition, the rise of a viable labor force capable of protecting its own interests, and the concern for society's welfare and the ability to provide for that welfare demonstrate the evolution. Nor is Rostow's requirement of a specific amount set aside from national income to be reinvested particularly relevant. Investments are important, but they are based on the utility of invested monies — a concept to be discussed within macroeconomic terms in chapter 6.

What is required is a concerted effort by the governments and the peoples of these developing countries to upgrade their technological capabilities and move up to the stage of the postindustrial countries. This cannot be done merely by copying the systems and the attitudes of the postindustrial societies. Such copying is beneficial in the learning process because it aids understanding of how these societies are oriented, how they function, and on what bases they provide for the development of viable technologies. But applying these very same procedures in the developing countries is not very efficient and often leads to both economic and social distortions. The histories, national characters, and evolved attitudes of the postindustrial societies differ among themselves and certainly differ from those of the developing economies. The governments and peoples of the developing societies must therefore develop their own technological infrastructures and provide the foundations for research and the applications of the products derived from such research. This does not necessarily mean that governments must accept the responsibility for such research. Indeed, where governments are too involved in developing economies, the entire process of economic growth tends toward politicization, with the result being that the emphasis becomes focused on politics rather than on the quality of research. In this situation there is a tendency for many political parties to be formed as the focus on political power becomes intense. This leads to the disutility of money as many parties seek to gather funds for their own political ideas. Electioneering is costly, and where the emphasis should be placed on research and development, it is directed instead to gaining the public's vote and using the small parties as leverages against the bigger parties to obtain their own special interests and public financing. This statement is, of course, not an attempt to deride the democratic processes, for it is held here that democracy is necessary for economic growth; a healthy growing country must be internally competitive, and this also holds for politics and the exchange of political ideas. But a balance must be struck between democratic politics and the utility of money, for if too much money is directed toward supporting government officials instead of into research, the technological breakthroughs necessary for the countries to move into the postindustrial stage will be withheld. Hence governments, while they are important in financing research, must not become too involved. It is up to industries and academic institutions to support research, and because these countries have moved into the development stage, their resources are that much greater than they were during the emerging stage. In the advance of unique technologies, therefore, industries and academic institutions have to be involved in order to maintain these countries' competitive postures.

As for the postindustrial societies, both internal and foreign competition are extremely rigorous. When markets are saturated, further liquidity necessary for innovation is difficult and costly to come by. Moreover, under policies of the previous social time easy money for risky investments was made available by banks and savings and loan institutions, many of which were brought to bankruptcy when loans were not paid back because of the failure of the investments for which the borrowing was granted. Among the postindustrial societies this has generated a serious debt situation that has been aggrevated by their investments in those emerging and developing economies who in turn could not repay the investments and the interest according to the terms under which the investments were made.

These internal and external financial problems have resulted in a new frugality on the part of postindustrial governments and their peoples. However, this has led to another serious difficulty, one that is contributing to the depth of the current recession and will be responsible for the very slow movement upward of all subsequent business cycles. As money has become tight and a greater conservatism in its spending has been practiced by both governments and their citizens, the welfare situation has worsened. Job training is required for the unemployed to gain an understanding of the new industrial realities. Businesses that once employed many people and used auxiliary businesses as suppliers and for transportation and distribution have closed down, threatening the existence of those still operating because of the decline in general consuming power. People on the unemployment rolls are increasing in number, and governments are having to finance the unemployment. This burden on the governments is a financial strain with little or no utility, depending on the results of long-term job retraining programs. Competition in the aggregate has thus declined, and what remains becomes even more strenuous as further labor cuts are initiated to keep production costs as low as possible so that profits can be made and competition maintained.

Moreover, because of the rigors or external competition for markets both in other postindustrial societies and in those of the developing and emerging economies, foreign trade is becoming more multinational-corporation oriented to cut production and shipping costs and to concentrate in the general areas in which markets exist or are being developed. This multinational-corporation phenomenon began during the Industrial Revolution, in which foreign-based industries had branches in domestic economies. But in that era, although competition was strenuous between the foreign-based companies and the domestic companies producing similar products, there was no serious paradoxical situation in which the major industries were affected. In our era, however, because of the extensive technological developments and the abilities of the postindustrial economies to absorb these developments regardless of the countries in which they originate, the production of similar products and the export of these products into countries whose industries are also competitive for these products result in a paradox. This is the paradox of industrialization, and it is affecting the further growth of the postindustrial societies as they now exist.

The paradox can be expressed as follows. The U.S., British, German, and French economies produce automobiles. Their production processes reflect their internal and external competitive positions, so that they have to produce automobiles with the latest technological and safety features. However, for their full lines of production, and because of rigorous internal competition, the production lines of these companies are programed to supply their share of the domestic market and to produce exports as well. But in order to export automobiles, these countries must receive imports from the other automobile-producing countries, and these exports are in kind. Hence if countries are to sell their automobiles, they must offer discounts and rebates and appeal to patriotism, while their foreign competitors, to protect their interests, must use the same policies. The consequences of such rigorous domestic and foreign competition are reductions in sales for the individual companies, the necessity to lay off workers, the decline in consumption of materials and parts necessary to manufacture, which causes further layoffs in the auxiliary industries, and the serious decline in liquidity required for further research and production of next-generation automobiles with still more advances in their technologies.

The paradox of modern industrialization, therefore, is that the more technological industry becomes, the more competitive it has to be; the greater the competition, both domestic and foreign, the lower the revenues and net profits. As these decline, so does the labor force that works the industries, and this spreads throughout the auxiliary industries, resulting in a downswing of the business cycle as aggregate consumption declines due to the layoffs in industries. Hence competition has resulted in unemployment and the closure of businesses that once were mainstays of the postindustrial societies. This decline in consumption affects the total production of postindustrial societies and also affects the exporting countries as consumption of their products also declines. The spreading of unemployment in one postindustrial society generates the negative employment effect, so that all postindustrial societies experience declining consumption and further unemployment, placing a burden on their welfare systems. The paradox is realized glaringly when in highly technological and industrial societies the unemployment lines are long and industries are operating at low levels, while other industries and businesses that supported them are closing down. This paradox and its declining business cycle will be discussed further in chapter 8.

Hence, unlike Rostow's five stages of economic growth, three stages are to be considered here: the emerging countries, the developing countries, and the postindustrial countries. The latter stage does not reflect the mature economy, in which a Say-like situation of aggregate demand being met with an equivalent aggregate supply exists. Each of these stages is dynamic; the first two aspire to the third, and the third advances technologically due to internal and external competition. A mature-state condition of sorts exists in the postindustrial societies when the cycle moves into the downswing recession phase of the cycle as innovation — a term yet to be clarified — slows down and market saturation sets in. Recession sets in as a result of the paradox of industrialization, and when the cycle begins its upward movements, it is because this paradox is no longer valid.

If countries had the leisure to develop at their own paces, then perhaps Rostow's descriptions would be valid. But in the real world of both political and economic changes, especially during our social time when the great empire of the Soviet Union has collapsed and its former member countries have formed an uncertain confederation of independent states with signs of border conflicts and hostilities emerging from the breakup, countries lack the leisure time to move from traditionalist societies to those of high mass consumption. But people want to work, to earn, and to achieve the luxuries that money can purchase; they are unwilling to undergo separate industrial revolutions, especially when the technologies exist for establishing viable production lines and for achieving high growth. The time element is relevant when these technologies have to be transplanted and knowledge about the workings of such technologies has to be gained.

This is the process of emerging into the technological conditions for genuine internal and foreign competition, and for developing economies to enter the third stage of the postindustrial societies by making their own viable technological contributions and exploiting them within their own industrial infrastructures.

These points will be discussed further in part III, Chapter 8, of this work. What now needs to be considered, however, is the single economic factor that unites the three stages of growth. This is the business cycle, and its uniting force is seen by noting that when the postindustrial economies decline, then so do the emerging and developing economies that are dependent on them. When the postindustrial business cycles rise, then so do those of the emerging and developing economies. This is not a two-sided relationship in which the emerging and developing economies affect the postindustrial economic cycles; it is strictly one-sided because of the dependence of the emerging and developing countries who can no longer engage in big-power playoffs against the superpowers now that the Soviet Union has collapsed and its former member countries have become reliant on the postindustrial societies. It is the business cycle that is the uniting economic factor, and this cycle and its implications for the emerging and developing countries must now be discussed.

NOTES

1. W.W. Rostow, *The Stages of Economic Growth: A Non-Communist Manifesto* (New York: Cambridge University Press, 1961), p. 16.

2. Jürgen Habermas, "The Uncoupling of System and Lifeworld," in *Jürgen Habermas on Society and Politics,* ed. Steven Seidman (Boston: Beacon Press, 1989), p. 194.

3. Rostow, *Stages of Economic Growth,* p. 1.

4. The immigration of talented peoples to the postindustrial societies is understandable to those who have lived in emerging or developing economies. Thus sending young, talented people to the postindustrial societies entails the risk they will not return and reside permanently in their countries of origin. The attraction is certainly strong to move to the postindustrial societies, but in unified Germany, France with its strict immigration laws, Great Britain, which has an obligation to citizens of the Commonwealth but observes it reluctantly, and the United States which has begun strengthening its immigration laws and is cracking down on illegal immigrants, this attraction has its price. Legal foreign residents are granted their status because they have come to these countries for a purpose; overstaying their time or seeking citizenship in their residence countries is difficult.

The emigration of talent, however, does not pertain to the migration from the emerging and developing countries to the postindustrial societies only. Often there is migration from one postindustrial society to another because of job opportunities, cultural affiliations, or personal reasons. Such migration does not come under the title of 'brain drain,' however, because the migration of talented peoples among the postindustrial societies has no serious effect on their development, while for the emerging and developing countries this loss is significant.

Chapter 5

THE BUSINESS CYCLE: CONCEPTS AND TOOLS

> Macro policies should, to be sure, seek to stabilize expectations of the course of the economy, a task scarcely separable from that of stabilizing the actual course. This cannot be done by sticking to rules of policy that insulate it from feedbacks of information about the economy or from observations and expectations of other shocks. How it can be done, better than in the past, is a quest that continues to deserve the attention of economic theorists and econometricians.
>
> James Tobin,
> *Asset Accumulation and Economic Activity*₁

PRELIMINARY REMARKS

A strong indicator for assessing whether a people has abandoned its stagnant and strict traditionalist commitments is whether its society is undergoing change and the semblance of a business cycle is being formed. The transition from a strict traditionalist social structure to that of an emerging economy may take on various degrees of subtlety that are perhaps unrecognizable to an outside observer, but the beginnings of a business cycle are certainly recognizable, and this is an indication that the social structure is undergoing changes sufficient to allow for private commerce, the establishment of economic infrastructure, and the beginnings of competition. It indicates also that a labor force is forming to protect its own interests in this dynamic situation. This is the real transition from the traditionalist society to the emerging economy in our contemporary era, not the transition described by Rostow. These countries require assistance and aid in order to speed up the process. The profit motive in the newly established businesses provides for the competition necessary to stimulate consumption and the rise of auxiliary businesses and also results in the development of increased infrastructure on the part of government. Moreover, as in all businesses, the profit motive is based on expectations founded on the feedback of information within the domestic and foreign markets, the very information at the disposal of a government whose policies indicate its own awareness and interpretation of this information with respect to its expectations.

The transition to the status of a developing economy requires the sophistication necessary to apply advanced technologies within industry. This sophistication is gained through internal competition as businesses seek to improve their output, expand their markets, and lower their costs by the efficient use of available technologies to better their positions. Because competition is general within the economy, all businesses will seek such advanced technologies and the understanding of their applications in their striving for profits. A developing economy is one that has the capability to apply advanced technologies to a certain extent, but cannot yet compete with their applications in the developed postindustrial societies, nor can it yet formulate technologies that can be applicable in the postindustrial societies as well as its own to any extent.

It was understood in the writing of Adam Smith that even in elementary market conditions a business cycle of sorts is established. These conditions in the emerging economy are far more sophisticated, because its status of emergence requires a high level of competition and opposing forces both within the business sectors and among the sectors of industry and labor. The "invisible-hand" model that Smith described is therefore not relevant in the modern emerging economy. The government serves as a regulator of the economy, even though competition regulates the market forces for each business sector. Thus the government has to protect the country's welfare, provide viable and continuing infrastructural growth, and regulate the economy's rudimentary business-cycle fluctuations.[2]

The developing economy's business cycle is more sophisticated than that of the emerging economy's cycle because of the applications of technologies, the heightened competition among the country's businesses, the export of technologically based products to other developing economies, and the attempt to enter the postindustrial markets with cost-competitive products. The expansion of its domestic economy requires greater sophistication in the banking and stock-exchange sectors, which are influential in the productive sectors and which are markets themselves, subject to their own fluctuations that are derived from the general liquidity and the utility of investment for specific periods.

The concept of credit becomes applicable in the developing economies as business expansion in general and the attempts of individual firms to establish secure markets in particular are subject to the forces of their business cycles. Hence credit has to be established for protection against unforeseen circumstances, and this depends on the ratio of equity to debt. Where such debts exist, if for any reason there is a reduction in revenues, with profits declining and perhaps turning negative, businesses have to continue servicing their debts or close down. Credit based on the business's equity is established in the developing economy, and the lower the ratio of debt to equity, the greater the business's ability to withstand cyclical fluctuations and the impact of increased competition.[3]

The postindustrial societies' business cycle is far more sophisticated and complex. The cycles of the emerging and developing economies tend to be macroeconomic in scale, with each sector affected in the same way. A cyclical rise brings the entire economy up, and a decline affects all sectors equally. In the postindustrial economies there is a tendency for this to occur, but each sector is sufficiently strong to withstand these generalized trends. It is only when market saturation approaches all sectors at the same time that the cycle's motion becomes macroeconomic in scope and affects the economies in this general manner. Moreover, it is only when such macroeconomic cycles occur that they generate international cyclical effects in other postindustrial economies and move also to the developing and emerging economies. This is because the general consumption liquidity declines, reducing consumption, which reduces production, bringing about a further liquidity decline because of the unemployment that is generated. This affects the amount of trade among the three types of economies negatively as the postindustrial economies reduce their consumption, allowing businesses to use their available liquidity for debt servicing, for further market intervention (a point that will be discussed in the next chapter), or both, depending on each business's individual liquidity position with respect to its current markets and its projected markets when the cycle once again begins its motion upward.

When trade is affected, aid is also affected as the amount is reduced according to each postindustrial economy's aggregate liquidity position. This, in turn, limits the amount of liquidity in the emerging and developing economies, bringing them also to slowdown in their growth, thereby generating the cycle of the postindustrial economies in their economies as well.

From the postindustrial economies' positions of relative economic strength, as determined by the quantity and quality of aggregate production and the economies' abilities to innovate and apply new technologies, it can be readily seen that this is a one-sided relationship. It is the postindustrial economies, therefore, that establish the general cyclical patterns, which operate in turn throughout the economic spheres of all countries.

The concepts and tools to be discussed here are, first, utility and entropy, and then liquidity, according to Keynesian orientation and then with respect to utility. Modern economies rely on these concepts and tools for economic growth and development, regardless of their status with respect to the three stages of growth. In Chapters 7 and 8 these concepts and tools will be applied to the business cycle.

DECISION MAKING AND THE THEORY OF VALUE: UTILITY AND ENTROPY

In economic literature the notion of "economic man" is the individual who, when confronted with decisions and choices, acts strictly in a rational manner. The economic man's judgments with respect to his options and choices are supposed to be without ambiguity, and he always opts for the best among competing alternatives in the decision-making process. Therefore, the economic man is one who acts only according to his best interests given his options and choices, and only he knows what is best for him among the available opportunities.

The very concept of the person acting rationally and in his best interests given alternative choices provides the basis of neoclassical economic theory. This is supported by the more fundamental concept of an economy fluctuating in dynamic equilibrium, so that at one time one set of alternatives is attractive as choices for an individual, and at another time a different set of choices will be available. Eventually a set of choices resembling the first set will appear better, while later a set resembling the second set will appear better, and so on in a recurring cyclical pattern. The economic man, according to his current economic situation at any one time, is confronted with these alternative options and will act according to his best interests at the time, only to be confronted with different choices in the future. Action with respect to these changing options may very well negate earlier decisions. According to neoclassical economic thinking, the macro economy is not in an optimum position when better bergaining positions are formed and alternative options shift in nuance. The presence of shifting nuances results in decisions that are made and then reconsidered as these nuances present differing options. The allocation of resources into these changing alternatives is not a reflection of the dynamic equilibrium aspect of the neoclassical cycle, but within the terms of the "economic man" notion changes in decisions are made with respect to changes in alternatives. Nuance shifts present new alternatives that the economic man will then act upon. This approach demonstrates the reduction in resource utility with respect to the neoclassical macro economy as resources are being shifted according to the rational decision-making process of the economic man.

Of course, it could be argued that one of the decisions confronting economic man is to maintain his position regardless of the shifts in nuances. This appears to be a rational position, but on closer inspection it is somewhat contradictory. Acting in a rational manner is necessarily connected with the circumstances of decision making. Given certain conditions, the economic man, as a rational being, will decide in one manner, but as these conditions change, different actions are thus required. The economic world is far from stagnant, and its dynamics influence conditions quite frequently. The economic man, acting rationally, chooses one policy, perhaps requiring extensive investment; when circumstances change, he acts another way, perhaps in a manner that affects his prior decision. The contradiction here is that rapidly changing conditions result in rapid decisions, perhaps negating earlier and very recent decisions. This changing of decisions may be rational with respect to the context of the new circumstances, but it is certainly irrational with respect to the real world and to investments and other consequences of decisions that are already made.

There is certainly a different approach to the individual as decision maker in our complex and dynamic economic world. The individual as a member of his or her society, regardless of the stage of economic growth of the society, makes economic decisions based on his or her standard of living, occupation, and family size. Also important are the expectations to be derived from the decisions taken. Expectation is not rational in the sense of preference ordering according to given and immutable conditions within the economy; expectation has a sense of uncertainty that is derived from the element of the unknowable associated with every economic venture. Whatever the stage of growth, the individual is the basic economic unit, as it were, and act in the manner he or she considers best. This concept of the individual is expanded, however, to relate to information systems and his or her situation with respect to these systems, and it is on the basis of these relevant systems that the individual decides and acts.

The contemporary individual as contemporary decision maker is rational and operates in all economic circumstances in a manner that, given the specific conditions and the available knowledge, seeks optimum utility according to his or her understanding and liquidity positions. Thus the contemporary individual deals with information that may be scanty in which case the choice may be to avoid decisions, or detailed, in which case the decision to relate to the information or avoid it will be made with a degree of assurance that corresponds to the levels and quality of the information.

Information comes in three forms. It may be informal and loose, scanty and far from complete, in which case its value in the decision-making process is minimal at best. Information may be detailed, systematic, and available to the individual as an information system that can therefore be analyzed and evaluated with respect to the alternatives, and from which conclusions can be drawn and decisions made. Information can also be acquired by the contemporary individual from sources that seem unrelated, but are assembled by the individual for his or her own use, and it can be acted upon by either avoiding it or accepting it within the decision-making process.

Whatever the form information takes, with respect to economics it is relevant only if it is of utility to the contemporary individual as decision maker. For this to be the case the information must take the form of either a closed or open system. A closed system in time **t** may not remain closed in time **t** + 1, but this is not a reflexive relationship, for an open information system will always remain so until it ceases to function. This is because by its very openness the system's information is dynamic and changing according to the situation to which it relates.

The contemporary individual, as opposed to the concept of the economic man, is important in the emerging and developing economies, as well as in the postindustrial economies. It is invalid to compare the emerging and developing economies to the neoclassical economic situations in which the concept of the economic man perhaps had some validity. The neoclassical economic situation was one that existed prior to the Great Depression, and neoclassical theory was developed to explain and analyze the problems and profitability of the firm in its production and competition. To perceive the emerging and developing economies as Industrial Revolution economies is invalid, and the concept of the economic man that held sway is equally so.

Emerging economies, for example, are those that have an already-established industrial infrastructure, a labor force concerned with its own interests, industry that is concerned with competition and expansion, and a governmental economic policy formulated on the basis of postdepression economics, in which the problems of inflation, welfare, and preventing unemployment are foremost, to be handled in a manner that will not prevent the economy from moving into the position of being able to apply new technologies in the production process and to utilize new educational techniques for training skilled workers. The individuals in the economy must have the best and most accurate information, regardless of the sector, to make decisions that will benefit themselves and therefore the economy in general. The contradictory situation of the economic man is thus avoided, as it is outdated with respect to the emerging economy's situation. Acting rationally means acting with respect to the information systems available. For the closed system in the emerging economy the degrees of sophistication are limited to the general sophistication of the specific economies. As the emerging economy expands its infrastructure, industrial output, and labor skills to work the industries, closed systems contain conditions comparable to the economies' abilities with respect to their increasing sophistication and their movement toward the stage of the developing economies.

Open information systems are less likely in the emerging economies because these economies lack sufficient dynamics for their formulation. Agreements are made on the basis of the specific economic conditions that exist, but because the economies are emerging, they lack the inner dynamics that change these conditions fairly rapidly. The only real dynamic that can exert an influence is that of political instability including invasions, either from within the economy or sponsored from without. In these cases it is most likely that neither closed nor open information systems will hold. Because of the relative economic weakness of these economies, they are viewed to be easy prey by those countries of equal weakness who seek their resources, or by stronger countries who also seek their resources. Internal usurpation of power may be rolled back as international pressure is brought to bear on the opportunistic politicians. External usurpation in the form of invasion or sponsorship may also be met with international reaction, forcing the invaders or the external forces to withdraw. This depends on how the policies of these emerging countries are viewed internationally with respect to safeguarding human rights and assuring economic growth. This is part of the legacy of World War II as it has been manifested in our contemporary era and our social time. No postindustrial country will mourn the downfall of a dictator, and dictators have certainly fallen in the emerging economies, Idi Amin, the barbarous dictator of Uganda, being just one notorious example. But the postindustrial leaders in politics, business, and labor would certainly not tolerate coups or invasions against countries that are encouraging economic activity and are concerned for the welfare of their citizens. Economic growth in the emerging economies is necessary to ward off such attacks and coups, and the closed and open information systems on which economic decisions by contemporary individuals in these societies are made assist in the processes of growth and the movement toward the stage of the developing economies.

Because information systems are related to the economies in which they are formulated, the closed information system in an emerging economy has a very limited time span and information content. The financial institutions operating in the emerging economy have the degree of sophistication necessary for economic expansion, but the stock, bond, and commodities markets are very small and limited in scope. Closed information systems pertaining to issues are thus of short duration. The content of open information systems pertains to programs that are formulated for economic expansion and hence personal profit for those who take advantage of these systems. Of course, the investment may be great and the actual returns may be disappointing, but this is the consequence of using venture capital when alternative uses exist that may not promise high returns if they are successful.

Moreover, in emerging economies the risks of investment are higher than in the developing or postindustrial economies. Solid economic infrastructures for each branch of intensive economic activity have still to be established, the velocity of money is high (the velocity of money will be discussed in chapter 6), and much of the industrial financing comes from government sources that must maintain a distance from the industrial decision-making processes or else stifle economic growth by way of bureaucratic and political interference and favoritism, a difficult undertaking in the best of circumstances. Information systems in these economies, be they closed or open, thus reflect the economies' limitations, but while the closed system assumes certain conditions during the time limit set for the system based on circumstances as they now exist and are projected to exist at the system's termination, the open systems allow for flexibility and, based on the premise of a dynamic economic situation, provide for growth but also contain the element of risk, uncontrolled by the systems' openness.

The information systems of the emerging economies often target specific aspects of the economies because of the restricted opportunities that these economies have to offer. But by acting on the information systems, by investing in industrial development, and by provideing technologies and the training to use them in the industrial processes of production and market expansion, these economies eventually move to the stage of developing economies.

The information systems of the developing economies are vaster in scope and market orientation than the emerging economies' systems. The developing economies provide closed systems to relate to specific projects over defined time limits, projects that, unlike the emerging economies' closed information systems, may also pertain to international endeavors. This is because developing economies are involved in international commerce. They gain technologies from the postindustrial economies either through trade or aid, and through the incorporation of these technologies into their own industrial bases they produce both for their domestic markets and for international commerce.

Their open-ended information systems also pertain to the domestic and international markets. While the closed information systems pertain to specific projects and their validity exists for the delimited duration stated within the systems, the open-ended systems allow for unexpected dynamics within their defined markets, as well as for flexibility as the markets develop and expand. This holds both domestically and for foreign-oriented projects, which are often extensions of the domestic markets because goods and services developed domestically are often exported, bearing the uniqueness of the developing country of origin. In this case, in foreign markets, where there is heavy competition among similar goods and services, the country's prestige adds to the products' commercial appeal and hence to marketability and sales.

Economies in the stage of developing have achieved sufficient wealth to expand their uses of current technologies. This expansion is expressed in their information systems. The extent of the closed system is far greater in the developing economy than in the emerging economy, if only because the existing wealth allows for geater opportunities. The time limit may be of short duration, but the system's content is greater. Moreover, for the open system the dynamics are such that the system's content may change due to changes in the areas for which it is stated, but a greater resilience exists, allowing the system's viability to prevail for longer periods.

This applies to a far greater extent in the postindustrial economies, where new technologies are being introduced into the manufacturing proceses and financial operations, and where training of workers is necessary for the use of these technologies, as well as their installation and maintenance. Both closed and open information systems are far more complex than their counterparts in the emerging economies and, to a lesser extent, in the developing economies. This is because of far greater levels of national and industrial wealth and the intense information systems required to expand this wealth still further. This intensity is due to the competitive positions among the various domestic industrial sectors for consumer liquidity, as well as the competitive situations of firms within the same industries, and is heightened still further because of the development of international markets. Here both competition among the firms for foreign markets and international consumer liquidity and the foreign markets' responses in terms of their own competitive situations are significant. This is so especially since many foreign competitors base their products on imitative responses to those that are brought into their markets. This international imitation effect will be treated later in chapter 10. But first, utility and entropy must be discussed, and the dynamics of the information system must be explored. The business cycle will then be analyzed, and its effects on developing and emerging societies and their responses to the dynamics of the postindustrial economies, specifically with respect to imitation, will be discussed.

Whatever the stage of economic growth, the information available to the contemporary individual, be it in the form of an open, a closed, or even an informal information system, depends on the objective conditions of the economic situation to which the information system relates. The utility of this information, however, depends on the quality and quantity of the information and on the individual's subjective interpretation of this information. This interpretation may be affected by his or her peers or by personal economic aspirations. Because the contemporary individual is the basic economic unit, it is as a result of his or her decisions, taken in summation to form the total decisions and their influences on the economy, that policies are made on the level of industry, on the decisions of the labor movement, and on the formulation of political policy.

As the information's utility depends on the objective information and its subjective interpretation, information — even in its most rigidly closed systems — has different utility schedules for $n > 1$ persons. This allows for the ordering of utility schedules for the individuals involved. These schedules are expressions of preference for the various information systems and indicate their utilities and entropies for the contemporary individual. However, because information is both objectively and subjectively interpreted, utility and entropy must also be considered objectively and subjectively.

Regardless of the economic stage of development, the dynamics for information systems are the same. The differences among these systems for the three stages of economic development are in their content and its extent, as both content and its extent are related directly to the economies' growth positions.

A closed information system is one that is bounded by a time signature and is isolated from the influences of data that could otherwise alter its contents. Any additional data incorporated into a closed system are redundant and unnecessary; moreover, this system is consistent and without ambiguities. An example that holds for economies in the three stages of growth is that on a certain day a transaction occurs in which a specific sum of money is exchanged between two identified individuals, each representing a firm, with the money exchanged concluding a production and marketing merger. Investors who have access to the information on the merger can determine the objective utility as well as their subjective utilities of investing in the new firm. This information is closed because the merger is completed, with the strategies of cooperation and continuation having been formulated prior to the completion of the merger, so that at the time of the system's closure all further information is redundant and of no value in the investors' decision-making processes.

Because the closed information system is time bound and isolated from data that could otherwise alter its contents, the system's subjective utility varies from one contemporary individual to another. Hence utility in general depends on the system's objective probability and the individual's subjective probability. The objective utility $S_t = [s_1, s_2, \ldots, s_n]_t$, where S_t is the system in toto in time t, and $s_1, s_2, \ldots, s_n$ are the individual statements composing the system, is assessed by setting each of its statements in turn within the maximum and minimum boundaries, respectively, so that for statement $0 < s_1 < 1$, which means that the information statement in question lies between the boundaries of utility and entropy, and its position with respect to each of these limits determines its viability within the system in general. Thus, for the closed system S_t, $0 < S_t < 1$ is valid for the duration of the stated time signature. In addition to the objective probabilistic assessment, for the contemporary individual this system must also relate to his or her preferences. In the example of the merger, for instance, the individual as decision maker must be acquainted to some extent with the relevant people and their respective firms, as well as the procedures involved in the proposed production and marketing processes. While the individual may not doubt the information system's content, he or she may be skeptical concerning the production policies and/or the marketing techniques, given the specific economic conditions to which the system relates. This skepticism may be due to the individual's consideration of other such systems pertaining to similar projects and his or her awareness of the possible short time lag before close competitors enter the market and reduce profits. Alternatively, the individual may also be considering other projects for investment and with limited funds may therefore place this specific project low on his or her preference schedule, even though the project is objectively sound. Another person may have a different opinion while possessing the same information about the market, the state of the economy for which the project is proposed, and the time-lag potential for close competitors to enter the market. This person may assign a high subjective probability in toto to the information system and place his or her investment at the disposal of one or both firms engaged in the transaction.

An incomplete system, that is, an open information system, is one in which one or both of two types of conditions occur: Either the system has been infiltrated by information elements of other systems, or there is a lack of sufficient data within the system to reduce or eliminate the uncertainty concerning the system's validity and utlity, thereby limiting the ability to make specific decisions. The system, being open, is by definition incomplete and thus not subject to a bounding time signature. Should a time signature be placed on an open system, it is merely for clarification of the specific time under consideration; this clarification is not strict, however, because of the system's dynamics. For example, consider the system A in which are incorporated the elements a_1, a_2, . . ., a_n, b_1, b_2, c_2, c_3, d_4 of information systems B, C, and D, respectively (it makes no difference whether B, C, and D are closed or open). Such a system exists for firms in developing or postindustrial economies engaging in foreign commerce prior to the finance minister's announcement of the proposed annual budget in one or both countries, when the investor's decision to place his or her money at the disposal of the exporting firm and/or that firm's representative in the importing company must consider not only the firm's present financial situations, but also the possible effect the announcements and the budgets may have on their enactment of the project. This information includes the firms' positions, information from other systems such as possible economic forecasts and their impact on the economies and trade, and the political systems of the countries involved. Because the information system is open and the time is prior to one or both budgets being announced, also included are projections into the future based on expected budgetary considerations. Moreover, an open information system is subject to conflicting information statements and therefore to contradictions; as both firms' managers and investors work with the same objective open-ended information system, they must assess the subjective and objective probabilities with respect to certainty determined by the utilities of the known information statements as they are evaluated and by yet to be determined probabilistic assessments of the utilities of those statements that will enter the system at future dates.

When an individual deals with a closed system, he or she relates to this system's subjective and objective probabilities in toto. This is because while each of the system's statements is unique as an expression of a specific point, this system has no inconsistencies or contradictions, and thus each statement depends on the others for meaning. The system's general probability depends on the subjective and objective probabilities of each of its statements (that is, elements). The objective probability refers to the facts to which the system relates, that is, to the information as presented, and is available to those to whom it is directed for their subjective evaluations with respect to alternative information systems and the choice of leaving their liquidity idle.[4] Hence significant for the interpretation and understanding of these facts is the subjective probability, and this pertains to each individual's specific requirements for the duration of the information system's pertinence as stated by its time signature. A closed system may be of utility for some people and be of little or no utility for others in the same sector or peer group even though its objective propability approaches maximum utility. It is on the basis of both these probabilities, each with its own weight in the decision-making process, that the contemporary individual orders his or her preferences. Hence a difficulty arises when the statements agreed to by an individual stand in contradiction to other statements within the system. Another individual agreeing to the same statements may also agree to other statements that the first person rejected as being untenable. Also, probabilities are often assigned to combinations of statements because they provide a fuller expression of expectations. Taken in combination, these statements may be accepted by some while they are rejected by others because their recombinations with still-different statements provide subjective contradictions. Nevertheless, on the basis of the available information systems, the contemporary individual must make choices and assign personal preference scales in order to relate the information presented to the reality of the situation as it is understood, thereby bringing the subjective interpretation as close as possible to objective probability and enabling a sound judgment based on the information to be made.

The difficulties of subjective evaluation can be minimized by assigning boundaries of verisimilitude according to expectations and allowing these boundaries to represent the utilities and entropies on which decisions are made. With the upper boundary designated by 1 and the lower boundary by 0, these limits can never be reached, but they can be approached. In the extreme, the upper boundary signifies complete verisimilitude as understood both objectively and subjectively (the latter even though it may be placed on a low preference scale for personal reasons), whether the system is closed and complete or open and incomplete, as a working model defining and delineating a situation, with the system's language corresponding as much as possible to reality. The lower boundary signifies the total absence of a relationship between an information system's language and the reality it purports to describe. For each decision maker, each information system lies between these limits, and a system's position with respect to these limits may be either stationary or fluctuating; the system's position within these boundaries determines its state of utility or entropy. By analyzing the system within these limits, the decision maker combines the highly subjective interpretation and its strong influence on personal expectations with the objective analysis of reality and the system's language as it relates to the reality.

For the closed system the assessment of the system's utility or entropy is a fairly uncomplicated process. Because of the system's closure, the decision maker confronts an either-or situation in which the information system describes its stated domain accurately or fails to do so. As the system's time signature states the duration of the system's presumed validity, this can be assessed with respect to the domain of reality to which the system relates. Based on this assessment, each of the system's statements can be broken down into its components, which can then be matched with the specific aspects of reality to which the statement relates, subjecting each statement to utility and entropy neasurements, thereby determining the statements' relations to reality. As no ambiguities or contradictions exist in the closed system, the system can be taken in toto and placed between the limits of 0 and 1; but while this determines the system's objective status, the contemporary individual as decision maker has to assess his or her preference with respect to this objective rating. The individual's expectations may have presented attitudes not allowed for by the information system, but the system's status may allow for revised attitudes. Alternatively, expectations may have been reinforced by the system's status and placed on still firmer ground. In any case, once the information system's position has been established objectively with respect to utility and entropy, the individual as decision maker concerned with this system must act on the basis of this knowledge.

Because of the possibility of contradictory information statements, and because information from other systems not necessarily relevant may intrude into the open-ended information system, such a system has a degree of complication lacking in the closed information system. The time signature placed on the open-ended system nevertheless is significant because it isolates a system that is dynamic and thereby allows some control over it. The system S in time t_1 may or may not be equal in the quantity or quality of statements to S_{t_2}; this can be determined only by analysis, given the system's dynamic nature. This situation is complicated further because an information statement existing in both t_1 and t_2 may have its nuances altered so that its identity in both times is only superficial with respect to the contexts of the systems. Moreover, because of the influences of new statements, those in the original S_t may be found to be contradictory in S_{t_2}. The dynamics of the system require that it be broken down and analyzed to determine which statements are necessary for the system and which are (or have become) superfluous and can therefore be eliminated without affecting the system's objective utility — a process that may entail breaking down specific statements and reformulating them so that their troublesome parts are removed.

For both closed and open information systems objective utility determines the extent to which a system describes reality accurately. This requires assessing the system's probability for its relation to its reality. Probability depends on the system's information content and is represented by the letter I, with the expression I/S_t representing the probability rating of system S at time t. I/S_t is the general expression of the probability $SI_S = P(S_t)$, where the left-hand side of the equation means the probability of S with respect to its statements s_1, s_2, ..., s_n, and the right-hand side of the equation represents the total information system. S_t's utility is thus assessed by focusing on each statement and determining its relationship to the aspect of reality within the general system for which it was formulated. As the probability of an open-ended information system tends to vary over time, with S_{t_1}, being equal or not equal to S_{t_2} in both information content and objective utility, S_t's utility must be revalued when one acts on its information content at different times. Moreover, because of this system's tendency to vary over time, there is a chance that decisions taken on the basis of this information at one time will yield consequences not considered at that time.

Such is the situation when an individual invests in a firm that presents itself as a dynamic organization producing for the domestic markets and exporting its diversified products into the markets of several foreign countries, adjusting the quantity of exports according to its targeted markets' needs and using its excess capital for retooling and engaging in innovative and imitative projects for further domestic and foreign market expansion.[5] When an individual becomes acquainted with the firm's internal situation and its domestic and foreign markets as stated in its prospectus and with the firm's performance on the stock exchange, he or she is able to decide if investing in the firm is a sound decision. However, because the firm presents its open-ended information system bound by a time signature stated in the prospectus, its future prominence in both the domestic and international markets and on the stock exchange cannot be determined, because this information is excluded from the prospectus. While projections may be offered, there is no guarantee that they will in fact be achieved. This situation is complicated still further by the possibility of new government policies in either the domestic or foreign economies in which the firm trades that will bear on its share price. Internal difficulties may also arise that may bear directly on its performance domestically and internationally. Even though the system is open, its time signature closes it, making it complete at the time it is presented; because the firm is dynamic, however, the total picture is incomplete, and it is the system on which the individual acts. As the information system changes, the individual must revise his or her calculations, taking each system as if it were time bound, even though it fluctuates. The time signature is thus placed by the individual on the basis of the information content at his or her disposal, while the reality is in fluctuation.

Two individuals working with a closed information system may choose to act on the system, thereby contributing to the dynamics that the system generates. This system may also be rejected by one or both people, who then make their decision in favor of other systems. While the degree of objective uncertainty is certainly greater in the open system than in the closed system because the closed system is static and the open system is dynamic and fluid, the individual treats both systems as closed in order to assess their objective utilities and subjective preference ratings. Both systems have time signatures when the decision is taken, so that when each individual assesses their utilities, he or she takes into consideration his or her subjective utility preference rating and makes the decision with regard to the desired consequences.

To the extent that the actual consequences are those that the individual seeks, subjective utility thus reflects the projected results that the individual desires. When individual desires are compared to future projections, the degrees of uncertainty are related directly to the degrees determined by subjective utility. This utility is derived from and determines the individual's ordering preferences, and personal preference ordering is derived from the information system, which is evaluated with respect to alternative systems. The consequences of future uncertainty are very important in this evaluation.

Preference ordering requires that each alternative system under consideration be ranked, first with regard to its objective utility, and then in terms of personal subjective utility. The significance of this ordering for both domestic markets and international trade is that government programs and business operations in these markets are information systems. The objective utilities of these systems can be determined within the time signatures prevalent for their durations and through consideration of current domestic and international issues in the relevant trading countries. The subjective utility preference ratings present another set of difficulties because government planners, when they are devising and considering alternative economic programs, cannot take into account the subjective assessments of the individuals involved, but there are other ways for determining somewhat the influences of these programs, and these will be discussed in chapter 8 pertaining to the welfare utility function and growth. It must be noted here, however, that a relationship exists between subjective utility as determined by the individual and subjective utility as determined by the assessment of the system's probability. If the individual acts to support the system, then this relationship is positive; a rejection of the system for other systems means that the individual finds the relationship to be negative. Economic activity is generated by the quantity of positive relationships among individuals and information systems, for by using these systems individuals give life to programs by investing money and making both domestic and international purchases. Those information systems that are inactive soon succumb to entropy. Those of little activity can develop into systems that attract individuals, but this depends on the acumen of the firms' managers.

Whether these relationships are positive or negative depends on individuals' purposes for considering the systems and the systems' objective information contents. If a person has an established goal and the information system in question fails to provide an inducement toward the realization of this goal, then the person will avoid the system. It is most likely, however, that the contemporary individual will have established modified goals in the form of a second-best situation in the event that the best goals become unrealistic with regard to the available alternative information systems and their realities. Again, this requires an ordering preference on the basis of utility: The individual acts on that system that provides the best future situation as determined by his or her goal modification, with the revised goal then becoming the best case.

Schematically, the objective-subjective relationship can be stated thus: $EuS_t = F(P, S)$, that is, the subjective or expected utility of the information system S_t is a function of S with regard to its objective probability. When S_t's objective utility approaches the maximum limit of 1, this does not necessarily bear on EuS_t, that is, on the expected subjective utility of S, because objectively S_t may yield consequences irrelevant or unwanted to the contemporary individual. Hence, while for one individual considering the specific information system, $EuS_t = [F(P, S)_{t+1}] \to 1$, another person considering the same system may have expectations that yield $EuS_t = [F(P, S)_{t+1}] \to 0$, with the subscript $t+1$ referring to the next time period that would occur when the system is acted upon. These subjective assessments are not necessarily permanent over time, as they are often altered over time because of the acquisition of greater comprehension, or because shifts in the systems themselves allow for reconsideration. Subjective preferences may also be shifted. In the second case, where shifts in systems allow for reconsideration, the S's are not identical, but often these shifts are insignificant where subjective preference ordering is concerned; in this situation the equation sign becomes an approximation sign. Of course, where such shifts are major, the system becomes entropic if it is not salvaged. Hence, while S_t may have been rejected in $t+1$ because of low subjective utility due to expectations, in a different time period t_n $(n > 2)$ the subjective reordering and possible shifts in S_t's information content, with S being open-ended, may result in the system's receiving a very high subjective ordering position.

The sum total of decisions based on objective-subjective utility and hence on preference ordering at any one time period can be considered to be the sum total of domestic and foreign economic activity for that time. Moreover, because the utilities of open-ended information systems are reduced over time because of their inherent instability due to the infiltration of information from other systems and because they fluctuate according to changes made within them, acting on these systems also brings about changes in their content. For example, a domestic firm investing in the development of foreign markets through representatives in these markets may bring about a decline in the rate of return on the investment as the demand for investment declines. If these foreign representatives deal in imitative markets, the rate of profit also declines according to the competition and new entries into the market line. This reduction of utility is entropy.

In its objective sense information entropy is the measurement of disinformation in an information system. It illustrates the extent to which the system's elements, its statements, fail to relate to their objective realities, thereby enhancing subjective discrimination in the consideration of alternative systems. Symbolized by the letter H, the entropy of a system S_t indicates the extent to which some or all of the system's statements no longer correspond to the realities for which they were designed and intended. Just as utility is measured between the upper and lower boundaries, so is entropy, thus making it the negation of utility, because when $S_t \rightarrow 1$, entropy is either at a minimum or of such slight import as to be insignificant; when $S_t \rightarrow 0$, utility has declined to the extent that the system's identity is threatened.

Because the closed system designates a reality relevant only for the period stated by its time signature, the only way it can be subjected to entropy is if its reality is altered and revised. For example, the system containing facts $1, 2, \ldots, n$ is bound by a specific future date. If one or more of these statements (elements) has to be altered to correspond to changes in the realities due on that date, the system can become entropic; however, this can be rectified by a reformulation of the affected statements in light of the changed realities. This adjustment is technical, restoring the system to utility in light of the changes.

It is possible that such a shift in reality could be so extreme that the information system could not be salvaged and would have to be abandoned completely. In investment in a firm engaging in both domestic and foreign enterprise, if one of the firm's directors should suddenly pass away, bringing instability to the firm and uncertainty in its domestic and foreign markets, the investment transactions would most likely be placed on hold and might even be terminated if it is not too late to do so until the board of directors could replace the director with a person of equal competence to regenerate confidence in the firm's ability to perform as stated in its prospectus, which might have to be redrafted to the investors' and foreign partners' satisfaction. In this type of situation there is no time signature, and objective entropy has replaced utility, thereby breaking down the information system entirely. The system can, however, be reformulated and revised so that its utility is once again at the maximum.

For the open information system objective analysis must be based on S_t's utility being dependent on te probability of all its statements relating to their realities as stated by the system, so that the information I of St equals the probability of S_t being relevant, that is, $I/Sl_t = P[S_t]$, with S at t_1 containing a set number of statements indicated by the time signature. If the probability assessment shows that there is absolutely no relationship between the set of statements and their indicated realities, then $I=H$, and the entire system is devoid of utility. If the probabilities of the system's statements correspond totally to their realities during the time period, then $I=-H$, and the system enjoys full objective utility.

This either-or situation in which either utility or entropy exists is the best of all possible worlds, and for utility it is difficult to achieve for more than a brief period of time. Because open information systems are formulated to correspond to their realities, it is unlikely that they will be totally irrelevant or absolutely perfect, especially after a reasonable period of time and usage. More than likely, some degree of entropy will set in fairly rapidly because of slight shifts in reality. This entropy is minor, however, and poses no threat to the system as such.

For the bound, that is, closed information system absolute utility is far easier to achieve because the changes in the realities for which its statements are relevant are very small. Absolute entropy during the time limit is also very difficult to come by because radical shifts in the realities are unlikely to occur. It is only when the time signature has expired, or in case of a crisis or a totally unexpected situation when the realities are altered, that bound systems become entropic (to be abandoned) and an alternative system (or systems) should be sought.

Objective determination of an open system's entropy level is achieved by assessing the probabilities of a system's statements with respect to the realities for which they were constructed. For example, when stated, $S_t \rightarrow 1$. If this were not the case, the system would not have been formulated as is. Over time periods 1 and 2 changes occur in either S's content or its reality or perhaps in both. Because the assessment of entropy or utility requires the evaluation of S's statements with respect to their realities, it may be found that some of these statements contain glaring inadequacies that can be corrected within the system, or if this is unfeasible, cast out completely. It is likely that these inadequacies are due to the incorporation of additional statements over t_1-t_2 that have a better definitive relationship to their realities; once the inferior statements are removed, S's utility will be strengthened.

Difficulties arise when statements exist whose subtle discrepancies seriously affect S_t's utility and are not subject to alterations because alterations would result in the system being drastically changed, perhaps to the extent of bringing the system into serious entropy and making its dissolution a possibility. This is due to the cumulative influence of shifting statements and/or realities, rendering S_t as such of little utility. For example, a firm may undertake to export a product that has succeeded in the domestic market and has thus established its information system to attract investors and develop foreign markets. There may be discrepancies between the exporting plans and the exporting process because of changes in either domestic or foreign policies or both. The consequence is that while the product is still successful domestically, exporting plans are not quite fulfilled, and the information system moves into an entropic situation because the system contains information about both the domestic and foreign market operations. If the movement toward entropy is compensated for in time, it will not be serious, and S_t can be revised to cope with the differing conditions prevailing in the targeted domestic and foreign markets. The information system can thus be reformulated with the entropy temporarily removed, so that S_{t_1}, S_{t_2}, with the revised $S_{t_1} \rightarrow 1$.

The dynamics of both the domestic markets and international trade are such, however, that new discrepancies will arise that are not accounted for by S_{t_2}, so that over time this system will also become entropic. Reconstruction of the system with respect to changing internal information and shifts in the system's defined and delineated realities continues until a situation is reached where the entropic conditions that finally evolve will render the entire system not worth the effort or the cost to reconstruct it still further. For example, increasing competition for the same markets with similar products may lower the firm's profit/cost ratio to the extent that any new changes in the products' marketing, performance, or composition in either its domestic markets, foreign markets, or both would be offset by the production costs involved in making these changes due to declining sales. The domestic and/or export markets may be so saturated that the product line can be maintained only at break-even costs and profits or, at worst case, at a loss, no matter what changes are undertaken to make it more attractive. The decision must then be made, whether to maintain production for its markets at its current profit/cost ratio, to maintain marketing incentives and advertising at a level sufficient to hold current sales in light of the strenuous competition, or to phase out the line and allocate the resources otherwise. If the choice is to maintain the product, then S_t is acted upon to retain its viability within its utility boundaries at worst case, and to move to maximum utility at best case. If the product is abandoned, then entropy is immediately introduced within the system, which is then rendered beyond reconstruction. The latter decision is final, bringing the system into complete entropy, while the former decision still preserves the product's dynamic, which will remain active in its markets until a decision is taken to phase it out, or until both domestic and international consumer demand and the economies' general dynamics no longer provide support for the product but encourage the allocation of resources to other projects.

Discrepancies exist also as a direct result of the information system. For example, revised plans for the product to make it more competitive if its position is threatened in the domestic market, the international market, or both, no matter how slight the revisions, result in difficulties not inclued previously in the system. Different production and/or distribution techniques, instituted to gain economies will incur such difficulties as moving the product in its directed markets. Another difficulty is the reallocation of resources required by the revised system in terms of the firm's previous and future priorities. Still a further difficulty, especially in highly competitive markets, but existing also in new markets, is that when revision results in cost reductions that are passed on to the consumer, it may very well be that these reductions are not a sufficient incentive for consumers because of their prior commitments of their liquidities according to their utility- ordering preferences. Further, as prices are reduced to move stock, aggregate demand may be so scheduled that profits are reduced more than planned (entropy), so that nevertheless the product's viability becomes questionable. While lower production and/or distribution costs may result in lower prices in both the domestic and foreign markets, in light of this, aggregate demand must still warrant a sufficient profit; otherwise the product will be abandoned. In this case the advantages proposed by cost reductions must be projected onto both domestic and foreign markets and assessed for their utility. If projections indicate that reductions will yield sufficient profits, then the markets will be maintained; if not, then either they will be maintained as a loss-leader incentive to continue in the markets with other products being introduced, or they will be abandoned. This decision will be based on projected utilities and entropies. If the changes are introduced and the resulting difficulties are overcome, this will generate similar changes in close competitors' thinking; the initial changes will introduce entropy into their information systems, and they must calculate their positions accordingly.

As for open-ended information systems, even though they are bound by their time signatures, they may be subject to various levels and intensities of other information at all times during their durations because their realities and information statements change. Changes may also occur during the periods of repair, thereby affecting the probabilities of these statements or of the system in toto. While the time signature indicates a system's duration, it indicates as well its position with respect to utility and entropy during this period. As time changes, so do these positions, and only through analysis can the extent of these changes be understood and the reasons for them be comprehended. Measurements of a system's positions are taken periodically, especially when there is reason to suspect that disinformation has entered the system. Nevertheless, changes occur because of the alterations that take place in the system's defined area and/or languages, changes that are detectable only by proper assessment.

Unlike objective entropy, subjective entropy is not necessarily relexive; that is, it is not necessarily in response to real alterations that may occur in the realm of internal structuring. For example, an information system may be approaching maximum objective utility, yet it may be considered entropic by an individual with a different preference ordering for the area that the system defines. The individual will choose to work with an alternative system — one with lower objective utility and therefore of higher risk — rather than a system with a higher objective but a lower personal subjective utility, providing, of course, that the chosen system is not entropic or in danger of becoming so. As the contemporary individual is considered rational economically in his or her preference ordering, and as his or her reasons for choosing the alternative system may or may not be understood by others working with the accepted system, this subjective entropy in the form of the choice for the alternative system will most likely pose no threat to the other system. There are situations where, the person subjectively prefers not to act at all but to wait and see what happens over a self-set time span, in which case this behavior is as if all the competing systems are subjectively entropic, regardless of their objective status. This decision, both personal and rational, depends on the individual's liquidity position and his or her understanding of the possibilities in the time considered significant for waiting before acting.

Subjective entropy is therefore due to personal assessment and depends on preference ordering with respect to the psychological aspect of expectation. Expectation is related to reality by the comprehension of current events and how these events may influence the future; preferring to work with an information system or choosing not to are based on the individual's best understanding of the reality. Hence there is no contradiction in the situation where $S_{ot} \to 1$ and $S_{st} \to 0$ (the subscripts o and s meaning objective and subjective). Furthermore, S_{t_n} may have a very high utility rating, with **tn** being a time in the subjectively assigned future beyond the length indicated by the time signature.[6]

Unlike their objective counterparts, subjective utility and entropy cannot be analyzed with respect to the probabilities of the system's information statements in relation to their various aspects of the system's defining and delineating area. Subjective entropy may be due to personal whims, values, or tastes, improper and incomplete understanding of the information or the area, or even an assigned period of waiting for alternative systems that are expected to be of greater utility, but may not materialize when the future is finally reached. As there is no real and objective accounting for personal tastes, preferences for information systems provide expression for those idiosyncrasies that economic activity seeks to control and channel by focusing on consumer products, investment opportunities, production processes, and both domestic and foreign markets.

Nevertheless, subjective entropy also has an impact on the direction economic activity takes. Since the decision to operate within one information system is made at the expense of using alternative competing systems — a decision limited and influenced by personal or corporate liquidity — the impact made by working with a system influences its statements, perhaps to the extent of altering their relationship to their area's realities. Rejecting a system because of subjective entropy will affect the system objectively. For the closed system this rejection inhibits the realization of that system's dynamics, which would certainly be more active by the influences of the individual's participation. Because a closed system defines and delineates a specific set of circumstances that are valid for the period indicated by the time signature, the system will undergo a decline in its objective utility if it is not used because of the subjective entropy of the targeted populace. This situation is usually extreme, but the extent of objective entropy with regard to the system's relevance with respect to its targeted populace will be determined by the extent of the response of that part of the populace willing to opt for the system. A system without sufficient takers, no matter how efficient it is internally, will collapse.

The open information system is in a different situation because it is constructed to relate to an area unclosable by the system's statements for a specific and yet uncertain period of time. Dynamics within the delineated area require that the system's statements be revised or discarded if their entropy is too serious, and also that the system take on new statements to relate to any area changes if the existing statements as they stand are inadequate. In this sense the system depends on the populace that works with it. For example, consider the extreme case of an open-ended information system without anyone working with it, the system will soon collapse because of the objective entropy generated for its area that will not be corrected. Subjective entropy, based on the preference ordering that allows the targeted populace to avoid the system, will therefore result in objective entropy and the system's rapid dissolution. This extreme case is unlikely, however, because managers and directors are realistic in their judgments and are not likely to construct systems they think will not attract. Nevertheless, what has been shown is the extent to which objective entropy is dependent on subjective entropy and the system's use.

There is a qualification that has to be made, this being that subjective entropy in its (nearby) extreme intensity is not the only way a system can be brought down, in the sense stated in the example just given. For example, the system does not have to be avoided entirely, but can be used by a very small minority of the targeted populace that, because of its size, is either too defensive and resists changes in the area or overcompensates too much in light of the need for changes; in either case their actions will bring about objective entropy in the system because their subjective evaluations are based on their numbered supporters and the need to maintain the system. Still, subjective entropy can act on objective entropy, bringing the system down before its time signature expires. For example, a closed system states that on a specific date conditions **a, b,** and **c** will occur; a disagreement ensues over the system's terminology and statements after its construction, with one individual acting to render the system entropic before the others involved realize this action. The dissenting person acts to prevent one of the system's conditions — say **c** — from being fulfilled. Since the closed system is so constructed that all its statements hold together and relate to their realities exactly as expressed in the system, altering the **c** statement will bring down the entire system. Subjective entropy can thus bring about actions that generate objective entropy, resulting in the project's collapse, the cancellation of a foreign deal, or whatever the situation may be.

For the open system this condition is no different. Assuming that the open system is nearing maximum utility, so that it is free from destructive entropy, an individual may reject the specific relationship and its reality, resulting in this person's changing the statement without sufficient consideration for the new statement's probability relationship. This will move the statement further away from the previously existing probability rating. Over time enough dynamics will be generated to require alterations in the statements, a process that will continue and will eventually bring the system into extreme entropy and its natural decline. But tampering with a statement in a system of high utility to suit a person's preferences brings a system into decline faster by generating entropy prematurely.

It is assumed that contemporary individuals participating in economic activity, whether as manufacturers or importers, exporters of consumers, act rationally according to their preference ordering. These people have their preferences as derived from their subjective and objective utilities and entropies, influencing and in turn influenced by their understanding of their information systems and their realities as they are so defined. The economist must deal with decision making, be it subjective, objective, or based, as is most likely, on combined considerations. However, just as people's individual realities change, so their perceptions of their information systems are altered; systems change due to realistic considerations and to personal considerations. Nevertheless, on the basis of these systems, choices are ordered and decisions made.

THE DYNAMICS OF THE INFORMATION SYSTEM

Open and closed information systems must be considered further because of their impact on entropy. It is impossible to discuss utility without taking into account entropy as the dissolution of utility and without examining the methods of repair to the information systems. These methods serve to maintain the systems' integrities until they are beyond repair and are abandoned or until they are replaced by systems lacking in entropy and capable of performing as stated.

In both the closed and open systems the elements define and delineate their respective realities; their elements are therefore information statements about the realities for which they are constructed, and because of the definition and delineation, they also tell what these realities do not contain. These information elements or statements are isomorphic, with each statement relating only to that aspect of reality within the area, the scope of which is contained only within the statement. This relationship is reflexive in the sense that each statement relates only to its specific aspect of reality and this aspect relates only to its unique statement. When these systems are first established, they lack the difficulties of ambiguity and of metalanguages and metainformation that usually develop through use.

In general, the information system contains the elements of information and reality to which these elements relate. Thus system S_t is viable if and only if it relates to R as stated within the system, with $\mathbf{R}$ being the defined and delineated reality, so that $S_{t_0} = [\mathbf{S}, \mathbf{R}]_{t_0}$, where the subscript t_0 is the time of origin during which the statements in $\mathbf{S}$ correspond isomorphically and reflexively with the particles in $\mathbf{R}$. There is no entropy at this time of origin, and the system has yet to be worked upon.

In the closed information system entropy sets in only when the reality is altered and the statements no longer retain their isomorphism. This may be caused by a de facto shift in reality or by subjective entropy on the part of an individual changing reality and thus bringing about objective entropy. As an example of a shift in reality, consider a project of manufacturing machinery, part of which is to be exported to an emerging country. The number of pieces to be exported has been agreed to, the delivery time established, and the terms and amount of payment set. Moreover, these conditions are finalized in a contract that serves as the basis for attracting potential investors in the emerging country. While the project is in operation, an unsuspected coup occurs in the emerging country, bringing the entire information system into unsalvageable entropy. The system's elements no longer relate to the area particles, and no reconstruction can redeem the system. When order is reestablished, whichever government is then formed may be interested in importing the machinery, but the importing will be under the terms of a different contract and perhaps by a different manufacturing and exporting company.

With respect to subjective entropy, a person involved in formulating a closed information system, such as a prospectus for manufacturing a new product, may seek to improve his or her personal position by rewriting the prospectus to provide a different slant, or by renegotiating the terms of the contract for the investors in the project before the production processes begin. If this person's position in the company is important, then the contract may be rewritten, thereby negating the previous contract and the prospectus on which the investors based their decisions to support the project. Subjective entropy may be due to altruistic considerations, such as realizing that a better contract can be obtained without personal gain, so that the terms in reality to which the contract is directed are altered, rendering it invalid. The point is that the reality is altered so that the system no longer refers in toto to the reality, rendering its information entropic.

It is important to note how the change is made. If **R'** is set as the new reality, the system **S** must also be altered, thereby allowing for a new system to be constructed. Consider the relationship **sdr,** that is, the information element **s** defines and delineates the area particle of reality **r.** When **r** is altered to become **r',** its defining element must also be altered to become **s',** because **s** itself has become entropic due to the shift of **r** to **r'.** Entropy can be reversed by combining **s** with relevant information and by casting out that part of **s** that is no longer adequate without destroying its general defining import. Hence, with **s** altered to **s'** and with the general import still intact, **r'** is valid, and the relationship still maintains its viability.

The situation considered here is a slight shift in **R** where only a single **r** particle is affected. If there is a radical shift in the closed system's reality, thereby affecting the majority of the relationships, then either **S** will be abandoned due to the extent of entropy, or a new relationship between **S** and **R** will be constructed, with parts of the previous system that were untainted by the entropy being incorporated into the new system. However, if such a reconstruction is considered not worthwhile because of the new reality's instability or uncertainty, then further research and planning will be abandoned and no attempt at reconstruction will be undertaken.

While for the closed information system only the reality is subject to alteration, for the open information system both the defining elements and their realities can change. It is because of the system's openness that the likelihood for entropy at any given moment is greater than in the closed system. When entropy does enter the open system, however, it is not as devistating as it is with the closed system, because its openness provides it with the ability to be altered and expanded and thus be salvaged when entropy enters.

Three reasons for entropy entering a system must be considered. Frist, a change may occur in the area's reality defined by the system's **r** particles. As S_t contains the elements of **S** and the **R** particles, $R_t = [S/S_dR]_t$; when both **S** and **R** are open-ended, the definitive relation holds only for the period bound by the time signature. At time t_0, **n** relationships exist within the system, and at time t_1, the **eth** particle in **n** is altered due to the reality shift of this particle, but the extent of the alteration is such that **e**'s identity is not totally destroyed. To compensate for **e**'s alteration, the defining element must also be altered, but in the open-ended system care must be taken not to interfere with the other relationships. This situation is similar to, but not identical with, changes that occur in the closed system; while the difference is one of nuance, it is significant because changes in the reality of the particle being considered can be brought about by changes in other relationships within the system. These changes may be due to improved information in the area of reality that may threaten the entire relationship. They may be due to the deterioration of the significance of one or more reality particles, thereby requiring different defining elements. They may also be due to the merger of two or more reality particles because of information being incorporated that eliminates the reason for the separation in definition and delineation. The specific instances of change need to be met with the appropriate alterations in the defining elements and their corresponding reality particles if the invading entropy is to be eliminated and the system's viability maintained.

An example of this is a developing country with fairly scarce natural resources and a highly developed agricultural base as a legacy from its earlier stage of emergence — a country that requires intensive importing and exporting activity to enhance its development and economic expansion. This country's government seeks to maintain development while issuing decrees and policies in light of the inherent economic instability, brought about by the uncertainties of growth. A firm engaged in importing and exporting in this situation has to maintain its information system open-ended for its investors, foreign suppliers, and those in foreign countries to whom the firm ships finished products of the country's industry and agriculture. Both the domestic and importing-exporting economies are subject to change, rendering parts of the firm's information system entropic. Changes have to be introduced in the firm's information system to account for these shifting realities. If these changes become too great, the information system loses its identity and becomes intensively entropic. The firm may formulate another system, or if its dependence on its previous system was too strong, the consequence of maintaining the entropic system may be the firm's closing because of its inability to cope with the changing realities.

The second reason for entropy in the open information system is the improved quality of the defining statements and the manner in which this improvement brings about a break in the isomorphic and reflexive relationships with the corresponding area particles. The result is that the statement $s_d r$, that is, is constructed s defines and delineates r if and only if r is so related to s by being defined and delineated by s that any change in s must be met by a corresponding change in the area reality particle if the isomorphic and reflexive relationships are to be maintained. The element s may change due to a greater understanding over the time period, while the reality particle remains stable. The sharpening of the s language opens new vistas for dealing with its reality. When decisions to enter new markets — be they domestic, foreign, or both — are considered, the system's defining and delineating elements are sharpened by the accumulation of greater understanding and experience, even though its reality remains as projected within the system. As the dynamics of the system are worked out through its usage, further understanding of the situation requires some problem redefinition; differences in the nuances in the system's operations, such as market responses to imported products as compared to the domestic market response, and the competition these products generate in both markets, have to be revised, while the basic reality for which the system was constructed remains unchanged.

The third reason for entropy in the open information system is that alterations occur in the s elements due to the refinement of information and in the system's realities independent of, and not corresponding to, changes in the s elements. For this condition appropriate adjustments have to be made on both sides of the definition if the relationships affected by these changes, and ultimately the system itself, are to be maintained. For example, an innovative product is exported to a country of similar economic structure and output (it makes no difference here if the country is developing or is in its postindustrial growth stage). The product is successful, and shifts in consumer liquidity in the targeted country result in greater purchases of the product than expected. The reality has been altered by the product's success, and further output is required to meet the foreign demand. The system is revised to take these dynamics into consideration and also to allow for further consequences in the targeted country such as tariffs, the country's business cycle, and the exporter's ability to meet new demand. Because such changes are made with the intent of increasing the product's production and increasing exports and stimulating marginal consumption according to the abilities of the domestic and importing economies to absorb the product, the system's financing procedures have to be restructured to correspond to this new reality. This results in the relevant alteration in both the s and r sides. The system is preserved and the reality changes as entropy on both sides of the definition is removed.

In both the closed and open information systems entropy is at its most destructive form when these systems are unable to handle changes in their respective realities through the reconstruction of their defining elements and area particles. In the long run the consequences of entropy are either constant reconstruction until the system loses its original purpose and intention, or the retention of the system, no matter how extensive the modifications, until a better system, one clean of entropy and of greater utility, can be constructed. Information systems for businesses engaged in both domestic markets and foreign markets have to be reconstructed when the economic conditions within the domestic market and for importing to the targeted country and that country's ability to absorb imports are altered.

The point is that for every information system S_t, given a change in either s or r — and, in the case of the open system only, both — the system's viability is maintained as a total information system. If these alterations are neglected, the entropy that has set in increases throughout the system, weakening it for further entropy to enter and thereby bringing about the system's decline. Economic activity requires that the necessary alterations be made when entropy is noticed. This is less certain when foreign markets are involved because of the lack of control one economy has over another. Information systems pertaining specifically to international trade are the most likely to become entropic rapidly because of the differences in domestic dynamics such as the positions on the business cycle, fluctuations in currency values, and the potential effects of internal political situations. These factors have to be included in the systems, either as statements or as parameters, to be reckoned with if and when they become potentially influential.

NOTES

1. James Tobin, *Asset Accumulation and Economic Activity* (Chicago: University of Chicago Press, 1980), p. 46.

2. Smith's argument was that if each merchant acted in his best interest, the best interest of the economy — not society — would be served. When excess production occurred, this would be removed by the lowering of prices so that people would purchase more. When demand exceeded supply, this would be offset at first by higher prices and then by greater production. In this manner the "invisible hand" would regulate the economy.

The emerging countries, however, are not concerned only with their economies, but with their social development as well. During the time in which Smith wrote, social and economic development were considered handmaidens. Now, however, with the lessons learned from the Industrial Revolution and the Great Depression that closed that historical era, this connection is even stronger.

See Adam Smith, *An Inquiry into the Nature and Causes of the Wealth of Nations,* ed. Edwin Cannan (London: Methuen, 1950).

See also Kenneth Lux, *Adam Smith's Mistake* (Boston: Shambhala Press, 1990). Lux argued that Smith merged the self-interest of individuals with the benevolence of human nature that is necessary for society to develop. This does seem paradoxical, especially as Smith was also a moral philosopher. This paradox is resolved, however, when it is considered that no matter how dismal the science of economics may seem, there is a little part of the preacher in every economist, and indeed the inquiry into the causes and the nature of wealth and its distribution is one reason why people enter the field of economics. Without a reasonable distribution of wealth, there would be no great consumption; without this consumption, production would be seriously lacking. In a world of highly competitive economies this distribution of wealth is important, and on it is based the very foundation of welfare economics and the economics of development. This is also a serious problem for the emerging countries, in which the middle class is forming to bridge the gap between the wealthy and the very poor. This is accomplished by establishing a middle productive class that can employ and provide salaries for consumption, which is done only on the basis of self-interest. Where social benevolence is important is in the maintaining of the welfare system that allows the economy to expand — this on the basis of personal self-interest. See also David Z. Rich, *The Economics of Welfare: A Contemporary Analysis* (New York: Praeger, 1989).

3. Tim Congdon discussed this same point:

A company's vulnerability to unforeseen adversity depends largely on the ratio of liquidity to debt. If for any reason cash flow suddenly weakens and turns negative, it has to continue to service its debt until the position improves. If it cannot service the debt, it has to close down. The purpose of equity is to give it the resources to see it through such periods of negative cash flow. Equity therefore acts as a buffer against shocks; the lower the ratio of debt to equity, the greater is the corporate sector's resilience when confronted by untoward economic fluctuations. 'The capacity to borrow rests on the foundation of equity capital. Without sufficient equity, private money and bond markets could not function.'

See Tim Congdon *The Debt Threat* (New York: Basil Blackwell, 1988), p. 185. This is an important book and is relevant today. Congdon quotes Henry Kaufman, *Interest Rates, the Markets, and the New Financial World* (New York: Times Books, 1986), p. 102. This holds also, moreover, when the cycle moves into its downswing, expectedly or otherwise, for then the debt/liquidity ratio is important for financing debts to weather the downswing.

4. This choice may be for tax reasons or for personal and therefore noneconomic reasons.

5. Innovation and imitation, already mentioned in this work, will be discussed further with respect to the business cycle in disequilibrium. These terms were introduced in an earlier work by this writer, *Contemporary Economics: A Unifying Approach* (New York: Praeger, 1986). See chaps. 6-9, pp. 90-143.

6. Also, the case may exist where $0 < S_{o_t} < 1$ and $S_{s_t} \rightarrow 1$; that is, objectively S_t has been invaded by entropy, while subjectively it is highly preferred. This subjectivity is based on the objective reality of the situation, but the relationship between objectivity and subjectivity is often very loose.

Chapter 6

THE LIQUIDITY FUNCTION: MONEY, PRICES, AND INTEREST

What, then, is liquidity? It is a defense against uncertainty.
G.L.S. Shackle,
                    "New Tracks for Economic Theory, 1926-1939"[1]

INTRODUCTORY COMMENTS

In his discussion on the theory of prices J.M. Keynes stated that the importance of money is due essentially to its being a strong link between the present and the future.[2] If we take this point further, it can be seen that one aspect of money's importance is its being the link between the past and the future. Just as the past contained a specific and historically unique set of circumstances — to be considered as an era or social time, depending on which aspects of the past are being examined — that determined the purchasing power of money, today's circumstances and those of the future are the factors that are the determinants of the power of money within the specific historical conditions.

Another aspect of money is its domestic purchasing power in the aggregate as compared with the purchasing power of other currencies in their countries. This, purchasing power, of course, reflects the stage of a country's development and the strength of its currency internationally and is the basis on which trade is undertaken with respect to an agreed-upon currency. On the basis of this purchasing power inflation is gauged, markets are developed, and products for which trade is conducted are manufactured for the domestic markets and, in some instances, at a better quality for the international markets.[3]

Hence the function of money, its socioeconomic purpose, remains constant over time, this being that money serves as a means of exchange. Savings programs and investment opportunities that provide for **monetary** remuneration at fixed and future dates in return for risk taking and abstention from use are sophisticated refinements of the means-of-exchange function that money plays in society, no matter what the position is with respect to the stages of growth.

The function of money remains constant, and saving and investing provide economic growth and sociological development in those countries that have obtained political stability. Nevertheless, the historical differences of events that determine the purchasing power of money cannot be overlooked. The uses of money have led to the search for common denominators as a basis for curtailing excessively rapid economic expansion and too severe a slowdown in economic activity. The economist today searches for historical similarities to explain our current worldwide recession. Because our current period has no precedent other than the Great Depression, economists sometimes seek similarities between these two periods of historical economic crisis and analyze once again the theories that led to the easing of the crisis of the past to determine their merits in relating to our current historical economic situation.

During the Great Depression and the current economic recession the problem was and is both institutional and theoretical. Institutionally, large amounts of productive capital were lying idle while unemployment was high. This is the situation now as industries cut back on employment to compensate for the decline in aggregate demand, thereby remaining with idle productive capital, a situation not eased by the growing numbers of people relying on unemployment insurance and welfare. Moreover, because of the interdependence that has developed among the world's economies in their various stages of growth, and because of the influence of the postindustrial economies on the developing and emerging economies, prolonged recession in the postindustrial economies such as exists now has a stifling effect on the economic activity of the developing and emerging economies. This is because of their need for economic support, for markets, and for aid from the postindustrial economies that is not readily available because of the dampened economic activity and the reduced production and hence liquidity in the postindustrial societies.

During the Great Depression, however, the currencies were so deflated that major attempts by private industry to retool for new production programs were unprofitable and the necessary investment from the private sector was not forthcoming. The institutional problem was getting industry in motion to absorb the unproductive unemployed labor force and generate demand through increased production and general increased liquidity in the form of wages. Keynes offered the advice of placing people in jobs to do whatever tasks could be found, thereby giving them purchasing power in the form of wages. Aggregate increased purchasing power would pressure industry to increase inventories, which in turn would require an adequate labor force for stocking these inventories. By reemploying the unemployed recovery would set in and the depression would be eliminated as newly injected money by way of demand resulted in greater employment and a work force capable of investing, purchasing, and bringing the economy into a healthy and productive position.

To accomplish this revival, Keynes advocated that governments become active participants in economic affairs, and he thereby revolutionized the institutional and theoretical basis of economics. Prior to *The General Theory of Employment Interest and Money,* the solutions offered for resolving the Great Depression were steeped in the laissez-faire doctrine established in economics by Adam Smith and his followers and strengthened by Thomas Jefferson's dictum that the government that governs best governs least. This was an ideological imposition accepted by the classical and neoclassical economists, and it prevented them from taking the bold and necessary step of advocating an active yet limited role for government in economic policy to provide the basis for recovery. Hence the neoclassical economists posited their explanations of the crisis and its duration on various themes of restricted economic activity. Either the government restricts economic activity through too much influence in the workings of the market, or unions restrict labor mobility and fix artificial wage levels, thereby preventing the market forces from determining the wage and price levels necessary for securing employment levels required for maintaining efficient resource allocation, or both the government and the unions are responsible for the severity of the crisis in varying degrees.

In *The General Theory* Keynes commented on several of these arguments, devoting much time to Arthur C. Pigou's theory of unemployment. While he respected Pigou's theory, describing it as the most comprehensive analysis of neoclassical theory, he nevertheless criticized the theory for not recognizing the instability of investment, significant in the fluctuation of employment but neglected as such by neoclassical economists.[4] This neoclassical failure of recognition was responsible for the doctrine that cyclical fluctuations are natural in capitalist economics. The mechanism of fluctuation was the level of inventories; as they were depleted — so the theory went — a state of depression would exist until new demand for goods and services required retooling and restocking; as inventories were replenished to the point of saturation, employment would decline and prices would fall until stocks could be moved and retooling could be begun anew, resulting in renewed employment to meet the demand for inventory restocking. This mechanistic argument failed to consider that goods and services will be consumed, no matter how slow the rate, but that the retooling and restocking of inventories depend on investment, and investment at insignificant levels would not bring the cycle out of its depressed condition.

This indeed was the case that Keynes argued. Uncertainty over the market situation and the general state of the economy prohibited the necessary funds from being invested to stimulate industrial output that would allow existing inventories to be moved and new inventories to be accumulated. Innovations that could generate new markets through demand were kept at extremely low levels because the necessary investments to finance them were slow in forthcoming. Products with low profit margins were phased out, increasing the unemployment level and reducing demand still further through the decline in consumer liquidity, while the unions sought as much as possible to protect their constituents. The obvious conclusion, yet one that clashed with the classical and neoclassical ideology, was drawn out by Keynes when he argued that the private sector would not or could not provide investments at levels sufficient to move the cycle upward; the public sector, that is, the government, had to undertake the investment to increase aggregate liquidity for retooling and restocking of inventories, thereby generating demand and establishing renewed confidence in the economy.

The theoretical problem that Keynes dealt with was the difficulty of formulating an economic theory that would not only explain the reasons for the Great Depression, but would also provide a basis of reasoning that would resolve the crisis and establish guidelines for institutional, that is, governmental, decision making in light of all further economic fluctuations. This Keynes sought in his treatment of employment, interest, and money. He attacked the neoclassical theoretical basis of employment as merely a function of the supply and demand for labor and criticied Say's law of markets as the philosophical foundation for this reasoning. Keynes formulated his theory emphasizing investment and saving as the monetary sources of industrial activity and hence of employment, thereby giving credence to his institutional argument that if such investment is not forthcoming from the private sector, then only the public sector can bear the responsibility for maintaining economic activity through the uses of monetary instruments to stimulate the climate for investment. Hence Keynes demonstrated that the theoretical and institutional problems are inseparable, that policy must be related to theory, and that theory must be such that it yields appropriate decision-making policy relevant for each situation.

Keynes posited another methodological point, that a theory is relevant only for its specific conditions. He argued this in the beginning of *The General Theory,* where in the very brief first chapter he wrote: "I shall argue that the postulates of the classical theory are applicable to a special case only and not to the general case, the situation which it assumes being a limiting point of the possible positions of equilibrium."[5] Indeed, similarities among situations must be recognized for what they are, and not as identities. Therefore, seeking points of comparison between the Great Depression and the present economic situation, especially in our changing world, with the postindustrial economies in a recession, can yield instructive guidelines, but certainly not identical prescriptions or cures. The most common and obvious factors are unemployment and idle capital. Then, however, there was deflation, while now the postindustrial economies and the developing and emerging economies are struggling to maintain inflation at reasonable levels. Then the banks and exchange markets were outside the regulation of governmental bodies; today they are very much regulated and subject to government control, as when the government closed the markets in light of the October 19, 1987, stock-market crash that affected the world's exchange markets. However, the manner in which Keynes's dictum that the government should assume an active role to stimulate investment, maintain interest rates, and contribute to aggregate consumer liquidity was stated was sound for the problems with which he dealt. Then the economies of the world were in a severe depression, and governments sought to move the business cycle upward. Keynes's theoretical arguments concerning money and interest must be replaced by theorems relevant to the contemporary world economic situation, for the theory of economics that Keynes stated is appropriate only for the special conditions of the crisis with which he was concerned.

THE LIQUIDITY FUNCTION: ON MONEY AND LIQUIDITY

In his discussion of prices Keynes commented that some economists concerned with the theory of value who teach that prices are determined by supply and demand and by the elasticities of short-run supply and changes in marginal costs with respect to demand very quickly lapse into jargon when they discuss the theory of money and prices, embarking on discourses on the velocity of income, time changes, the quantity theory of money, and every other concept that can possibly be associated with it. While Keynes's comment is valid, he did not mention the reason for it. In its broadest sense a theory of value must pertain to the relationship between money and the goods and services it can purchase. This concerns the relationship between consumption and prices and the analysis of the elasticities of supply and demand during short and long-run fluctuations as well as changes in wage structures. The theory must also take into account the quantity of the money supply, the level of savings and investments, and the current governmental fiscal and monetary policies and the manner in which these policies affect the other factors, as well as the available quantities of goods and services, both of domestic and of foreign origin, acquirable through monetary transactions.

In his chapter on prices Keynes formulated a velocity theory of money from which price elasticities, output, wages, and employment could be determined. This is not an association of loosely connected concepts, but a theorem within his general theory that allows for a process of derivation, hence overcoming that very criticism he levelled against other economists.

Keynes's formula is **MV** = **D**, where **M** is the quantity of money and **V** is its income velocity, the value of which is dependent on the institutional factors of banking, on social habits, on the social income distribution, and on the effective cost of holding cash as opposed to investing. The effective cost of holding cash is itself determined by available personal holdings and by the interest rate. Further, Keynes defined money as consisting of two parts: M_1 for precautionary holdings and transactions and M_2 as the amount held for speculative motives. Therefore, $(M_1 - M_2)$ $V = D$, where D is the effective demand for money as determined by these components of money and the income velocity, which is the social and institutional component of the equation.

Further, Keynes stated that $M = M_1 + M_2 = L_1(Y) + L_2(r)$, where L_1 is his liquidity function corresponding to an income Y, which determines M_1; L_2 is the liquidity function of the rate of interest r, which determines M_2.[6] Substituting L_1 and L_2 for M_1 and M_2 in his velocity theory shows that the velocity at which money circulates in a domestic economy is equal to the effective demand for goods and services in that economy, both of which are functions of income and the interest rate.

From this formula Keynes derived the elasticities of employment, wages, output, and demand, keeping true to his claim that he joined a quantity theory of money to elasticity. This he accomplished by differentiating each factor with respect to the standard elasticity equation, so that elasticity e for demand D and prices p is stated as $e = Ddp/pdD$, and so forth. Elasticity is a micro concept, and this macro-micro dichotomy remains in Keynes's treatment. He could not remove this dichotomy because, as he maintained, money is the economic connection between the past and the future; elasticities show only short-run movement, while the effects of the money supply and its velocity of circulation are long-run and concern foreign and domestic investment and liquidity that cannot be measured by elasticity, but must be considered from a different view.

This dichotomy can be resolved, however, by the formula $M_t = Y_t$, that is, by equating money in the economy to the national income, including foreign money invested in terms of the domestic currency, and with the time signature indicating the specific period under consideration. Y_t is broken down into three components: $Y_t = Y_p + Y_g + Y_f$. Y_p corresponds to Keynes's M_1 and M_2; that is, it is money for personal transactions and precautions such as sound savings and investments in the form of government bonds and blue-chip shares; these are programs in which only marginal risks are involved and dividends are paid according to the demand for money for these investments and savings and in relation to the demand for other savings and investment programs. Included in this classification is speculation in which both the risks and the remuneration on investments are high. Y_p (personal income) is derived from wages, inheritances, profits on investments and savings, and other money sources at the individual's disposal. The Y_g income, generated by the government, is that income that the government has at its disposal as a result of tax collections, payments on loans from foreign countries, gains from bond purchases, and grants and/or loans from foreign countries and international monetary bodies, a factor of great importance for the developing and emerging countries. Also included in Y_g is the difference in the values of currencies, based on the domestic currency, being held as reserves, allowing greater or lesser amounts of domestic currency into the market with respect to its international value. Y_f, the firm's income, is net profits from business transactions, monies from government grants, loans from government and nongovernmental sources, and monies gained from mergers and from stock and bond issues.

Because $M = Y$, $M_p = Y_p$, $M_g = Y_g$, and $M_f = Y_f$. This formulation leads very easily to a theory of value relating the micro aspects of price changes to the macro aspect of the velocity of money. This will be demonstrated in a later section of this chapter; for further clarification, maximizing and satisficing must now be discussed, after which the liquidity function can be derived.

MAXIMIZING AND SATISFICING

It is important to note that the term "profit," traditionally used in the business sector to mean revenue that remains after costs are deducted, has another meaning in this discussion. It is used here to mean the achievement of objectives after the alternative costs and business expenses have been deducted. Hence, when the term is used in the discussion of profits in decision making, it refers to business profits and government profits, where alternative costs, that is, business costs for the entire economy, are considered. The profit motive, as used here, contrasts with the concept of maximizing. This is so because of the prevailing conditions of economic development.

In the changing economic world, especially in the developing economies that broke away from the Soviet Union, and in those in South America, Africa, and the Middle East, the concept of profits has to take on another meaning, one different from the neoclassical approach of revenue after costs are deducted. Such alternative costs as those of imports and exports, the accumulation of resources that are far scarcer than in the postindustrial economies, the need for ad hoc government policies to steer an economy that seems to be heading into a chaotic situation such as hyperinflation and unemployment, and, in the case of Western Europe, the need to absorb mass immigration without disrupting the normal flow of economic activity, as well as the paradox of industrialization that confronts the postindustrial societies (to be discussed in chapter 9), require a different approach to the concept of profits with respect to maximizing.[7]

According to neoclassical theory, the ideal situation for a business is when its profits are maximized and its costs are maintained at a low, economically efficient level. Neoclassical theory treats the firm as sufficiently small and its manager, the entrepreneur, as alert for new market trends and new projects. As the "economic man," the neoclassical manager is motivated strictly by those projects that yield the highest profits. The profit motive brings him into as many diversified areas as his business can support.

The neoclassical investor seeks to place his liquidity in those projects that offer the highest yield for the lowest risk, so that the profit motive here is the only driving force and the investor, also an economic man, seeks projects that provide the highest profit-to-risk ratio, rejecting alternative projects because either profits are too low or risks are too high. Speculation in neoclassical theory is offset by hedging against alternative projects. The economic man as investor will not place all his liquidity in one project, but will distribute it according to profit-to-risk ratios of the various investment opportunities.

In our current situation, however, some economists claim that the profit motive has lost its position as the prime hedonistic mover in economic activity. The complexities of contemporary markets in the postindustrialized economies, coupled with intense competition, have reduced the "lion's share" approach to entrepreneurial activity to that of satisficing. This approach has been further enhanced by the swift retooling activities of close competitors due to the uses of increasingly sophisticated technologies. Accurate market projections reduce the element of risk when close imitative substitutes are projected for innovative markets, so that entrepreneurial innovation is an extremely short-run affair and profits are registered accordingly. The status of profit maximization, so revered in neoclassical theory, has fallen, to be replaced by satisficing.

Satisficing, according to Robing Marris, is that behavior

> in which the subject, faced with a difficult problem to solve,
> prefers to sacrifice some of the rewards of the optimum solution
> in order to reduce the pains incurred in searching for it. Rather
> than maximise, he chooses to 'satisfice', i.e., to accept some
> solution which is 'good enough' in relation to various criteria
> such as survival, aspiration or avoidance of shame.[8]

That a psychological concept has become a part of our current economic thinking is shown by an article by H.A. Simon, one of the pioneers of satisficing in economics. Simon wrote that models of satisficing are richer than those of maximizing behavior because they deal not only with equilibrium but also with methods of reaching equilibrium. In the satisficing models the decision maker's aspiration level defines a natural zero point on the utility scale, while in the neoclassical approach, according to Simon, the aspiration level is arbitrary. Because the neoclassical decision maker is identified with the entrepreneur, his aspiration level is that of his firm's, so that the entrepreneur's maximum aspiration level limits his firm's goals to those projects that yield only the maximum utility. Opting for the satisficing position, however, can allow the entrepreneur to develop strategies that provide the firm with optimum positions instead of seeking only the maximum, which is too often unobtainable. Hence the difference between neoclassical economics and the economics of managerial decision making that concerned Marris and Simon is that neoclassical theory stresses only profit maximization, while the proponents of managerial economics argue that the conditions are such that maximization is unobtainable and must be replaced by optimal conditions. According to Simon:

> When the firm has alternatives open to it that are at or above its aspiration level, the theory predicts that it will choose the best of those known to be available. When none of the available alternatives satisfies current aspirations, the theory predicts qualitatively different behavior: in the short run, search behavior and the revision of targets; in the longer run, what we have called above emotional behavior, and what the psychologist would be inclined to call neurosis.[9]

Placing psychoses and neuroses aside, Marris described one way in which a firm satisfices. This is when a firm maintains a sustainable but nonoptimal growth rate by deliberately setting an above-optimum retention ratio — the ratio between net and gross earnings — thereby providing the maximum sustainable growth rate at a level lower than that which can be achieved and thus increasing the ratio of the firm's market value to its net assets and operating with this value as assessed. This ratio can be passed on in the future in the form of higher prices demanded for new share issues, allowing for the increase in the ratio of liabilities to assets, which is the gearing ratio, and according to the market demand for these shares.[10]

For Simon, the satisficing models are the only models valid for describing the contemporary firm's operations. Seeking the optimum solution for the firm's problems, as mentioned by Marris, is legitimate and indeed operable in the decision-making processes in the firms of the postindustrial economies and those in the developing and emerging economies. Moreover, the developing and emerging economies take on models of the postindustrial firms and apply them whenever possible, adapting them to the specific conditions of their respective economies. The theory of the contemporary firm is important in welfare economies to determine under what circumstances the firm's behavior contributes to the efficient allocation of resources in the economy.[11] From this, Simon commented that "the satisficing model vitiates all the conclusions about resource allocation and are derivable from the maximizing model when perfect competition is assumed. Similarly, a dynamic theory of the firm sizes... has different implications for public policies dealing with concentration than a theory that assumes firms to be in static equilibrium."[12]

In this comment Simon identified the problem with satisficing — that it is effective only when dynamic equilibrium prevails, for in such a setting firms of different sizes compete, and equilibrium is maintained in spite of each firm's ability to control its resource potential and its share of the market. By maintaining that welfare economics is a static branch of this discipline, he implied that the allocation of resources for welfare recipients is affected by those conditions in the equilibrium economy that bring about change. According to the conditions of dynamic equilibrium, the necessity for resource allocation exists and is controlled by the dynamic conditions necessary for maintaining growth and stability — whatever the stage of development — underwritten by governmental monetary and fiscal policies.

Yet the question here is not one of dynamics and statics for those firms whose policies have necessary implications for the distribution of wealth, the composition and level of aggregate employment, and the structure and distribution of productive capital. In the Keynesian, and to a lesser extent the Chicago school's, domination of post-World War II economics the uses of statics have been merely for analysis and not for micro or macro policy formation. The de facto dynamics have been those not of equilibrium, but of disequilibrium — a point that will be argued in the following chapters — and of welfare considerations changing according to the business cycle and the conditions brought about by its motion. The difficulty with the satisficing approach to contemporary decision making is accepting that since postwar economics the areas of concern have been the generation of market dynamics for new products in both domestic and foreign markets, maintaining production and distribution of those products that retain an acceptable profit-to-cost ratio, and the phasing out of those products whose profit-to-cost ratio is unacceptable. The derivation of satisficing conditions from maximizing models where near-perfect competition is assumed is, again, a technique for analysis, one important, perhaps, in formulating policies, but no more than that. Releasing the near-perfect-competition restraint brings the model closer to reality and allows greater flexibility between maximizing and satisficing. But the closer the model approaches realistic conditions, the closer maximizing and satisficing become.

Consider Marris's firm that maintains a substantial but nonoptimal growth rate, achieved by raising the retention ratio. The consequence is the reduction of the potentially maximum growth rate, the purpose of which is to exert influence on the gearing ratio — the ratio of liabilities less liquid assets to gross assets. This results in increased liquidity and consequently a trade-off between liquidity and growth. Because no economic actions are taken without external and internal reasons, the logic of this trade-off is apparent: A sluggish market leading to declining sales, for example, results in a growth rate lower than optimum. Lower sales mean lower profits, reducing liquidity necessary for financing other projects. A higher retention ratio — retained earnings to earnings — than otherwise available when left strictly to market forces allows for the release of greater resources and hence provides for more flexibility in programing and producing. By raising the retention ratio to its optimum, the firm is thus in a more viable competitive position that allows for the shifting of production priorities according to market conditions, placing it in a better position for generating new markets where product and consumer response warrant.

By raising the retention ratio, the firm increases its viability, thereby improving its competitive position with respect to other firms. With this increased viability comes an increase in the firm's maximizing position. Thus, if the retention ratio remains fixed in terms of present, that is, static, market conditions, the firm will be in a position of dynamic equilibrium, shifting its policies as the markets change. The firm will not, however, be in control of the market because its equilibrium condition places it in an isomorphic dependence on its markets.

This shows that it is incorrect to argue that by increasing the retention ratio, satisficing is obtained. What is achieved is a maximal position of the firm as a dynamic force in the economy, in which the retention ratio is raised to the level that allows for the greatest flexibility for the firm and hence the maximum level of achievable profits, restrained only by the market conditions and both consumer and competitive responses to the firm's policies. Raising the retention ratio prevents the firm's decision-making processes from becoming entirely dependent on the market conditions in both its domestic and foreign activities and permits policies to be established that will allow consumers to try the firm's products and divert their liquidity according to their individual preferences. If strict satisficing were the case, the firm would be entirely at the market's mercy, being deprived of the ability to exert an independent influence. However, the dynamic firm in disequilibrium brings new products into the market, stabilizing the products that show acceptable profit levels and phasing out those products whose profit levels are unacceptable. This disequilibrium and dynamic situation demonstrate that satisficing is in fact maximizing, for the firm establishes policies that will obtain the highest profit levels, given the constraints placed on the firm by its internal and external conditions.

The case with investments is similar. In a dynamic disequilibrium market hedging and investing in short-and long-term projects depend on the expected utilities of these projects. An informed investor will diversify his or her portfolio according to the proposals at his or her disposal and the conditions of the market. Instead of receiving maximum yields on one investment by placing his or her liquidity entirely in that project and risking losses that may occur if the market becomes fickle, the investor will spread his or her liquidity, thereby ensuring the highest aggregate returns with the greatest maneuverability to cope with market changes. Where maximizing calls for seeking the highest profits, the wise investor avoids seeking such profits in a single investment project. Instead, satisficing is the strategy used, seeking acceptable profits from each project that, when taken in the aggregate, provide the highest maximum profit rate. Moreover, the ability to maneuver ensures the freedom to maintain this profit level despite changes affecting the investments.

It is only because of utility that satisficing is equated with maximizing in operative behavior. In rational economic behavior — rational in terms of the contemporary individual's ordering preference — it is economic utility that is sought. In the example of investing, placing total liquidity in a single portfolio to maintain that portfolio's highest investment return subjects both the investor and the investment to the whims of the market. The investor is left with little maneuverability thereby exposing his or her money to the risk of a decline in value, which will render the investment entropic.

In the case of contemporary decision making the situation is similar. Utility equates maximizing and satisficing, as in the earlier example with the retention ratio. By setting the retention ratio to the level that provides the greatest flexibility and hence the maximum achievable profits, the decision maker can obtain sufficient maneuverability to formulate and act upon projects that could not have been undertaken had the retention ratio remained unaltered. This is a manifestation of utility, for by altering the retention ratio, the decision maker is provided with greater scope, and his or her competitive performance is enhanced. Indeed, the main reason for initiating this policy is to overcome entropic conditions that eixst either as potential threats or as real factors confronting the firm and reducing its viability as a profit-making organization. Whether a business is in an emerging economy, a developing economy, or a postindustrial economy, the firm's and the investor's economic positions depend on specific decision-making processes and the economy's response to these processes, given the restraints on the economy because of its development and cyclic position. Utility and entropy are both responses to, and determining factors of, the firm, the investor, and the economy, which in turn places constraints on the decision maker's maneuverabilities. Those government officials concerned with economics are also concerned with maximized satisficing, because the constraints within which they are able to maneuver are those of the general macroeconomic situation. This will be discussed in chapter 8, in the section on the Welfare Utility Function and Dynamic Disequilibrium, but both government and business working with labor — each from its own perspectives and interests — must act together in a situation of economic disequilibrium to maintain a healthy economy.

THE THEORY OF VALUE AND LIQUIDITY

A favorite theme in works of economics is seeking to determine the causes of value and the reasons why people purchase certain products and searching out the mysterious manner in which value is imputed to an object or event. A difficulty in determing economic value is that economics is a discipline with analytic, descriptive, and predictive force, while value seems subjective and not subject to quantification. But this subjective and intangible concept of value still persists in economic thinking.

A theory in science must be both relevant and workable; in economics a theory is relevant only if it is applicable. The concepts of supply and demand, while forming the foundation of economic thinking, cannot provide a theory of value because of their vagueness, clarified only in models or realistic situations, but still leaving room for more than one interpretation of their dynamics within the micro and the macro contexts. Even the barter process in the marketplace cannot offer a satisfactory theory of value because, although a selling price is agreed upon, the question remains unanswered why the barter was undertaken in the first place. This question is one that a theory of value must answer.

The concepts of utility and entropy in their expression of satisficing and maximizing form a theory of value that meets the scientific requirement of being derived from reality and being used to explain it. Utility is both subjective and objective. In its subjective form it affects the economy only when the individual acts according to his or her preference ordering. Objective utility is that which is derived from the information system and forms the basis for individual actions and preference orderings from which these actions are initiated. Entropy is manifested through the subjective choosing of alternative systems, thereby supporting some at the expense of others. Objectively, entropy is introduced into a system by way of disinformation, or by information not adequately covered by the system, or by shifts in the system's languages that have not been corrected. But supporting one system over another provides it with use and hence dynamic changes that can be treated by the necessary repairs; a system that is not so used will not readily respond to its internal and external changes by its users, so that entropy tends to be more intensive in these systems. The concepts of utility and entropy in their expression of maximizing and satisficing meet the requirement of deriving a theory from reality and applying it to its reality. Indeed, objective value is nothing more than the total of utility and entropy schedules as maximizing is undertaken by people acting in their economic capacities, subject to the satisficing constraints. This, then, is the impact that these total utility and entropy schedules have on the economy, regardless of its stage of growth and development, as people seek the maximum, constrained by satisficing.

With respect to liquidity, in Keynes's equation **MV = D**, if the velocity of money is constant, changes in prices will be proportional to changes in the money supply, providing that the change with respect to demand is unity; this notion of elasticity explains the situation after prices change and provides no guidance concerning the dynamics of such changes. However, for the equation $M = Y$, part of the money in the economy, that is, part of the Y component, will be held as liquid assets. This is liquidity not in circulation, so that the equation can be written $M = y_c + y_d$, with y_c being money that is in circulation, and y_d being money withheld from circulation. The variable y_d is the liquidity element of money and is money held for personal disposable income, income held by firms that is not used for investments or debt payment, and money held by the government that is not used in the economy. It is to this liquidity that the value theory must apply.

This is because all changes in prices, wages, output, and employment in each economy, regardless of its stage of growth, affect the preference for holding liquidity as opposed to consuming, investing and saving, or using it for debt servicing. Upward price changes bring a lower disposable income and hence a reduced short-term liquidity holding expressed in altered and then stable demand. This upward price movement has a short-term effect on wages, employment, and output that is even more significant in the medium and long run when disposable income is further reduced and the aggregate liquidity preference is altered by the multiplying effects of inflation. Unless wages are adjusted upward so that the value of liquidity has the same expected utility as before, output will be affected by labor unrest, with a consequent decline in employment as efforts are made to maintain the semblance of the present wage level. When the existing wage structure or even an increased structure for the small employment level is maintained, unemployment — its seasonal fluctuations are taken into account — will result in inflation because of the competing consumer disposable income for the same goods and services. The value of disposable income will decline along with the decline in liquidity because a greater proportion of income is required for consumption. Also, the quantity of goods and services will either remain stable or will decline because of unemployment, and production will be maintained by technology instead of manpower and also by the reduced programs of imitation and innovation inspired by the business community's cautious outlook in both the productive and financial aspects of business, manifested in the preference to hold liquidity rather than to place it in investments and production.

In contrast, an overall decrease in the general price level will result in an increase in the value of disposable income. Businesses will become more active with respect to imitation and innovation, engaging in more products to increase their profit levels and hence the aggregate profit level. Either a steady rate or an increased rate of investments will result, affecting the borrowers' interest rates. Price reductions are due in part to increased competition, but these usually mean lower variable costs such as those of supplies and basic materials, as these also are influenced by competition. Competition increases consumer liquidity, with lower prices leading to higher levels of liquidity that in turn can be channeled into investment, consumption, and or increased production.

With respect to business, price reductions offered, resulting in greater sales and turnover of merchandise, may result in greater liquidity, but businesses may not be able to exploit this liquidity because of market uncertainty, which led to the price reductions. This uncertainty is manifested in the unknown effects of the change in the value of money brought about by the lower aggregate prices on interest rates and on innovating new products, as well as on consumer response to the expanding and hitherto successful programs. There are two reasons for this. One is that since the Great Depression, and especially on the emerging and developing countries, governments, maintaining Keynes's dictum, have played extensive roles in economic affairs, establishing a reliance of industry on governmental monetary and fiscal policies. Industry's hesitance to carry out projects during periods of uncertainty is thus due in part to waiting for government action and observing the consequences of such action when it indeed comes about. This is Keynesian in orientation and will be discussed further in chapter 8 when the welfare utility function is explained. Therefore — and this is the second reason — the difficulty of initiating both imitative and innovative projects is compounded by the time lag between government action and the consequences of this action, expected or otherwise.

A program of injecting more money into the economy requires a period of time before the consequences of this injection are felt. One possible consequence of this injection is greater industrial liquidity that may not yield the government's desired result of greater industrial activity; instead, industrial managers may hold this liquidity until they consider the markets ready to absorb products that are competitive with those already existing, and products that are new and different. The added liquidity at the consumers' disposal may not go into further purchases that would be a signal for the clearing of the markets, but may go to pay off debts incurred or into investing as a hedge against further uncertainty.

During periods of inflationary pressure governments will act to reduce the money supply and, through the banks, to reduce credit. In the emerging countries where output is limited to the industrial base and its auxiliary businesses, the setting in of inflation is a fairly rapid process. The business cycle is far from developed, and the industrial base remains fairly stable — a feature that distinguishes this type of economy from the developing and certainly from the postindustrial economies. Inflation results from government policies in trying to regulate the economy and taking liquidity from the consumers in the forms of taxation, higher charges for basic government and city services, health, and education, and regulating the amount of currency in circulation. Consumer liquidity declines, but industry and businesses have to maintain their standards and their levels of employment. The consequence is a higher across-the-board price rise, while wages remain stable or rise slightly as a result of organized labor's pressure in certain key economic sectors. Consumption will be reduced fairly rapidly, however, and industry and businesses will yield by reducing their costs in the form of increasing unemployemnt. This type of economy has not achieved the sophistication necessary for coping with inflation by firms increasing their gearing ratios and by offering better terms for institutional lenders willing to invest in spite of the macro restrictions. The institutional lenders are government corporations that follow the lead of the finance ministers who set in motion these policies. Inflation is thus reduced, but the economy is revitalized by injecting more money and by foreign assistance providing the leverage of reserves in the form of hard currencies, allowing the financial backing for easing the economic restraints and for businesses and industry to resume their activities, perhaps with innovative programs with respect to the economy's ability to absorb new products.

The government policies in the developing countries will be the same in periods of inflationary pressure: higher taxes, higher government fees, and the macro reduction of consumer liquidity. Business and industrial activity will certainly be reduced as consumption declines because of higher prices passed on to consumers. Marginally profitable products are phased out of production as businesses seek to increase their liquidity. This newly gained liquidity, together with raising the gearing ratio, allows these businesses to maintain the production of more profitable goods and services and to limit their price increases, thereby seeking an edge on their competitors. But as competing businesses and industrial firms follow the same defensive practices, prices tend to be lowered generally after the initial aggregate price increases. However, the government, operating in a Keynesian framework, has an important function here. As the overseers of the economy, if the financial leaders, for whatever reasons, seek to maintain low consumer liquidity, they can increase taxes, add and/or increase value-added taxes on the production of goods and services, or issue price-fixing regulations to maintain low consumer liquidity. These restraints on the recession phase of the developing country's business cycle may be effective in the very short run as consumer liquidity is indeed maintained at a low level; they have, however, uncertain longer-term effects, such as the uncertainty generated with respect to government policies by businesses, which then take their liquidity — legally or illegally — into other countries' markets. Also, low consumer liquidity tends to increase emigration either to other developing countries that offer better conditions or, as is usually the case, to the postindustrial economies where the economic opportunities are far better and government policies certainly less oppressive.[13] In any case, business is revived when the constraints are either eased significantly or removed altogether, making production profitable and allowing the economy to expand as innovative and imitative products enter the market in competition for consumer liquidity.

The postindustrial economies are usually the economies that set the cyclical patterns that the developing and emerging economies follow. These economies will be discussed in chapter 9, where the paradox of industrialization will be examined within the dynamic disequilibrium business cycle. It suffices here to state that one of the factors that bring about the recession phase of the cycle and indeed is a determinant of its intensity and duration is the international competition among the postindustrial economies for one another's markets and for those of the emerging and developing economies seeking to achieve economic sophistication and growth and development. Hence industrialization and its increasing sophistication generate an international imitation effect among those countries that have adequate and similar economic infrastructures. This imitation is highly competitive, but as these economies are advanced in development, recession is not excessive. Depressions, especially those of the duration and intensity of the Great Depression, have been politically ruled out, and our present economic sophistication is such that fiscal and monetary measures exist to prevent them. Instead, recession serves as a market-clearing mechanism and a corvective economic force that continues until economic distortions are rectified.

Such a distortion was the emphasis on finance in the 1980s at the expense of production and genuine innovative and imitative competition. In the United States, for example, this allowed other postindustrialized economies, such as Japan, to make headway into the productive aspects of international competition and eventually into the U.S. economy itself. The financial aspects certainly followed, but only as necessary consequences of developing and expanding the industrializing processes. The Japanese trade laws are not as liberal, and the United States has again begun to focus on production to regain its position. The recession phase of the cycle, however, has led to serious economic revisions and retrenchment, bringing about revaluations by union and government officials. But, because of their extreme intricaces and interrelations, postindustrial economies must wait to be discussed in chapter 8. Then the business-cycle dynamics for the emerging and developing countries can be analyzed, as they are involved with those of the postindustrial economies.

With respect to money in the emerging, developing, and postindustrial economies, the equation $\mathbf{M} = \mathbf{y}_c + \mathbf{y}_d$ holds. This is so even when the element of international trade is considered, but in the emerging and developing economies, with their thriving black markets for foreign currencies, the official calculations of the amounts of this black-market currency circulation are usually erroneous, and the impact of this circulation on the domestic economy is usually marginal because the money is either hoarded or shipped out of the country to be held in offshore investments, which are tax free and very private.

Nevertheless, the velocity of money in circulation is a function of its utility, that is, $VM = u(M)$. Hence, if markets are such that consumption is high — and this includes investments as a consumer product — then the velocity of money in circulation will also be high because the aggregate consumption is high. This occurs when incomes in the aggregate are sufficient to afford both consumption and liquidity, and in this situation liquidity is that aspect of income both held and invested but available upon demand. The velocity of money in circulation is thus high when the economy is prosperous, and for the three types of economies this means that markets are expanding, with new products entering the markets and with competing products vying for consumer preference manifested in purchases. In each type of economy the consumer's budget is broken down into transactions accounting for purchases made and debts paid, as well as disposable income for savings and investments; this second category, disposable income, determines the individual consumer's liquidity ratio. Consumers judge how to spend their money on the basis of their utility preference ordering. Since the velocity of money is also a function of utility, firms seek to formulate their projects, either as products or as information systems, to achieve the highest appeal to their prospective consumers.

Investments and savings are means by which firms acquire liquidity, and if they attract a sufficient level of consumes patronage, their reliance on outside investors and savers declines and their financing is primarily internal, either by accepting per product profit and higher liquidity through higher sales, or by means of internal maneuvering such as increasing the retention ratio, the basis of net profits. Nevertheless, firms must seek to attract consumer liquidity, and because the consumer may calculate that his or her liquidity in closed savings programs or may diversify and increase both consumption and investments, the managers of firms must relate to the aggregate utility of liquidity as it affects the velocity of money in circulation. They must do this by offering products that attract consumers' attention so that these products will be placed high on consumers' utility ratings.

The money-income equation can be stated another way: $M = (L_\xi)Y$, which means that money is equal to income of which liquidity is a component. Liquidity is derived from the uses of money, such as from wages and returns on investments and savings programs. Expressed as disposable income, this liquidity is transferred into working money in the form of savings and investments that are then loaned and receive interest, or in the form of purchases, in which case the money directed toward consumption goes into meeting costs and providing profits. As disposable income, liquidity must be included in national income because it is a factor to which projects and advertising are directed. Although liquidity is money not yet used, it stimulates economic activity to absorb it. Hence the extent of liquidity also depends on the level of income — a factor determined by the price level.

Because **VM** = **u(M)**, and **M** = **Y**, the velocity of money is a function of money and of national income. Because the velocity of money depends on its utility, the theory of value is a utility theory. It determines the products that will be consumed and also which types of projects economic managers should strive to innovate and imitate, if the markets for these products have already been pioneered.[14] Because the velocity of money is a function of income of which disposable liquidity is a component, the rate at which money moves within the economy depends on the rate at which disposable income is placed in the economy, either through direct consumption or indirectly in the form of savings and investments. The preference for holding money for interest or in place of goods and services determines its velocity; this is the expression of individual utility preferences. Hence, contrary to Keynes's approach, the value of money here is an expression of the theory of value as a utility concept, making possible the choice between holding money as liquidity or exchanging it for goods and services. This allows for individual utility preferences, thereby giving rise to an aggregate utility ordering that can be tapped through innovation and imitation.

LIQUIDITY AND THE INTEREST RATE

How does this utility theory of value apply to the interest rate? Historically, classical and neoclassical economists have held that the interest rate is that rate that equates the supply of money with the demand for money for either short-term or long-term liquidity, so that at any one moment in time the macro supply and demand for money are held in equilibrium by the interest rate. Keynes pointed out that the interest rate is not a magic instrument for maintaining an economy or its money supply in balance, nor is it a part of the macro economy that can be examined validly in isolation. Keynes explained the interest rate in terms of liquidity, with the preference for holding liquid assets as an inverse determinant to the interest rate. The higher the interest rate, the lower the amount of liquid money held; the lower the interest rate, the greater the liquidity.

In his chapter on the theory of interest Keynes stated a functional relationship **M** = **L(r)**; that is, money is a liquidity-preference function that he stated is a potential or functional tendency that fixes the quantity of money the public will hold when the interest rate is given, and **M** is the quantity of money.[15] He commented that this relationship explains how the quantity of money enters the economic scheme. A high interest rate brings about a decline in disposable income because liquidity is saved and invested at high rates of return. Keynes maintained that this results in at least a stable demand while the money acquired through the high interest rate (reflecting its scarcity at that rate) is used ultimately to generate production. The mechanism is such that when demand is sufficiently stable, the newly increased aggregate supply of goods and services resulting from the new production induced by the money injected into production by the high interest rates reduces aggregate prices, leading soon after to decreased consumption due to the decline in consumption utility. Interest rates decline accordingly as the demand for money for industrial expansion falls, with all further expansion for this period financed by sales earnings and not from borrowing; money is then released for further consumption and liquidity. This continues until inventories begin to approach depletion and the demand for money to replenish stocks increases. Firms lack sufficient financing to draw on the reserves from their sales to accomplish this, and the result is that interest rates rise again as firms compete for liquidity from investments and savings. This system is one of movement around a general equilibrium position, for money is either saved or invested or held liquid as disposable income, depending on the economy's requirements.

Keynes wrote during the Great Depression, when the problems of emerging and developing economies were not considered. He therefore recognized that this system was not infallible and that as a consequence of its breaking down, the government had to take measures to initiate manifold and diversified projects to inject money into the economy — money that had the backing of output and employment to maintain its value. Potential demand would then be converted into effective demand as purchases increased, placing pressure on industry to retool and restock. Money would then absorbed by the interest rate, thus maintaining inflation at a reasonable rate after the seriously deflated depression.

The problems of inflation and those of the emerging and developing countries, as well as the rigorous competition among the postindustrial countries, certainly differ from those problems that existed at the time that Keynes wrote. His approach to the interest rate was geared to reviving consumption by converting potential to effective demand. Our contemporary situation is unique in that the preference to hold liquidity is not being aligned with the industrial demand for money by being regulated solely by the interest rate, so that instead of production being at the level where aggregate demand brings about reduced or stable prices according to production costs and profit margins, production now has to compete with investment and the contemporary individual's profit considerations as to how his or her money is to be used.[16] Of course, Keynes's point that the nature of the interest rate can be understood within the context of macroeconomics is still valid. The difference today is that the nature of the interest rate for the emerging, developing, and postindustrial economies itself has changed in accordance with the changing economic situation. To clarify this, consider the interest rate's role in microeconomics.

From large industries to the small business firm the interest rate is treated as the return on investments that can attract funds from being used for other purposes. Thus for business managers the interest rate is the rate of return calculated for attracting these funds for project financing. This rate of return is based on projected production and distribution costs, advertising expenditures, and taxes, thereby allowing for the return on investments to be included in the overall costing but not in profits. The rate of return should be attractive enough to compete with other firms and sources vying for this liquidity, with the projected inflation rate considered as a factor in this calculation. Computation of interest must be such that the rate offered is competitive yet sufficiently low so as not to affect firms' operations through repayment.

In his *Treatise on Money* Keynes defined what he called the natural rate of interest as that rate that preserves the equality between the rates of savings and investments.[17] While this book provided the basis for his general theory of money, prices, and interest in *The General Theory,* however, he argued that this definition was an attempt to clarify Knut Wicksell's position of the natural rate of interest and that as each society has a different set of rates, the concept of the natural rate of interest is no longer useful.[18] However, the point is surely not that each society has its own set of interest rates between savings and investments that can be unified statistically and that fluctuates in response to the economy's macro conditions and the changing political and economic world situation. If a global interest rate is determined, it may be useful to those econometricians who are seeking to find international economic activity and flows of monies among the various countries in response to the nuances of their cycles. But the significant point of the interest rate is that for each investment opportunity the rate of return at which the investment is made reflects the investment's utility as considered by the firm's managerial board in its planning, costing, and bargaining for available funds, as well as the investor's individual utility preference. If a natural rate of interest exists, it reflects the actual utilities for savings and investments and for holding liquidity as determined by individuals who place their monies in various programs and by business managers who construct these programs. The econometrician, examining the statistically derived global interest rate, could derive general conclusions about capital flows and the internal macro utility of money within each economy; for these conclusions to have practical relevance, howver, it is necessary to examine on the micro levels each proposal for investments and savings and the corresponding conversion of liquidity to investments and savings to draw rigorous conclusions and recommendations from this study.

Thus, what must be considerd by both investor and business manager is the savings program's and investment's utility. From the managerial position the utility is assessed by the product's potential success as determined by its costing and expected returns as projected by market research. The investor or saver, however, must consider alternative sources for placing his or her money held in liquidity. He or she must diversify his or her portfolios to ensure the highest obtainable rate of return, calculating the proposed interest rates offered among competing alternatives against the risks involved in saving and investing. The utility rate of interest is that rate of return offered by management to investors and savers for placing their monies after considering the most profitable investment and savings programs and the trade-off batween holding liquidity and portfolios.

No economic mystique surrounds the utility rate of interest. It is unlike Wicksell's natural rate of interest that determines the equilibrium rate of interest for savings and investments and projects. The utility rate of interest fluctuates according to the utility placed on it by investors, savers, and business managers.

If economic activity is slowing down and if liquidity is scarce and in demand by businesses seeking funding, the utility of money will increase and the interest rates, on the aggregate, will rise. These rates tend to fall if business managers reduce the number of projects presented to investors, thereby reducing the utility of investment money. If the demand for money due to increased business activity exceed the amount people are willing to spend, the utility of investing will increase as the interest rates rise to acquire money for business funding. While sufficient liquidity is absorbed into savings and investments, the interest rate tends to decline as the utility of holding money from investments declines, thereby releasing liquidity for consumption. However, it must be stressed that these movements are tendencies, and that no necessity is implied. Interest rates may decline, for example, during the initial phases of economic activity as businesses use idle liquidity already at their disposal, thereby reducing the need to pay interest on borrowed funds. During periods of declining activity interest rates may increase as businesses seek liquidity for realizing projects when the slowdown ends and thus acquire money at rates lower than they would be when activity increases. The utility of money and the interest rate depend on specific circumstances and personal preference orderings and do not rely on economic "mechanics."

Contrary to the utility rate of interest, the natural and neutral rates of interest — the latter is said to exist during periods of full employment[19] — are strictly macroeconomic and equilibrium oriented. They are based mechanically on de facto functions and tend to be self-regulatory, like Adam Smith's "invisible hand" that regulates the markets when each person acts in self-interest. In this view the natural rate of interest is supposed to correspond to that aspect of the invisible hand that regulates the supply and demand for loanable funds, maintaining these factors in equilibrium. However, were such equilibrium indeed operable, there would be no serious problem with these factors, for macroequilibrium approaches such as the Harrod-Domar model for economic growth and development to be discussed in the next chapter could be employed, maintaining the economy, be it emerging, developing, or postindustrial, on a continuing equilibrium growth path.

The utility rate of interest is not intended as a balancing force between the supply and demand for loanable funds, but depends on each project for the liquidity of each investor and saver. The investment and savings transactions will be made at an interest rate set by the individual's acceptance of the project's utility and by management's offering the rate according to its demand for liquidity and the prospective sales and profits derivable from the project.

How is this utility rate of interest to be compounded? In *The General Theory* Keynes stated a formula for the computation of the interest rate. He argued that if 1^dr is the present value of one pound sterling deferred for r years, and it is known that n^dr will be the value of one pound in the year n for r deferred years, then the interest rate for the pound sterling is $n^dr = 1^dn+r/1^dn$. He also stated that if the future rate of interest is uncertain, it cannot be safely inferred that the equation will hold when the time comes.[20] It is understood that a degree of uncertainty always exists in economic activity because even the best information systems are influenced by forces unexpected and uncontrollable by individuals and businesses. Nevertheless, given our current economic situation, the computation of the interest rate must be revised. Some degree of certainty can be found in our changing and uncertain world.

Business considerations relate not only to planning and executing production programs, but also to financial matters such as returns paid on investments as well as savers' and investors' considerations as to the uses of their liquidity. The interest-rate computation must be revised, becoming $E/U_i^dnr/1^dn$), with E/U being that part of utility expected by both the saver's and investor's and the business manager's sides; the d is Keynes's deferment, and the 1 refers to the unit of currency in question. When this expectation on utility on both sides is equal, then the saving or investment is made, and the formula determines the rate of return offered.

From this formula the liquidity function can be derived. The liquidity function is an expression of whether utility is high or low. As liquidity is disposable income, if we set that part of disposable income for savings and investments as L_1, then $L_1 = F(E/U)_1$, and liquidity for consumption is a function of the utility preference, also based on expectations. If we set liquidity for consumption as L_2, then $L_2 = F(E/U)_2$, derived from the utility preference as expressed by either holding liquidity or converting it into consumption, forms the liquidity function. Hence in the aggregate $\Sigma L(1+2)_t = [F(E/U)]1+2]_t$. The time signature here is of extreme importance because it reflects the phase of the business cycle. When the cycle is low, liquidity is also low, so that L_1 is reduced, while L_2 is diverted mainly into consumption. Aggregate savings and investments depend on the availability of money, and as money is directed into consumption due to unemployment because of the recessed cyclic phase, the velocity of money is very high, to be absorbed by high prices due to reduced sales. During recovery the velocity of money is somewhat eased as employment increases and money is directed in part into savings, investments, and, of course, consumption. Recovery results in greater savings and investments, while the utility of consumption on the aggregate increases only slightly, which assists in bringing the cycle down once again.

During the downswing sales remain fairly stable at first, but then decline as unemployment increases, reducing the amount of liquidity for savings and investments. Ultimately, consumption declines significantly, and the velocity of money in circulation increases once again in the form of money being absorbed by high prices for consumption as businesses seek to protect themselves from the recession.

In each phase of the cycle the expected utility of liquidity varies according to personal preferences and the general economic conditions. The utility of holding liquidity as opposed to investing or consuming, of course, is an individual calculation, but the economic trends dictate the parameters of the utilites. Interest rates vary for each investment and savings plan, as determined by the individuals and businesses involved. Because the interest rate is the expected rate of return as determined by the individual as investor and saver and by the businesses competing for individual liquidity, the concept of expected utility is extremely important, for it allows the individual and the businessperson the leeway to choose alternatives for investment, savings, and production. Indeed, it is the expected utility that allows for preference ordering, and preference ordering is based on previous returns and projected results.

With respect to the interest rate and equilibrium, before placing their money, savers and investors must compute their expected utilities, ordering them according to the possibilities available and their desired rate of return on their money for saving and investment. Business managers have their own computations regarding the rate of return they are willing to pay for the use of the liquidity. The savers' and investors' calculations take into account the objective market conditions and realities, while the business managers' calculations are based on their projected and analyzed models of their future market dynamics. When the savers' and investors' objective and expected utilities reach agreement with the objective utilities as assumed by market analysis and expected utilities established by management, the monies are placed at contracted terms — at the interest rate r. If the utilities of both sides are not in agreement, the transaction will not be made, and the liquidity will not be absorbed by the interest rate until one or both sides alter their utility orderings. Hence no mechanism is involved in maintaining equilibrium because the interest rate is based on both objective conditions and expected utilities as manifested in bargaining.

The extreme case may occur where high interest rates are offered but savers and investors prefer to hold their money liquid because no economic necessity exists dictating that objective utility as expressed by the high rates should overcome expected utility ordering. Each saver's and investor's utility preference cannot be quantified economically; although when savings and investments are made, the interest rate signifies the utility of the transaction, equating the objective and subjective components on each side of the bargaining process.

In contemporary economies there is movement among projects, some being phased out while others are being developed. This is a manifestation of the profit motive expressed by the utility of saving and investing as directed into production, that is, of choosing liquidity or interest on money in light of new projects offering acceptable rates of return. In the model of a dynamic equilibrium economy the transfer of disposable income into savings and investments continue as long as the natural rate of interest for the economy prevails. The difficulty with this, however, it that it is a tautology, for the natural rate of interest is that rate that prevails. In a dynamic disequilibrium economy the transfer of disposable income into savings and investments continues as long as the utility for doing so remains. Once the utility is undermined by either one or both sides of the transaction, the relationship begins to break down and entropy sets in. In an economy in which the dynamic disequilibrium processes of growth are maintained, whatever its stage of development, investments are rescheduled according to the utility preferences and projects are phased out, while others are initiated. If business managers falter in the aggregate, employment and prices are affected as inflation chases after goods and services as they are reduced in quantity by reduced production and the resulting unemployment. As is the case in many of the emerging and developing countries now, inflation and near stagnation are the consequences. The postindustrial countries have a broad-enough industrial base to weather the recession, even though the consequences for these economies are very serious. But the model of dynamic equilibrium requires a nonindustrial, nonbusiness force to restimulate the economy. For the emerging and developing countries this force tends to be the government that has not yet found its way in its political motivation. The tendencies are for semidictatorship, military coups, and general instability, while for the postindustrial economies greater government influence in the managing of the economy is in order, perhaps tending to socialism and economic stagnation in the mature balanced economy. In the model of dynamic disequilibrium industry and businesses in general possess the inner dynamism to move the economy out of near stagnation through the processes of innovation and imitation. In this model the government's role is to ensure that these processes are maintained without actually becoming involved in the private sector of business activity.

COMMENTS ON LIQUIDITY, INTEREST, AND DEBT

Our present social time in our contemporary era can be defined and delineated with respect to the geopolitical events that are now occurring, in contrast to those events that existed previously. The Cold War has ceased, and its dynamic of setting big-power blocs and their surrogate countries against one another has lost its relevance. The tendency now is for the newly formed emerging and developing countries to try to fend for themselves politically and economically and to seek trade and aid from those countries that are sufficiently stable politically and strong economically to be of real and sustained assistance.

For the most part, the emerging countries, and to some extent the developing countries, still have to establish a general direction in their political and economic procedures and policies. But whatever direction they take, they need financial assistance and trading partners. The aspects of trade will be discussed in chapter 10; it is on assistance that the focus must here be placed.

During the Cold War the utility of money directed for international assistance was not the overriding consideration, as it is in business transactions. The utility of policy and of diplomacy in that climate was the important consideration. Injections of vast quantities of money were used to maintain surrogates during that period, but even then this was not always sufficient to ensure international support. The fickleness of countries during the Cold War period often led to such international competition for favoritism that both blocs paid a heavy price and ended up with uncertainty, and the monies were too often directed into the private and secret accounts of the rulers.

Prior to the cessation of the Cold War the postindustrialized countries embarked on internal policies of easy money with respect to credit and interest. Savings and loan associations in the United States and their equvalents in the other postindustrial countries provided loans at interest rates that may have been realistic, but the value of the collateral offered fluctuated with the market conditions. Money accumulation became the object instead of the means for a better and easier life, and the stock exchanges became more important than the real factors of wealth, those of production and consumption. Big industries approached insolvency within these countries, and the governments had to support them. Moreover, the "paper chase" that was the accumulation of money instead of real wealth could not continue, because the paper, based on the economies' output strength, was weakened as output declined with respect to the money in circulation. The savings and loan associations, together with many banks, suffered as interest and principal were found to be lacking the real value they had had previously. The October 19, 1987, stock-market crash that reverberated throughout the major stock exchanges demonstrated that the paper chase could no longer continue and that a reconsideration of policies had to be undertaken. The presence of the governments in these countries, acting out of the neo-Keynesian concept as backers of the economies, demonstrated that this crash could not be compared to the Great Depression, and that since 1929 the economies had gained an internal resilence that would carry them over the 1987 crash and similar crises that might occur. This, together with the break-up of a system that was untenable in the first place — that of communism as practiced in the Soviet Union — and the political changes that were being implemented in mainland China, brought about our new social time and its economic environment.

In our social time the utility of money has acquired a new significance. It is used with greater respect to preference ordering on the personal level, and on the level of foreign aid and assistance the big-power-bloc considerations have lost their importance. While on the personal level money was used in the paper chase, the October crash and echoes of the Great Depression brought about the awareness that money had a utility other than making more money; the concept of liquidity and expected utility became relevant once the market revived and those injured by the crash recovered. On the political level money was no longer to be used to buy off countries in the struggle of the big powers. The Soviet Union no longer existed, and those countries that had once composed it turned to the postindustrial countries for aid and assistance in their economic situations. They joined the ranks of countries in Africa, Asia, and South America as emerging and developing countries, and although they had some foundation of industry as a result of their past relationship with the central government in Moscow, their industrial output was controlled and the quality of their output often left much to be desired.[21] Their status as newly formed countries that have rejected Soviet communism and have opted for a system that they had never understood, that of capitalism, has placed them on the aid, assistance, and trade list of the postindustrial economies.

But in our social time there is a serious economic problem that was not recognized previously, this being debt. Credit has always existed in capitalist societies, originating in the agricultural sectors and being incorporated into the business sectors for those businesses that have sufficient collateral to back their credit ratings. Credit has also become an international concept, because aid to the emerging and developing countries is no longer based on big-power considerations, but on the genuine attempts to assist these countries in their economic growth and development. The granting of outright money has resulted in difficulties, especially, because the granting countries are unable to demand an accounting of how the money is used. This tends to lead to corruption, with those people really in need not receiving the funding. The concept of loans guaranteed by the donating countries is now being applied, thereby requiring these recipient countries to act responsibly in their uses of the money so that the interest on the loans, as well as the principal, can be met on time. This has resulted in the application of the concept of liquidity and the utility of money in the internal economy by both the governing bodies and the peoples in these countries. These countries' creditworthiness is therefore brought into the open as the debt of the loans is accepted by them. Their ability to return the money depends on their ability to apply the concepts of utility to preference ordering, both in industrial development and in personal disposition of income. This is important because it brings these countries into the new economic concept of market economies, a concept that they never considered in their existences when they were governed by socialistic governments that directed production, regulated the money supply with respect to output, and hence indirectly controlled the levels of consumption within their respective countries.

In our social time we are witnessing the interaction of two forces that are assisting us in our understanding of our current socioeconomic situation, as well as providing a different realism in our understanding of money and financing. In the first place, our current debt situation, inherited from the easy-money period of our previous social time, has left us with the burden of paying back these debts and of revaluing our basic economic structures. The government backing of deposits in savings and loan associations provided a false sense of security for depositors, one that was certainly needed after the Great Depression; nevertheless, when the savings and loan associations failed, it was governments restrained in their financial capabilities that had to make good. This resulted in increased taxes, while governments kept themselves well staffed. The consequence was that extra taxes affected consumption and contributed to the declining employment situation that had already begun with the business cycle's downturn. Savings in banks have also suffered to a large extent, and the entire banking system is under threat. In response to this, people sought utility in investing, mainly because the resilience of the stock exchanges after the October crash — granted, after some time had passed and government had reassured their peoples that echoes of the Great Depression were merely echoes — encouraged investors to return to these markets. But the paradox of industrialization had set in, together with speculation for profit, because this aspect of the paper chase had resumed to a certain extent.

The second force is related to the first, this being the move into our own social time with its tasks and challenges, as well as with the obligations of our time. The internal economies of the postindustrial countries are facing what seems to be an inherent stagnation, which affects both the emerging and developing countries because of their reliance on and need of assistance and aid, as well as partners for trade. However, monies are available for these countries, backed by the governments of the postindustrial countries. The emerging and developing countries therefore have the obligation to apply the financial support they receive in ways that are of the greatest utility in forming and expanding industrial output, improving infrastructure so that further advances can be made, bringing the educational levels to those of the postindustrial economies, and providing social and economic conditions that will allow for economic improvement to the extent that the appeal of emigration will weaken.

This movement into our social time has to be met with the obligation of debt repayment, removing the transgressions of the previous time from our systems of economic growth and development. It has also to be met with the wisdom and understanding of our events as they unfold before us and as we, as the participants of our time, act and respond to these events. We must become aware that our business cycle is unique, and that the opportunities that it provides us and that we ourselves make must be met, for our social time is unique in that the old orders have fallen, but new dictatorships may rise in their wakes. The greatest challenge, therefore, is the application of our economic understanding and knowledge to rid the world of the scourges of hunger and want and to bring the emerging and developing countries into our contemporary era and social time. Our business cycle is faced with the paradox of industrialization, which hampers its upward swing; confronting this paradox is part of our challenge. To accomplish this, the business cycle must be understood as it operates in our social time. The cycle will first be discussed within the context of dynamic equilibrium as expressed in three theories of growth, after which it will be treated in the context of dynamic disequilibrium and growth, which is the way it functions de facto in the emerging, developing, and postindustrial economies in our social time.

NOTES

1. G.L.S. Shackle, "New Tracks for Economic Theory, 1926-1939," in *Modern Economic Thought*, ed. Sidney Weintraub (Philadelphia: University of Pennsylvania Press, 1977), p. 32.

2. John Maynard Keynes, *The General Theory of Employment Interest and Money* (London: Macmillan, 1947), p. 293; *"For the importance of money essentially flows from its being a link between the present and the future."*

3. The extent to which an economy produces two levels of quality, one for domestic consumption, the other for export, serves as an indicator of its position with respect to its stage of economic development. Postindustrial economies do not have to rely on this procedure.

4. Pigou's work was critized by Keynes in *General Theory,* pp. 272-279. Keynes refered to the fourth edition of 1932, when the Great Depression was making its full impact. The rejection of automatic full employment, a pillar of classical and neoclassical thinking, was replaced by Keynes with the more realistic concept of fluctuating employment, dependent on the business cycle.

5. Keynes, *General Theory,* p. 3.

6. Keynes, *General Theory*, pp. 199-200.

7. Israel's absorption of Ethiopian and Soviet immigrants is a special case, for in spite of their cultural differences, there is still a common tie of brotherhood.

8. Robin Marris, *The Economic Theory of 'Managerial' Capitalism* (London: Macmillan, 1967), p. 108.

9. H.A. Simon, "Theories of Decision-making in Economics and Behavioral Science," *American Economic Review* 49, 1959: 253-283, quoted here from *Managerial Economics,* ed. G.P.E. Clarkson (Baltimore: Penguin, 1968), p. 26. In 20 to this page Simon wrote:

> Lest the last term [neurosis] appear fanciful, I should like to call attention to the phenomena of panic and broken morale, which are well known to observers of the stock market and of organizations but which have no reasonable interpretation in classical utility theory. I may also mention that psychologists use the theory described here in a straightforward way to produce experimental neurosis in animal and human subjects.

10. See Marris, *Economic Theory of 'Managerial' Capitalism,* pp. 247-248, where variations on this theme were thus stated.

11. Firms are part of industries, and industries are part of the general **I** component of the welfare utility function developed in David Z. Rich, *The Economics of Welfare: A Contemporary Analysis* (New York: Praeger, 1989), pp. 103-148. The welfare utility function is also analyzed and expressed as a component of the international utility function stated in David Z. Rich, *The Economics of International Trade: An Independent View* (New York: Quorum Books, 1992), pp. 111-142. Both utility functions will be discussed in this volume.

12. H.A. Simon, "Theories of Decision-making in Economics and Behavioral Science," p. 28.

13. Of course, the reason for such oppression in developing countries is to maintain the ruling party in office. The point is, however, that this oppression is maintained as a trade-off with real economic growth, which contributes to these countries' continuing reliance on aid and assistance without having taken sufficient measures, such as enacting liberal policies, for ensuring entrepreneurial activity and economic growth.

14. The term "pioneer," as used in this context, is Robin Marris's and will be treated in chapter 7.

15. This formula is found in Keynes, *General Theory*, p. 168.

16. The distinction between savings and investments as the terms are used here is that savings are institutional in the sense that they involve placing money in banking programs and government bonds, while investments pertain to placing money at the disposal of businesses. In either case the value of the money placed at the disposal of these receivers depends on the utility of money and its supply with respect to the demand for liquidity.

Regarding investment (and saving) behavior, Dale W. Jorgenson formulated an approach based on the neoclassical concept of optimal capital accumulation, in which the object is maximizing the present value, be it for an investor or for a firm. This value is derived by maximizing utility with regard to what he termed the consumption stream, subject to a fixed set of production possibilities and to fixed current and future prices and interest rates. His argument is demonstrated mathematically and holds for his main premise that investment behavior for a fixed time depends on the maximization of utility as determined by the interest rate — this on the neoclassical consideration that the demand for investment is a decreasing function of the interest rate. He thus cautioned:

> However, the demand for investment goods depends on the rate of interest through the comparison of alternative paths of capital accumulation, each continuous and each depending on the path of the rate of interest. Although this conclusion appears to be the reverse of that reached by Haavelmo, his approach to the demand for investment goods is through comparative statics, that is, of time. The demand function for investment goods cannot be derived by means of such comparisons. As a proposition in comparative statics, any elation between variations in the rate of investment and changes in the rate of interest is nonsensical.

Dale W. Jorgenson, "The Theory of Investment Behavior" in *Determinants of Investment Behavior,* ed. Robert Ferber, (New York: National Bureau of Economic Research, 1967), pp. 129-155, See T. Haavelmo, "The Inadequacy of Testing Dynamic Theory by Comparing Theoretical Solutions and Observed Cycles," *Econometrica* 8 (1940): 312-321.

17. See J.M. Keynes, *Treatise on Money* (London: Macmillan, 1936), for his discussion of interest, the various aspects of money, and his basic theory of money, interest, and value. His discussion of the trade cycle and the depletion and building of inventories is also interesting in light of the prevailing economic crisis of the Great Depression, for which he revised his theory in *General Theory*.

18. See Knut Wicksell, *Interest and Prices,* trans. B.R. Kahn, (1936; reprint, New York: Augustus M. Kelley, 1965), and J.M. Keynes, *General Theory,* p. 242.

19. Keynes wrote in *General Theory*:

> If there is any such rate of interest, which is unique and significant, it must be the rate which we might term the *neutral* rate of interest, namely, the natural rate in the above sense which is consistent with *full* employment, given the other parameters of the system; though this rate might be better described, perhaps, as the *optimum* rate.

The neutral rate of interest can be more strictly defined as the rate of interest which prevails in equilibrium when output and employment are such that the elasticity of employment as a whole is zero (p. 243).

20. Keynes's argument is stated in *General Theory,* p. 169.

21. The difficulties of the Soviet-style planned economy sometimes reached laughable proportions. A shoe-manufacturing government-owned firm in Moscow met its semiannual quota of output, conforming to the quantity that the firm was ordered to manufacture. There was a problem, however, as all the shoes' heels were placed squarely on the toe section.

Chapter 7

THE BUSINESS CYCLE: DYNAMIC EQUILIBRIUM AND THREE THEORIES OF GROWTH

The general identification of monetary policy with interest-rate control or manipulation pervades contemporary literature on business fluctuations.

Clark Warburton,
"The Misplaced Emphasis in Contemporary Business-Fluctuation Theory"[1]

INTRODUCTORY COMMENTS

"Economic theory is in its essence," wrote Gustav Cassel, "a theory of price. Its main function is to explain the whole process by which prices are fixed at their actual heights."[2] The manipulation of interest rates necessarily requires government intervention, and its purpose is to maintain the economy on an even keel of steady growth. The reasoning is that when interest rates are lowered, people will borrow more and inject this money into the economy to stimulate growth. Likewise, when interest rates are too low, that is, when there is too much money in the economy not backed by production, interest rates should be raised to reduce borrowing, with the existing money flow being reduced through consumption.

Of course, regulating the interest rate affects savings and investment. When rates are high, depending on the liquidity function, investments are made and savings are placed that can be used for loanable funds and for financing projects; when rates are low, depending on personal liquidity functions, the tendency is toward holding liquidity or using it for consumption but not for saving or investing. According to this approach, raising interest rates encourages reducing consumption because liquidity could be better placed in savings or investments; reducing the interest rate assists businesses in obtaining liquidity to finance projcts.

The purpose of regulating interest rates is to maintain the economy on an even growth path, eliminating as much as possible the disruptive business cycle. Moreover, when interest rates are regulated, prices are also influenced. When liquidity is greater in the economy, prices will rise to absorb it; when liquidity is less, prices will fall so that greater purchases can be made, profits can be accumulated, and restocking can be undertaken, assisted by the falling interest rate, initiated to stimulate further demand and steady growth.

However, during our current situation governments have reduced interest rates, lowered the ratio of reserve holdings to deposits, and maintained the levels of risk insurance on banks and covered savings institutions. These policies have demonstrated no great success in stimulating economic activity. Prices have not responded to the general economic situation and remain fairly high with respect to the decline in demand and to unemployment. The world's economies are still very sluggish, with signs of recovery being temporary, overwhelmed by the current stagnation.

Moreover, the general economic malaise is occurring at a time when the emerging and developing countries are turning to the postindustrial countries for assistance, aid, and trade to stimulate their own economic activity. The difficulty, however, is that with the emphasis on interest rates and prices — neoclassical economic policies that were of utility in the era of the Industrial Revolution — the world's economies will remain in their predicament until policies are adopted by governments, businesses, and labor to move the economies out of the doldrums. In this sense the specter of the Great Depression does hover over us, for then, with the help of Keynes's theory, we learned that cyclical downswings of such proportions lack the natural momentum to move upward again and must be skillfully assisted by governments. In our era, however, businesses, government, and labor have become so intricately involved, even though their interests are distinct and fairly well defined, that the business cycle's momentum is dependent on these three forces and their activities.

The emphasis should not be only on interest rates or prices in economic theory and practice, but on growth and development, with prices and interest rates being factors in this process. The problem, then, is how growth should be achieved. Can the world's economies be in an equilibrium position and still achieve growth?

Static equilibrium and growth and development are certainly inconsistent concepts. Static equilibrium requires motion in economics, but this motion always reverts back to the same point, with supply and demand being held in equilibrium, after the adjustments for this motion are made. This motion comes about when some of the economy's sectors are selling more than others, and those that are selling reduce their prices to attract demand. Liquidity is therefore moved to those sectors with the lower prices, and demand is reduced in the other sectors. The consequence is that the lower-priced sectors raise their prices to make profits and to regulate the supplies of their goods and services, bringing about reduced prices as demand is shifted back to the previous sectors. During this motion at one point all sectors are in equilibrium with respect to production, consumption, and supply and demand. There are, however, no new products introduced into the markets; indeed, no new markets are developed. No products are phased out, and international competition is either insignificant or nonexistent. This model maintains all sectors in equilibrium after the adjustments are made, with all motion returning to the equilibrium point. It is certainly not conducive to economic growth or to the development of an economy's various sectors.

A more serious type of model that has to be considered is that of dynamic equilibrium. This has become the watchword of the overseers of the world's economies because of the historical influence of the Great Depression, in which growth and development ceased, and in which the neoclassical concept of equilibrium broke down. This is also because of the uncertain conditions — both economic and political — that persist in many of the emerging and developing countries. Equilibrium means balance, and the very notion of balanced growth is psychologically pleasing in a still very chaotic world. Equilibrium and growth mean that many of the business cycle's natural disturbances have been removed, and while fluctuations exist, they are within the growth process and can be handled by policy formulations to correct them and to maintain growth in a balanced manner. Dynamic equilibrium will be examined in this chapter with respect to three growth models; but first, the basis of this approach, Say's law of markets, must be discussed briefly.

ON SAY'S LAW OF MARKETS

No economic law has held such celebrated status as the law of markets posited by J.B. Say, the French economist and follower of Adam Smith. This law is a refinement of the argument of his British predecessors. John Locke, for example, argued that a higher force (that is, a metaforce) regulated the overall balance between production and consumption. David Hume turned to international trade as the vestiges of mercantilism were yielding to more rational approaches to commerce. He stated that in the specie-goods flow imports tend to equal exports, and that all differences in balance, if they occur, are made up in currency payment.[3] Balance and equilibrium were the key concepts when Adam Smith wrote his *Wealth of Nations*. The nature of economic activity during Smith's time, as it was manifested in transactions, fortified his confidence in balance and equilibrium, both in domestic and international commerce.

Adam Smith's work, as well as delving into issues of international trade and· discussions of mercantilism and physiocracy, sought to explain the forces of economics in terms of their objective manifestations of supply and demand, emphasizing the division of labor as a means of achieving maximum productive efficiency, with the amount of labor employed being determined by the demand for the product. Hence in the economy as it was understood by Adam Smith, the "invisible hand" of supply and demand leads to the most efficient uses of resources and provides the markets with the greatest quantities of goods and services at the lowest — that is, the most competitive — prices. This efficient operation of market forces depends on the absence of government restrictions as well as on the lack of collusion on the part of both buyers and sellers in the transactions. The invisible hand was not considered by Smith and his followers to be a static force, for it brought about shifts in fortunes. The demand for product A, for example, would be of such intensity that many merchants would enter the market supplying A. This would result in a surplus of A because demand was not keeping pace with supply. Product B would be scarce because of the allocation of resources for A, so that its price would be relatively high compared to that of A. Profits from marketing B would be high, while those for A would be low because of the intensive competition. Merchants would then allocate resources into marketing B because of the high profits. A would still be produced, but at lower quantities, so that its price would rise relative to that of B, which would now be highly competitive. Fortunes would thus be made and lost, depending on the intensity of demand, the ability to sell at the lowest price for sufficiently long durations, and the ability to diversify and expand into other products that satisfy consumer demand. Given free markets, those businesses that could withstand the rigors of this competition would survive and prosper; those that were unable to would fail. The invisible hand certainly regulated the free markets, but in doing so it often wielded a sharp sword. The process that Adam Smith described was explained by Say.

While Smith treated the workings of the free market, he left unanswered the question that has presented itself to economic theory and practice ever since: How is demand created?[4] For markets to be regulated by supply and demand, free-market forces had to be generated. The question arose because of the basis on which supply and demand exist and because of their relationship to the markets, which is other than regulatory. Advertising is an example, and in the classical Smithian tradition, if advertising generates demand, then the allocation of consumer liquidity will be centered around the product advertised as well as those already known; the process already described will occur with that many more products involved. The invisible hand equating supply and demand will still prevail, but the difficulty remains as to how this equilibrium results in the moving of goods and services. Hence, while Smith described a process that demystified Locke's approach, he nevertheless failed to treat the questions raised in the *Wealth of Nations* as to how the forces came about.

This Say did in his law of markets. In his *Treatise on Political Economy* (1803) Say developed the concept of the entrepreneur (translated as "adventurer" in the English edition, but the term "entrepreneur" has been retained) as the person who establishes the markets, which are then cleared for production and consumption. His argument was that supply creates its own demand, so that as supply increases, so does demand, and as supply decreases, a corresponding decrease in demand occurs. A product is presented in the market and brought to the attention of econsumers, who allocate a part of their purchasing power (liquidity) to its consumption; the supply has generated demand, and the greater the demand, the greater the increase in production until no increase in supply or demand is warranted. If there is a radical shift in one or both sides of the transaction, then as the product is phased out, demand shifts toward other products and the supply-demand relationship is reinstated.[5]

This simple law of markets, posited for setting the invisible hand in motion, sparked this tirade by T.R. Malthus:

> Of all the opinions advanced by able and ingenious men which I have ever met with, the opinion of M. Say which states that, *un produit consommé ou détruit est un en débouché fermé* (I. i. ch. 15) appears to me to be the most directly opposed to just theory, and the most uniformly contradicted by experience. Yet it directly follows from the new doctrine, that commodities are to be considered only in their relation to each other, — not to the consumers. What, I would ask, would become of the demand for commodities, if all consumption except bread and water were suspended for the next half-year? What an accumulation of commodities! *Quels débouchés!* What a prodigious market would this event occasion![6]

In spite of the optimism of Say's law of markets — and not because of the type of criticism that Malthus levelled against Say — it did break down during the Great Depression. Its validity was brought into question by Keynes, who wrote that if Say's law were not the true law relating the aggregate demand and supply functions, "then there is a vitally important chapter of economic theory which remains to be rewritten and without which all discussions concerning the volume of aggregate employment are futile."[7]

It is important to understand Keynes's formal argument against Say's law, for this law appears in Keynes's own reasoning, as will be demonstrated. The argument against Say's law proceeds thus: Let Z be the aggregate supply price of output whose production requires N employees, with the relationship between Z and N being $Z = \varnothing(N)$, which is the aggregate supply function. Similarly, let D be the proceeds entrepreneurs expect to receive from N employees, so that $D = f(N)$, which is the aggregate demand function.

For a given value of **N**, if the expected proceeds are greater than the aggregate supply price, that is, if **D** is greater than **Z**, there will be an incentive to increase employment beyond **N** and if necessary to raise costs by competing for the factors of production up to the value of **N** for which **Z** becomes equal to **D**. At this point of intersection between the aggregate supply and demand functions the amount of employment is fixed; Keynes said that at this point the entrepreneur's expectation of profits (but not necessarily the profits themselves) will be maximized.

Keynes therefore challenged the classical argument: Say's law, stating that supply creates its own demand, involves a special assumption about the aggregate supply and demand functions, that being that f(**N**) and ∅(**N**) are equal for all values of **N** and that therefore an increase in **Z** = ∅(**N**) corresponding to an increase in **N** necessitates an increase in **D** = f(**N**) by the same amount of **Z**. This means that instead of having a unique equilibrium value, effective demand is at an infinite range of values, each equally admissible as equilibrium points. Furthermore, if this condition should hold, competition would always lead to the expansion of employment to the point where an increase in effective demand will no longer effect an increase in employment. Here Malthus's comment that Say's law is not in accordance with economic reasoning rings true, for the law of markets as analyzed by Keynes most certainly did not hold for the Great Depression.[8]

KEYNES'S ARGUMENT: SAY'S LAW REINSTATED IN EQUILIBRIUM

In spite of Keynes's critique of Say's law, his theory is not free from this law. Consider his argument that demand and supply schedules are equal in the aggregate and that as a result all points in the demand and supply schedules are equal. This, of course, was Say's point also — that demand and supply are equal for all output, and this depends on full employment. Keynes rightly stated that according to Say's argument, instead of a single equilibrium position, equilibrium would be general and total. But why should a single equilibrium position exist? Surely within the realm of Great Depression and postdepression economics — the problem area that Keynes and the Keynesians have dealt with — equilibrium did not exist even for a single market. Either supply or demand was excessive in relation to the other, but they were never in balance. Equilibrium describes the relations of economic forces when they are converging on a specific point of stability. Consider Tibor Scitovsky's statement:

> For price takers are people who can transact all the business they want to at the market price; and this means that for all the buyers and all the sellers in the market to be price takers at the same time, the quantities that the buyers want

to buy must add up exactly to the sum of the quantities that the sellers want to sell. If this condition is to be fulfilled, the market place must be such as to equate supply with demand.[9]

According to Keynes, where $Z = D$ for each product, there is equilibrium; when the aggregate supply and demand functions meet, then aggregate equilibrium exists. From the vantage of historical reasoning, the following comments can be made: First, to reach aggregate equilibrium, the supply and demand must be equal for each product. Second, although these schedules are not infinite, they are as many and as diversified as the products — of both domestic and foreign origin — that are available. Third, according to Keynes's argument, for Say's equilibrium to be reached for the supply and demand schedules, the amount of labor must be infinite to account for increased products on the markets and for the corresponding increased demand. Keynes failed to account for a fixed or slowly growing labor force, supplemented by increasingly sophisticated technology for increased production of diversified goods, thereby allowing consumers to direct a greater part of their liquidity toward demand. No necessary correlation exists between increased production, increased diversification of products and markets, and an increasing labor force equal to the requirements of production and diversification, for these can be and very often are offset by technologies.

Moreover, in contemporary economies, regardless of their stages of development, aggregate equilibrium cannot exist. It is ruled out by markets that are subject to changes, with some products being introduced, other being phased out, and others expanding domestically and internationally. Also, supply and demand schedules are not only for single products from a macro perspective, but for similar, that is, imitative, products that are manifold variations on a single-product theme. Here infinite production for a single product is prohibited by consumption of close substitutes and by the allocation of resources for developing other product lines. Furthermore, to say that $Z = D$ in aggregate equilibrium means that; $\Sigma(Z = D)$, and that for every market m and for every firm 1, 2, . . ., q, $Z = D$ for the market's product and its close substitutes. At each point of juncture for Z and D and in each specific market m, supply and demand are equal, with employment at a level sufficient to maintain this equality. Hence, even if technology's impacts on the labor market and on production are considered, the labor force must consume only what it produces, with the products marketed in toto. Here, therefore, is a situation of supply generating its own demand, as consumption must relate to production for each m and for each aggregate equilibrium. Say's law, criticized by Keynes, has nevertheless been reinstated by Keynes in the guise of equilibrium reasoning.

In all fairness to Keynes, however, another argument has been posited by Paul Wells, in which he asserted that Keynes's theory is both dynamic and a theory of disequilibrium. Wells's argument is technical and certainly interesting. He summarized it by stating that in both short — and long-term expectations aggregate supply and aggregate demand play equally important roles in Keynes's theory of employment. Also, Keynes's model determines both the actual or day-to-day level of employment and the short-run equilibrium level. Wells further stated that Keynes's theory is dynamic in that it contains an adjustment process describing the way in which employment and output respond to unrealized expectations and to changes in expectations, to aggregate supply and demand. On these points there is no disagreement. His fourth point, that in terms of structure, emphasis, and results, Keynes's model is a disequilibrium theory of employment and output, is the point of contention.[10]

For example, Keynes argued that as demand and employment are interrelated, when effective demand is deficient, there is underemployment in the sense that there are unemployed people who are willing to work for less than the prevailing wage rate.

> Consequently, as effective demand increases, employment increases, though at a real wage equal to or less than the existing one, until a point comes at which there is no surplus of labour available at the then existing real wage; i.e., no more men (or hours of labour) available unless money wages rise (from this point onwards) *faster* than prices.[11]

Effective demand depends on consumption and constant supply, which in turn depends on employment for both production and consumption.

When expenditures increase with full employment, distortions occur in the economy. Keynes maintained that for a while rising prices may delude entrepreneurs into thinking that they are earning higher proceeds from sales; as a result they increase employment beyond the profitability for so doing. Also, entrepreneurs can pass off rising costs to the rentier, since the rent payment is fixed and affected in real terms by the distortion. Higher employment means greater consumption in spite of the price rises, and Keynes's system, while certainly dynamic, tends to equilibrium with respect to consumption and production, which is indeed a Say-like condition. Hence Paul Wells's fourth point, that Keynes's model is a disequilibrium theory of employment and output, does not hold for Keynes's theory itself.

Entrepreneurs will more than likely continue to bring new products into the markets as inflation alters their profitability position. Those products that are only marginally profitable or are produced at break-even costs, or even at a loss, will be phased out. Those entrepreneurs who cannot bring new products into the markets will most likely become imitators, entering into established and fairly secure markets. This will continue until market saturation is reached, and when this occurs in the aggregate, the business cycle will turn downward. These are certainly point that Keynes did not treat sufficiently, since the problem area with which he dealt did not allow him to dwell to any great extent on the entrepreneur as initator and imitator in economic activity.

SAY'S LAW AND THE HARROD-DOMAR MODEL OF DYNAMIC EQUILIBRIUM

"Our comfortable belief in the efficacy of Say's Law," wrote Evsey Domar, "has been badly shaken in the last fifteen years. Both events and discussions have shown that supply does not automatically create its own demand. A part of income generated by the productive process may not be returned to it; this part may be saved or hoarded."[12] Money saved and invested in the accepted institutions will eventually be returned to the productive process, thereby generating the manufacturing of goods and services; on this point Say's law maintains a large degree of validity. Domar's comment that hoarding is a significant factor is questionable, because hoarding yields no rate of return and is usually practiced in countries whose economies are highly unstable. Moreover, in periods of inflation, hoarding, however marginally it occurs, is decreased as higher prices bring the money into circulation to compensate for the erosion of its value. Placing the focus on the money in circulation through consumption and also by the release of hoarded money merely brings Say's law to the fore again, as the money in circulation is the means of exchange on which production and consumption are based.

The Harrod-Domar model of growth is Keynesian in orientation, especially because of its emphasis on the role of government in economic activity. Nevertheless, it seeks to answer the basic question raised by Adam Smith, that of the origins and causes of the wealth of nations, a question significant for the emerging and developing countries in the aftermath of World War II.

The problem that confronted Harrod and Domar was how to maintain equilibrium growth while preserving expanding output and preventing serious cyclic fluctuations. The Harrod-Domar model is significant for two reasons. First, the Cold War and the instability of the defeated countries, as well as the emerging and developing countries formed after the war, required programs that when instituted would build up these countries in accordance with the competitive requirements of the Cold War as the big-power blocs sought political and strategic support and would make them consumer-oriented societies similar to the non-communist and postindustrial countries. This required a macro growth model that would eliminate distortions and prevent volatile economic situations that could be exploited by the Communist bloc. The defeated countries of Germany and Japan possessed skilled labor and technological potential for such redevelopment, for which the Harrod-Domar model provided a basis. It was not as if these countries had to begin anew psychologically, for the motivation to forget the trauma of the war and to begin reconstruction was certainly strong. A growth model in which equilibrium could be maintained served these countries' purpose. Under such a model investments would allow industries to be rebuilt, and people's inner drives would provide the wherewithal for doing the work.

The second reason for this model's added significance is that the countries established in the aftermath of World War II required a growth model that would aid in the channeling of investments into heavy industries without bringing about major economic upheavals that would leave them easy prey for foreign conquest and domination. Countries such as India, Pakistan, and the newly formed State of Israel each had their own specific problems, compounded by the search for foreign capital for building industries. The politics that evolved during the Cold War certainly played a role in these countries' considerations and calculations for the accumulation of capital, and these funds were used in the best way possible given the external and internal pressures upon them. In consequence, each country required a growth model that would allow for demand to increase with increased supply but that would ensure growth without major cyclical disruptions. Such a model as that of Harrod-Domar thus suited the occasion.

In light of the economic depression that existed prior to World War II, and because of the many economic problems in both the vanquished and victorious countries in the aftermath of the war, the Harrod-Domar model sought to establish economic determinants of growth necessary to ensure that aggregate demand and aggregate supply would develop in a manner that would continue growth on a pattern devoid as much as possible of serious cyclical fluctuations. The model emphasizes the role of capital investment in increasing productive capacity and the significance of investments (and savings) in generating income necessary for providing employment and hence maintaining aggregate supply and demand. The roles of productive capacity are such that they must be in balance, in equilibrium, if stable and constant growth is to be achieved. If productive capacity grows more rapidly than income, the result will be unemployment, since inventories will be moved at a slower rate than they are produced by the labor force, and labor will be reduced to compensate for the lack of sales. There will be unused resources due to increased production, with the consequence being reduced investments, because the amount of money available for investment is less. If, on the other hand, income increases faster than output, inflation results from excess purchasing power unaccompanied by increased output; the consequence of this is also reduced investments.

Hence increased investments increase both aggregate demand and aggregate supply. Stated notationally, increased investment Δ I leads to increased income Δ Y; this increase is in accordance with the standard multiplier equation $Y = I/\Delta$ 1-c, where c is the marginal propensity to consume.[13] This equation can also take the form $Y = \Delta I/s$, where s is the marginal propensity to save. The economy's additional capacity for output depends on the capital/output ratio, that is, the accelerator. If k dollars of investment are required for creating the capacity of one dollar additional output, $k \Delta Y$ dollars of investment will therefore be required to produce an output increment equal to ΔY, so that $I = k \Delta Y$ and therefore $\Delta Y = I/k$.

The equations in this model representing the marginal propensities to consume and save are the demand equations; those equations pertaining to investment and the accelerator represent the aggregate supply potential. This is aggregate supply potential because investment is undertaken with regard both to the economy's present state and to its prospects in the future — prospects that can only be expected. Moreover, sustained economic growth requires that these equations be equal, so that $\Delta I/s = 1/k$, that is, if there is to be equality between supply and demand, there must be growth at a rate equal to s/k. Since savings (and investment, after Keynes) are assumed to be a constant percentage of Y due to the marginal propensities to consume and save, the equation can be written thus: $\Delta Y/Y = s/k$.

This model purports no automatic self-regulating method for growth. This year's savings and investments (minus hoarding) result in increased incomes in the following year. Large savings produce large incomes that must be offset again by large savings if the process is to continue. The problems of consumption and production are interwoven in this model. Money is channeled into investments from consumption; moreover, when incomes increase, consumption also increases. This tends to deter money from investments, so that productive capacity must be regulated, if not by the free market and entrepreneurial activity, then by government intervention in the form of monetary and fiscal policies — a Keynesian proposal incorporated within the model to keep it on as even a keel as possible.

This model can clearly be seen to apply to the emerging and developing economies as well as the postindustrial economies, since it is of such a scope that its principles apply to the three types of economies providing that its parameters are adjusted so that the warranted and natural rates growth tend to equality, that is, so long as the potential and actual growth rates deviate little, if at all.

The Harrod-Domar model is a mixture of classical and neoclassical economics and Keynessian economics. The Keynesian influence is the requirement that the government act as economic regulator and maintain investment at levels sufficient to provide the basis of production and consumption whenever these fall short of, or exceed, the amount necessary to maintain the system's functioning within its equilibrium orientation. The classical influence is its very emphasis on equilibrium, striving to equate aggregate demand with aggregate supply. The neoclassical influence lies in this system's emphasis on marginalism in its investment and consumption equations.

In this model, as labor produces and consumes and as aggregate savings in the form of investments retool industry and finance the restocking of inventories, these producers and consumers have liquidity available for consumption equal to **1-s**, which is the marginal propensity to consume. When this equals aggregate supply, then aggregate demand and aggregate supply are in equilibrium, which is indeed a Say-like condition. Through the actions taken by businesspeople and the government, a set rate of economic growth can be planned and achieved, according to this model, with the risks of overproduction and underconsumption or excess inflation or deflation curtailed. In the Harrod-Domar model of growth, therefore, a post-Keynesian formulation is stated in which Say's law of markets has a definite and positive role.

ROBIN MARRIS ON MANAGERIAL CAPITALISM: SAY'S LAW IN MANAGERIAL CLOTHING

While economists such as Sir Roy Harrod and Evsey Domar were concerned with the problems of the macro economy in light of the trauma of the Great Depression and with respect to the emerging and developing countries in the Cold War atmosphere, a different approach to growth was taken by economists who sought to analyze and understand the dynamics of the corporation as it came to be and developed after the war. The resources and techniques of wartime production were converted to peacetime manufacturing. Computers, which provided new possibilities with increasingly sophisticated program techniques and memory banks, and the necessity for demobilized service people to become employed, opened new vistas for consumption and production. This required industrial reorganization for providing the most effective forms of resource exploitation at the lowest aggregate costs while yielding the highest possible profit margins in light of renewed and rigorous competition.

This was a period in which both individuality and conformity were stressed; it was a time of organizational approaches, of standardization of production and of thought, in which the conformity of the past military life was transformed into the working patterns of the lower levels and middle management. It was the beginning of our era of knowledge, of individuality and uniqueness, where innovative attitudes in business were needed to enter into new markets and to exploit to the limit of costs to profits of the existing ones. Thus one of the most important skills of upper management was to take into account this dualistic individuality and conformity, to mold employees and work with them in a manner that would open new markets, provide profit levels that would ease refinancing, and ensure employment and growth. The new economic system that subsequently rose from the ashes of World War II and that resulted in a reorganization and rehabilitation of industry is managerial capitalism, a system of which Robin Marris is one of the important theoreticians.

While this system is unique to the postwar era — indeed, so much so that it is being adopted by the emerging and developing countries — its tenets are steeped in Say's law of markets, as will be demonstrated in the argument to follow. Marris's work analyzed the corporation as it has developed in the postwar environment, and it is in this micro position of the firm that concepts of supply and demand do not reach macro proportions. Hence, while Say's law is a macro concept, it is important to analyze Marris's theory to demonstrate how the law of markets can nevertheless be derived, for he constructed his theory to treat the big corporations. While Marris limited his area of discussion to the economic systems of North America and Western Europe in the mid-twentieth century, in which the means of production are concentrated in the large joint-stock companies, his theory is being considered here because both the emerging and developing countries have their large corporations — large relative to the sizes of the respective economies — that function similarly to those of the postindustrial societies. This is the case because of the interdependence of these economies and their reliance on the postindustrial economies. The big corporations are studied; their production and marketing techniques are learned and are applied within the sociopolitical contexts of the emerging and developing countries.

Marris stated that managerial capitalism did not result from a managerial revolution, but from the transition from entrepreneurial activity of the classical entrepreneur of Smith and Say, evolving into the giant conglomerates where the division and specialization of labor necessitate a specific class of people to define market areas, provide programs of production, and establish production guidelines. Traditional economics can therefore be contrasted with managerial capitalism, for the earlier economics assumes that in many instances the decision maker has property rights over his capital, rights that are restricted by what the markets are able to handle and by the law that prescribes the extent to which the rights of other people and their positions can be infringed.[14] Furthermore, neoclassical (Marshallian) economics dictates that if the decision maker's behavior is such that his business operates at a loss, a point will be reached where production will be closed down.

For corporate managerial capitalism these conditions are not binding. Corporate managers are legally obligated to their shareholders, but the extent of this obligation has not been clearly defined, especially for conflicts concerning personal or corporate interests. Because of their size and product diversification, neither profit maximization nor breaking even is considered necessary for any specific product, as losses on products can be used for tax write-offs. Moreover, the inability to earn profits or to break even for one product may be resolved by underwriting the loss through channeling the profits from other products. Marris suggested that profit maximization may indeed be relegated to secondary importance, superseded by managements' seeking to maintain a good image for their corporations, so that policies of effective labor relations and pollution control can be implemented. Whereas in classical and neoclassical theory the firms are sufficiently small that their policies have little or no effect on the positions of secondary, that is, supportive, industries, the firms of managerial corporate capitalism, whether they act as individual units or in concert, influence directly the prices and strategies of the secondary industries.[15]

The differences between the classical and neoclassical theories, on the one hand, and the theory of managerial capitalism, on the other, result in different approaches to demand and supply. In earlier economic theory demand is considered monotonic and does not distinguish among the types of consumers, but merely among the types of products, their production costs, and their profitabilities. In managerial capitalism demand is stimulated and exploited as well as directed toward the many nuances of consumer groups, both actual and potential. Supply in the earlier theory is considered only in terms of output and its costs; in managerial capitalism supply is related directly to financing.

In his approach to managerial capitalism Marris discussed the firm and its relation to the markets it generates. First to be considered is the firm's growth position and its maximum profit rate. The maximum growth rate is expressed by the following equation: $\mathbf{C^{*\cdot}} = p \cdot (I{-}^i/_p \cdot \mathbf{g})/(1{-}\mathbf{g})$ where

$\mathbf{C^{*\cdot}}$ is the maximum financially permitted growth rate;

$\mathbf{I}$ is the investment rate;

$\mathbf{p}$ is the parameter of return after deducting taxes and the entrepreneur's (that is, the manager's) subsistence;

$\mathbf{i}$ is the average interest rate on debt; and

$\mathbf{g}$ is the maximum permitted leverage ratio, which is the gearing ratio, the ratio of money borrowed to money reinvested in capital structure.

Where p is the profit rate after tax deductions and managerial wages, the optimum rate of profit given the firm's maximum growth rate is $\mathbf{P^*} = [\mathbf{1/(1/f_C)} + (a_S/f_D)] + (\beta_S \cdot v/a_S \cdot f_D/f_C)$, where

$\mathbf{P^*}$ is the optimum growth rate and is associated with the maximum growth rate;

f_C is the reciprocal of the capital/output ratio, itself a function of d, the symbol for the diversification rate on which growth depends;

a_s is an adjustable parameter representing the slope of the supply-growth function, determined by the firm's existing money supply;

f_D is the function that represents the growth of demand for the firm's output with respect to diversification;

β_s is the stock market's influence on the firm's activity, which although not related dirctly to the demand for the firm's products, is related in directly because market conditions result in, and are reflected by the firm's diversification programs; and

v is the constrained valuation ratio, that is, the ratio of the market value to the net assets, constrained by being held constant.

The values v, f_C, and f_D make their appearances in other equations, namely, $C^{*\cdot} = (f_C/f_D \cdot \partial D \cdot / \partial C^{*\cdot}) \div (1 + \partial D \cdot / \partial C^{*\cdot})$, in which f_C and f_D retain their values and the expression $D\cdot / D^{*\cdot}$ is equal to $(1\text{-}m) \cdot f_D/m \cdot f_C$, with m being the profit margin as affected by policy decisions. The dotted values are changes in the ratio of capital to output with regard to diversification. The value of c in the equation $C^{*\cdot} = am/c\text{-}\beta v$ is determines by the equation $c = c(d)$, expressing the capital/output ratio as a function of diversification, with the ratio f_C/f_D being a highly sensitive function of diversification. Further, $D\cdot = D(d,m)$, $C\cdot = D\cdot$, and $C^{*\cdot} = D\cdot$. The conclusion is that $C^{*\cdot}$, which is the maximum financially permitted growth rate, dependent on net profits after the deduction of managerial costs and net interest on debts. Considering that the gearing ratio is equal to the relationship between diversification and profits, $C^{*\cdot}$ is the maximum financially permitted growth rate for both production and diversification as assessed by p^*, the optimum growth rate. Since $C^{*\cdot}$ depends on the demand for diversified output with prices set in accordance with the profit margin, this is another way of stating Say's law — that output generates consumption.

With respect to demand, Marris's theory accounts for two subclasses of consumers. In one class are the pioneers who experiment with products without being influenced by others in their experimentation. In the other class are what Marris called the "sheeplike consumers" who buy a product on the recommendation of others or because they have become acquainted with the product through their association with other people and their purchasing patterns. The aggregate demand function for the product i, therefore, takes the form $Q_i = N_p \cdot \varnothing_p \, \beta \, N_a \cdot \varnothing_s$, where N_p is the number of pioneers, N_a is the number of active consumers, and the functionals **op** and **os** represent the pioneer and sheeplike demand curves.

Aggregate demand for the group of consumers for the product **i** must meet one of these three conditions: (1) gestation, where $N_a = 0$, so that $Qi = N_p \cdot \oslash_p$; (2) saturation, in which $N_a = N_s$ and $Qi = N_s \cdot \oslash_s$; and (3) the explosion stage, where instability and fluctuation between gestation and saturation exist. With regard to a product's profitability, Marris stated that without diversification all the firm's products will reach saturation, and their profits will be determined by the economic conditions of the later stages of their market lives. These stages are likely to be less favorable than their early stages because with the passing of time their consumers are more aware of both the products and those of their competitors, and as a consequence there is a general decline of the products' utilities. Marris maintained that we may reasonably view a product's profitability over the entire history of gestation, explosion, and saturation as consisting of an early rise, followed by a flattening, then gradual and possibly asymptotic decline. He argued that the average profit contribution of young or youngish products must always exceed that of old products, and that the higher the proportion of moderately young products in the catalog at any given time, the higher the average rate of return, ceteris paribus.

> This effect, which is positively associated with the diversification rate, must be set against the negative effect of declining intrinsic utility. We may then suppose that at moderate rates of diversification, the average rate of return *increases* with the rate of diversification, then, as declining intrinsic utility sets in and becomes increasingly severe, the position is reversed. This is probably what is implied when business men say that diversification may sometimes enhance profitability.[16]

Hence the decline in profits results in production cutbacks. Reduced profits are brought about by rising costs and declining demand due to competition among producers' goods. Equality of $C^{*\cdot}$ and $D^{\cdot}$ means that a decline in $D^{\cdot}$ must, under static conditions — that is, where a single product is involved — bring about a decline in $C^{*\cdot}$.

The supply side of this equation is geared for maximum growth and depends on the stock market as well as on managerial activity and responses with respect to production and demand conditions. Another way in which Marris stated the maximum growth position is $C^{*\cdot} \simeq a.p - \beta \bar{v}$, where **p** substitutes for $\bar{g}$, which is the leverage or gearing ratio. Significant for this aproximation is the retention ratio, symbolized by the letter **r**, which is the ratio of retained earnings to gross earnings — gross earnings being profit less debt interest, with dividends on preferred shares included as debt, and retained earnings being gross earnings less dividends on ordinary stock, with all other shares not included at debt. The retention ratio thus defines profits, a definition necessary when the total picture of the corporate firm's growth position is considered. The coefficients in the approximation statement, **a** and β, are rigorously delineated by the firm's existing money supply, and the stock market's impact on the firm is fairly determinate. This statement becomes a close approximation when the uncertainty of the coefficients is reduced, thus allowing the firm's managerial staff to act with relative certainty in accordance with the firm's capabilities of output within the confines of the stock market.

The net profits delineated by the retention ratio allow the managers to plan further diversification and to seek capital for necessary additional financing. Investments provide the firm with greater degrees of freedom for further diversification and higher output targets. The newer products planned tend to have greater sales once they are marketed than existing and well-established products that have already been marketed over time and thereby confront competing products of other firms. Therefore, the greater the sales of the new products, the greater the profits yielded to the firm. If the firm's past experience has resulted in financial success, then its present drive for capital accumulation, ceteris paribus, will also be successful. The greater the production output and the wider the range of diversification, the higher the sales, with a possibly higher retention ratio; but this depends on current managerial strategy.

Marris's argument is that because the corporate firm's growth is determined by its money supply and its showing on the stock market, and because the firm's money supply is determined by profits and debts as the stock market makes its impact on the firm with respect to the firm's position in competition and its ability to attract consumers for its products, the firm's supply is related directly to its demand position. Thus, for the microeconomic situation of the corporate firm, Marris, perhaps unwittingly, established a Say-like condition in the mechanics of his managerial supply and demand concepts. In the macro sense Marris advocated equilibrium, be it static or dynamic, over the alternative of disequilibrium. He stated that if the vertical segment of the valuation curve, which represents the ratio of the market value to net assets and replaces the ratio of return as the variable dependent on the growth rate, when the firm will be in dynamic equilibrium. Marris maintained that if the firm is not in dynamic equilibrium, or at least the ideal conditions for ensuring economic health and prosperity — the "golden age" conditions — will not be met.[17] This is a projection of the composition of the aggregate of corporate firms on the economy, in which each firm maintains dynamic equilibrium, and, by inference, the entire economy is in a growth condition as determined by the total of the firms' output and total consumption. So long as diversification ensures a greater range of products in competition, these products, through marketing and sheeplike behavior, will be sold, thereby maintaining the economy in a state of equilibrium and growth. Therefore Marris's theory is Say's law of markets in managerial clothing.

A THEORY FOR CONTEMPORARY ECONOMIC CIRCUMSTANCES

Contemporary economic theory has incorporated Say's law of markets as a tacit axiom, founded in the principle of dynamic equilibrium. It exist in managerial economics as interpreted by Robin Marris and is inherent in the dynamics of the Harrod-Domar model of economic growth. This durable law, brought seriously into question by Keynes during the Great Depression, has been shown to have withstood all subsequent onslaughts. This is because it is taken as given that equilibrium is the best situation, and thus arguments are put forward to justify and explain equilibrium. This axiomatic argument considers the best economic system to be one in which supply is consumed in toto, with demand being of sufficient strength to move all existing goods and services to make room for further production and consumption.

If this were so, then recessions would have been abolished with the Keynesians. Their theories — all extensions of Keynes's monumental work — would provide the fine tuning to the system, maintaining its dynamism and equilibrium in a growth position. But amid the current events of the prevailing recession and the emerging and developing economies seeking their way, the hard world of the dismal science of economics remains removed from the esoteric theories of its practitioners. The axiom of equilibrium falls by the wayside when it is challenged by the current problems of high unemployment and stagnating production and by inflation levels that often threaten the very social fabric in which the economic systems operate.

The only valid way to understand and treat contemporary economic circumstances is to place them within a theoretical framework and draw out their consequences. This framework, however, must relate to the real world as much as abstraction allows. This requires that the basis for theory be not equilibrium but dynamic disequilibrium, in which new products enter the markets while others are phased out, and in which the money supply and general liquidity depend on the proposed utilities of investments and savings programs and on aggregate utility functions for production and consumption. The Harrod-Domar model demonstrated that, given the model's conditions, growth can be achieved without volatile cyclical fluctuations, but the postwar conditions for which the model was formulated required economic policies by fiat. While this is in keeping with Keynesian theory, it has been shown to be inoperable in controlling the business cycle, especially as industry has developed to meet existing demand and stimulate further demand. Marris certainly shed light on the contemporary corporate firm's inner dynamics; but when he related the firm to the macro economy, he was guilty of reinstating Say's law, albeit in more esoteric terms than those used by its originator.

Because of the existing integration and the tendency for further integration among the world's economies, among which the postindustrial economies provide the markets for the developing and emerging economies and stimulate the dynamics of these economies' industries and markets, business cycles are primarily oriented in the postindustrial economies, but spread to the secondary economies of the developing and emerging countries. This, of course, does not mean that these economies do not experience cyclical fluctuations due to their own economic processes, but the big cycles are generated by the stronger industrialized economies and spread to the rest. Recovery must therefore come from the postindustrial economies, because it too moves in cyclical fashion throughout the world's economies.

There can be only one theory for these countries, and this theory must relate to the contemporary economic conditions and the changing political situation. Equilibrium and stability, long sought after, are only chimeras, utopian and never to be achieved. Cyclical fluctuations are inherent in our system and can never be removed. The theory must relate to this instability as the postindustrial economies expand and as the emerging and developing countries seek wealth and prosperity. Poverty, hunger, and want are certainly not new in our era, but despite our advanced technologies, which are being studied and adopted in the developing and emerging countries, they remain as scourges in our societies. The wars that generate hunger are symptoms of instability, of which the pursuit of political power is perhaps the greatest manifestation. Power without economic strength, however, is a sham, enforced by military might and the police state that maintains poverty, hunger, and want and seeks to prohibit attempts to flee to better conditions. There is no conflict between economic stability and dynamic disequilibrium, as the postindustrial countries readily demonstrate. There is a conflict between economic growth and development and dictatorship, as was demonstrated by the collapse of the Soviet Union, and economic growth and development cannot exist in Say-like conditions. Dynamic equilibrium is perhaps necessary for model building, with the ceteris paribus clause attached to account for the lack of fluctuations. But if theory is to achieve a closer approximation to reality, especially our current reality in which countries are in search of identities and are seeking growth and prosperity, then dynamic disequilibrium must be introduced and explored in the processes of growth and development for the postindustrial economies and for the developing and emerging economies for which they set examples of prosperity.

NOTES

1. Clark Warburton, "The Misplaced Emphasis in Contemporary Business-Fluctuation Theory," *Journal of Business of the University of Chicago* 19 1946: 199-220, quoted here from F.A. Lutz and L.W. Mintz eds, *Readings in Monetary Theory* (Homewood, Ill.; Richard D. Irwin, 1962), p. 312.

2. Gustav Cassel, "The Rate of Interest, the Bank Rate, and the Stabilization of Prices," *Quarterly Journal of Economics 42* (1927-1928): 511-529, quoted here from Lutz and Mintz, *Reading in Monetary Theory,* 00p. 319.

3. See John Locke, *Several Papers Relating to Money, Interest, and Trade* (New York: Augustus M. Kelley, 1968), and David Hume, *Writings on Economics,* ed. Eugene Rotwein, (Salem, N.H.: Ayer Co., 1955).

4. The question of how demand is generated was never adequately dealt with by Smith and the classical and neoclassical economists, except Say. It existed as a given condition of the economy, and this perhaps justifies the existence of equilibrium. To say that supply generates its own demand, as Marris has demonstrated, is certainly insufficient for economic analysis. How this is done with respect to value, the dynamics of the firm, the psychological factors of marketing, product distribution and costing, and competition was analyzed by Marris. However, Marris avoided taking the important step of fully integrating the firm into the macro economy, which placed his theory in the realm of Say-like dynamic equilibrium. This will be discussed in the section of this chapter that deals with Marris's theory.

5. See J.B. Say, *Letters to Mr. Malthus on Several Subjects of Political Economy,* trans. John Richter (London: Sherwood, Neely, and Jones, 1821); and *Treatise on Political Economy,* trans. C.R. Prinsep (London: Longman, Hurst, Rees, Orme, and Brown, 1821).

6. T.R. Malthus, *Principles of Political Economy* 2nd ed. (London: William Pickering, 1836), p. 363 n.; quoted here from J.M. Keynes, *The General Theory of Employment Interest and Money* (London: Macmillan, 1947, pp. 363-364. Say certainly had an optimistic view of economic growth and development, while Malthus's view was pessimistic. Given the current situation in Somalia and the terrible conflict in Yugoslavia, the weight seems to be on the pessimistic side of Malthus's argument. Food is scarce, and population growth is certainly being hindered. Economic development is nonexistent. But these are largely man-made situations and can be rectified.

7. Keynes, *General Theory,* p. 26.

8. Oscar Lange argued that Say's law of markets precludes any monetary theory, but he drew the conclusion that the traditional procedure of the theory of money involves a contradiction: "Either Say's law is assumed or money and prices are indeterminate — but then *Say's law and hence the neutrality of money must be abandoned."* Oscar Lange, "Say's Law: A Restatement and Criticism," in *Studies in Mathematical Economics and Econometrics,* ed. O. Lange, F. McIntyre, and T.O. Yntema (Chicago: University of Chicago Press, 1942), pp. 67-68. Commenting on Lange's point, Franco Modigliani stated: "Lange's result seems due to the failure to distinguish between necessary and sufficient conditions. Say's law is a sufficient condition for the neutrality of money but not a necessary one. Lange

asks me to inform the reader that he agrees with my conclusion. This conclusion, however, does not invalidate his result that under Say's law money and prices are indeterminate." Franco Modigliani, "Liquidity Preference and the Theory of Interest and Money," *Econometrica 12* (1944): 45-88, quoted here from Lutz and Mintz, *Readings in Monetary Theory,* p. 217 n. 35.

9. Tibor Scitovsky, *Welfare and Competition* (Chicago: Richard D. Irwin, 1951), p. 231. Scitovsky was discussing here neoclassical perfect competition; his argument holds, however, for all forms of equilibrium.

10. See Paul Wells's interesting article, "Keynes Disequilibrium Theory of Employment," in *Modern Economic Thought,* ed. Sidney Weintraub (Philadelphia: University of Pennsylvania Press. 1977), pp. 93-101.

11. Keynes, *General Theory,* p. 289. Italics in the original text.

12. Evsey Domar, *Essays in the Theory of Economic Growth* (New York: Oxford University Press, 1957), p. 83. See also Sir Roy Harrod, "An Essay in Dynamic Theory," *Economic Journal* 40 (March 1939): 14-33; Kar Shell's discussion of models in his essay, "Neoclassical Growth Models," in Weintraub, *Modern Economic Thought,* pp. 347-367; Sir Roy Harrod, *Towards a Dynamic Economics* (London: Macmillan, 1958); and Daniel Hamberg's chapter, "Early Growth Theory: The Domar and Harrod Models," in Weintraub, *Modern Economic Thought,* pp. 333-345, including the bibliographical note on p. 345.

13. The paradoxes that result from marginalism were stated in David Z. Rich, *The Economics of International Trade: An Independent View* (New York: Quorum Books, 1992), pp. 55- 59, and resolved on pp. 85-87.

14. However, even for managerial capitalism there is also the financing of money and of productive capital, the financing of property, and the paying of dividends. The issue of ownership for the managerial capitalists is therefore not clear-cut.

15. A further distinction between traditional economics and managerial capitalism pertains to the demarcation between economic theory and social theory, which Marris maintained was false in its inception. This demarcation was useful for the development of economic theory because it enabled the focus to be placed on specific issues of economics without the complications from involving social dynamics; in managerial economics this demarcation must be dropped because, as Marris stated:

> A man's utility system is the result of his social situation, of the society around him and of the way it has moulded his psyche. But his social situation depends in turn on economic organisation. (The conventional separation of economic and social theory was false from birth.) For example, it is by no means obvious that action intended to maximise the utility of a company's stockholders is consistent with maximising the utility of action-takers, i.e., of the management.

However, it must be noted that a social system's economic organization depends on the very dynamics of the social system itself. Nevertheless, because there is a strong intertwining of these factors, they are extremely difficult, to isolate, if this can be done at all. Because the economic organizations of the emerging and developing countries tend to emulate those of the postindustrial countries, conflicts often arise between the social and traditional attitudes of the peoples in these countries and their striving for economic growth and development. The quote from Marris comes from chapter 1 of *The Economic Theory of 'Managerial'*

Capitalism London: Macmillan, 1967, p. 5. 'The Institutional Framework,' p. 5. This chapter provides a schema for the development of the corporate firm. It is interesting to note that this schema is perhaps correct for the emerging and developing countries, given their respective degrees of individual and economic freedom.

16. In this context G.L.S. Shackle's comment on equilibrium is relevant. He wrote that "equilibrium is a paradox, for in it each rival interest serves itself by offering advantages to all others." G.L.S. Shackle's "The Concept of Equilibrium," in S. Mittra, ed. *Dimensions in Macroeconomics,* (New York: Random House, 1971) p. 67. However, this paradox can be resolved by considering that if every sector, each rival interest, offers advantages to all others, then each sector or rival interest gains as much as it loses. The real problem with equilibrium is that it does not allow for real growth.

Chapter 8

THE BUSINESS CYCLE: DYNAMIC DISEQUILIBRIUM AND GROWTH

It is natural to wonder whether we shall ever find a mathematical means to predict the chaotic aspect of probabilistic behavior, just as we have found a means in statistics to predict the deterministic aspect of it. If we ever do discover such a means, then human behavior will be made to seem wholly deterministic, and we shall be able to foresee the entire future of our species and our universe. The probability of this ever happening might seem small to us now, but it is not zero. For precisely because one aspect of our behavior *is* chaotic, *is* unpredictable, the seemingly impossible will always be probable.

Michael Guillen,
"The Cloudy Crystal Ball"[1]

We, as a species, tend to find chaos an anathema. We seek to classify, to categorize, and to control our situations in a universe that often seems to be undergoing changes, the reasons for which we understand after the fact. The direction of these changes seems always highly uncertain, not subject to statistical laws or to mathematical probabilities. Even physics, once the paradigm of certainty, is confronted with indeterminacy that cannot be breached.[2] Still, we seek to impose our need for order on our chaotic world, adapting and adjusting to changes whenever they interrupt our ways of composure and coping.

Defining a discipline of human endeavor is such an attempt to impose order on our chaotic world. We delineate as much as possible our areas of concern, formulate our terms and languages for others working in these areas as a basis for communication, and then seek to explore our areas as we understand them, describing and defining further as a result of our understanding and the findings of our exploring. Nevertheless, for all our efforts, the unknown, the uncertain, and hence the chaotic always remain, unbound by our attempts at imposition and control.

Economics is such a discipline. It has existed in a nonrigorous form since humankind sought to impose order on nature and the means of production. The ancient Babylonian, Egyptian, Greek, Roman, and Israelite civilizations shared the common struggle to produce food, to engage in commerce, and to distribute their wares. The feudal systems of the Middle Ages were economically oriented to supply living quarters and food for the workers in exchange for their labor. Moreover, guilds protected the rights of the artisans whose wares were exchanged for the foods of the feudal manors, and standards were set on the quality of these wares and on the training and apprenticeships of those who sought to learn the crafts and join the guilds.

However, it was only with the writings of such thinkers as David Hume and Adam Smith, who dealt with the theories and problems of mercantilism and physiocracy, that modern economics came into its own as a discipline. Moreover, it was a discipline that was born with the certainty of the time of the beginnings of industrialization that resulted from the merger of science with the means of production that led to the Industrial Revolution.

While the classical and neoclassical body of economics developed on certainty, there were clouds of uncertainty produced by Thomas Malthus and David Ricardo — Malthus with his analysis of food production and population, and Ricardo in his treatment of the decline of value through use, especially where land is concerned. Nevertheless, as the Industrial Revolution advanced, the certainty and optimism that began with the Industrial Revolution were the rule in the general body of economic theory, from Adam Smith's "invisible hand" and Say's law of markets up to Keynes's *General Theory*. Business cycles were considered as the nature of overall economic activity, serving to bring goods and services for consumption and to clear inventories so that retooling and further production and consumption could continue. Even during the Great Depression the concept of full employment necessary for consumption and clearing the markets was maintained in spite of the realities of the breakdown of the system.

While Keynes challenged the concept of the necessity of full employment, he nevertheless developed his theory so that equilibrium in its dynamic form existed and served as the foundation for his contribution to economic theory. Keynes's importance in the development of economic theory cannot be denied, for he not only brought into perspective employment as a function of growth and development; he also instituted the role of government to maintain employment within the framework of the continuance of economic theory as it was inherited from Smith, Say, and the classical and neoclassical thinkers who followed in their tradition. Moreover, because equilibrium is dynamic, the role of government is especially important to maintain this dynamism when demand equals supply and no further growth is possible until the cycle moves downward once again and the markets are cleared for retooling and consumption.

However, economic theory is not constructed in a vacuum, but in response to problems that previous theories were unable to handle. The statement of classical theory, from Adam Smith to Alfred Marshall, responded to the inadequacies of mercantilism and physiocracy as well as to the challenges that the new industrialization offered.[3] From Marshall to Keynes the problems were of the firm and of its costing and production, expansion, and efficient distribution of products. The business cycles and welfare economics were offshoots of the macroeconomic approaches that had developed with respect to the firm and the deviations in employment.[4] Keynes's contribution in light of the Great Depression had provided macroeconomic thinkers with the possibilities of developing their theories either as refinements of Keynesian theory or as macroeconomic theories based on Keynesian contributions, such as the Harrod-Domar model.[5]

Our current economic situation poses problems that are not responsive to neo-Keynesian thinking. The sluggish response to lowered interest rates in the postindustrial economies — lowered by government decree to stimulate borrowing for investment — is just one indicator that neo-Keynesian thinking is inadequate for our current economic problem situation. Another sign is the high unemployment, as dynamic firms trim down their organizations to reduce their fixed costs and to become more competitive in highly lucrative yet competitive markets. Still a further sign is the lack of international monetary stability as hard currencies fluctuate wildly, especially within the European Economic Community, an organization formed to eliminate such currency fluctuations and high unemployment among its members as well as to provide an economic system that can compete viably with the United States and its free-trade bloc with Canada and Mexico, and to exploit effectively the markets of China and compete with South Korea and Japan.

The world's postindustrial economies are not responding to Keynesian theory because its inherent dynamic equilibrium is not in accordance with the market dynamics and cyclical fluctuations that have developed since World War II. The emphasis on dynamic equilibrium has been in error, and while it is sound within the traditional development of economic thinking, it has been shown to be unsound in the current situation as the world's economies do not respond to the policies that dynamic equilibrium presents. Neither neo-Keynesian theory nor the theories developed on the basis of Keynesian reasoning are adequate for dealing with our current economic crisis.

Our current crisis is not a depression, but a severe recession. This distinction is not merely one of semantics, but definitely reflects the world's economic situation. There are no trade barriers levelled against countries to protect national interests — no beggar-thy-neighbor policies that result in similar responses and a serious slowing down of international commerce. Moreover, there is a genuine interest among the postindustrial societies to provide assistance and trade to the emerging and developing countries, even though domestic issues in these postindustrial societies are severe and pressing. The world's political leaders understand that the instability in the newly formed states of the former Soviet Union can bring about serious troubles in the form of wars in which they will be involved, and that economic independence and national independence are intertwined in these countries. The Cold War adversaries no longer confront one another in these countries and in the countries of Asia, Africa, and South America; the situation is far more complicated now. The postindustrial societies are becoming involved in these countries through aid and trade within the perspective of their own vested interests. There is the danger that the old nationalism will be revived as these countries vie for influence in their client states, and that a new form of cold war will begin.

There are, therefore, two conflicting major strains in the geopolitical situation. One strain is that of unity, illustrated by the coming together of the European Economic Community, the North American Free Trade Area, the attempts at resolving the apartheid issue in South Africa, the Middle East peace talks, and the attempts at real Arab unification in the name of peace. At the same time there is the strain of separateness that is causing bloodshed in the newly formed Eastern European states, such as that in Yugoslavia's former possessions and in Georgia and other parts of the former Soviet Union.

A theory of economic growth and development must relate to these issues. Theories formulated to relate to the bygone period of the Great Depression or to the postwar situation in which countries were forming into Cold War blocs are no longer adequate. The geopolitical problems of these countries will be treated in chapter II of this work, but in the context of a theory based on the economics of dynamic disequilibrium, for equilibrium and growth, as demonstrated by our current crisis, have been shown to be incompatible. It is not growth and development that have to be revised, but the very economics on which they are formulated. This revision is the purpose of this chapter.

THE PARADOX OF INDUSTRIALIZATION

The paradox of industrialization not only affects the postindustrialized economies; it also hampers the growth and development of the emerging and developing economies. This paradox is the outcome of the Industrial Revolution, when the criteria of industrialization were established through the growth processes that occurred during industrialization. The paradox is a result of the "symbols of growth," of automobile manufacturing, of steel mills, and, since the beginning of our era, of high technology in the form of computer development and robotics.

The paradox of industrialization is also a result of the aid and technical assistance that the postindustrial societies have provided to the developing countries that brought them out of the state of emergence and allowed their industrial bases to become competitive, both domestically and internationally. It is this paradoxical situation that now confronts the emerging economies as they seek their foundations in the contemporary economic condition of independence and domestic and international competition. The paradox exists as follows: Postindustrial economies have moved from the stages of industrialization that they underwent during the Industrial Revolution and have developed their industries to the point that a union between mass production and high technology has been established and forms the basis of all production. This high technology is the manifestation of the merger of science with the means of production that occurred during the Industrial Revolution and is a feedback into the very scientific foundations that brought about industrial technology.

For example, the automobile was a product of Newtonian physics that merged with the processes of production; those companies that produced more effectively and distributed their product to a wider public maintained their competitive situations, while those companies that could not reduce production and distribution costs without affecting the quality of their automobiles closed down due to the decline in their sales. The automobile had become a symbol of industrialization, both in the resources required for its manufacturing and in its own contribution to industrialization in the forms of ease of transport, the movement of goods and services, and the distribution of plant for the means of production.

During the early stages of automobile production the industrializing countries manufactured their own automobiles for the conditions of their roads as they were paved and expanded to cope with this new form of private transport. Exports were limited, and domestic competition was fairly strong. Marketing was geared primarily for domestic consumption, and apart from the very expensive cars that were imported because of their status appeal and their quality, markets were limited to the domestic consumer who expressed his or her preference because of income, location, job prestige, and personal considerations of service and reliability.

In our era, however, developing countries have established sufficient industrial bases and integration to engage in the manufacturing of automobiles, both for domestic consumption and for export. South Korea, for example, raised itself up from the destruction of World War II and the Korean War to become a competing developing country in the world's markets. Its autos are exported to the postindustrialized countries as well as to other developing countries and to the emerging countries. But here the paradox of industrialization can be understood.

South Korea's industrial base is sufficiently productive to allow its auto manufacturers to compete not only with the postindustrial economies within its own country but also internationally, both with respect to price and to quality for its defined markets. Competition from South Korea lowers the sales of the other auto companies, requiring them to become even more competitive in terms of quality, pricing, payments, and servicing. This competition results in greater benefits to consumers initially, but indirectly the world's economies suffer, as is now the case. Again, it must be understood that the decline in auto sales by a specific company does not reflect the aggregate position of this market; we are not experiencing a recession in the classical and neoclassical sense. In this example the South Korea economy, although it is still developing and has not reached the postindustrial stage, is sufficiently productive and strong to have automobiles manufactured in the country and exported competitively to the world's markets. Of course, the consequence of this rigorous competition is declining sales, calculated by the auto companies' marketing boards. This results in lower employment levels as production costs are reduced for the competitive position to be maintained. Higher unemployment means both reduced consumption and a greater reliance on the government to prevent poverty. This is the situation that is occurring now in the United States and Japan (whose governments seek to protect their countries from foreign competition as far as possible by high tariffs) and in Great Britain, France, united Germany, and Italy. These heavily industrialized countries are competing, both internally and internationally, for the same markets, and this competition is a manifestation of their industrial strength. This strength is weakened through this competition when unemployment results.

The paradox of industrialization can be stated thus: The development of specific industries, from the Industrial Revolution to the present, is not only an indication of the economic strength of the countries that possess these industries; it also represents those countries' abilities to allocate efficiently their available resources for production and their competence to compete effectively both domestically and internationally. While this is the case, these countries are in competition for similar products, and the consumers of these products benefit, providing that tariffs are also competitive. Protected industries are indicators of the processes of industrialization, and in those countries with protected industries competition is not effective and consumers pay higher prices than they would in competitive markets.

Moreover, developing economies strive for the same markets as those established by the highly competitive postindustrial economies, with the emerging economies structuring their industries on patterns of the developing economies and seeking — as far as their resources and abilities allow them — to emulate as much as possible the standards of the postindustrial economies. Hence the competition, both domestically and internationally, tends to focus on specific products. This, of course, does not mean that other types of production, such as foods and clothing, are not part of the economic infrastructure. But much of the textile production for the postindustrial markets is conducted in the emerging and developing countries; this allows for employment in these countries, as well as the release of resources, including time, for the production of products that the emerging and developing economies are incapable of manufacturing or could manufacture only at great economic cost and hence without being competitive domestically and internationally. A major consequence of this industrialization is the integration of the economic factors, such as finance, transportation, employment, and the availability of alternative resources in competitive situations. These are certainly important, because the degree of integration determines the stage of development. Such integration as has already occurred in the postindustrial economies is not only strengthened, but also becomes increasingly sophisticated as computers and communications technologies ease commerce and industrial development and expansion. Indeed, in these countries industries that had begun as service industries have become ambiguous with respect to this definition. Computer industries, for example, were formed to provide the service of information and its swift retrieval; these industries have since become major users of resources such as financing, transportation, and time and provide not only the service of information and its retrieval, but computers that are indispensable for the functioning of finance and transportation, for the efficient uses of time in scientific and technological research, and for handling the affairs of business in an increasingly complex and competitive world. This is the result of the sophistication that has developed in the postindustrial societies, and the luxury of this sophistication is one of the aspirations of the emerging and developing societies.

While the processes of industrialization result from economic integration and sophistication, there is another consequence to industrialization. This is the employment effect that is required for integration and sophistication, and it is incorporated into the emerging, developing, and postindustrial economies that are expanding not only their competitive industrial bases, but also the levels of their economic sophistication.

The employment effect is manifested in the training of workers for the requirements of modern industries. This training itself requires the integration of economic and social resources, as well as knowledge that is state-of-the-art in the various fields of production, including management. When a well-trained and competitive work force is employed in industries that are exploiting existing markets, both domestically and internationally, the competition for these markets results in reduced prices that are met by reducing employment, which is a main cost factor. Thus employment allows for greater competition, and its reduction allows for the competitive position to be maintained in integrated and sophisticated economic structures. The employment effect is part of the paradox of industrialization because the development of industries relies on employees skilled in state-of-the-art production processes.

This is the predicament today. Our worldwide recession is not due to the cyclical downturn as understood by the classical and neoclassical economists; it is due to market saturation in those industries developed initially by the postindustrial societies that set the standards of production and opened the markets for the developing and emerging countries to enter once they achieved sufficient economic integration.

Nevertheless, the business cycle has turned downward and appears to be stuck at the recession level. Because this is a recession that is not within the conception of classical or neoclassical economic thinking, the business cycle must be reconsidered.

THE WELFARE UTILITY FUNCTION: THE BUSINESS CYCLE IN DYNAMIC DISEQUILIBRIUM

The consequences of the paradox of industrialization certainly resemble those of neoclassical recessions. Idle productive capital together with high unemployment and the uncertainty prevailing throughout the world's economies are not new. Policies that were successful for stimulating economic activity are being tried and their effects evaluated. For example, interest rates are being lowered to encourage investment in industry ad the business sector in general. Small businesses in local communities are encouraged to borrow on favorable terms to replenish inventories and stimulate sales. There is a reliance on the "natural" optimism that the business cycle will eventually gain sufficient momentum to begin its upward movement. Moreover, this optimism is based on government policies such as the lowering of interest rates for borrowing, increasing the money stock to increase spending, and lowering taxes to increase liquidity for both investments and spending[6]. With the social burden of unemployment increasing as industries reduce their production costs by laying off their employees, the emphasis on welfare has increased accordingly. The national works projects of the Great Depression period have not been considered, because trained workers will not accept these policies. Welfare programs that increase skills and allow learning while a worker earns are being adopted by various national, regional, and local welfare agencies. These programs, together with the traditional unemployment payments and welfare benefits, are being used to ease the situation.

They are, however, insufficient to move the cycle upward again, because consumption is marginal and investments are low in spite of the low-interest-rate incentives offered by the governments through their banking systems. With respect to the paradox of industrialization, the business cycle can be considered as a force generated by the dynamics of the closed-ended production cycles, and indeed the policies of governments to move the cycle upward have been based on this concept. Tax incentives and lower interest rates on borrowing to make money attractive are based on the Keynesian $M = VD$ equation, so that with an increase in the money supply through lower taxation and interest rates, the velocity of money in circulation will also increase, stimulating demand and the consequent retooling and restocking of inventories. This is intended to lead to reemployment and still further increases in demand, thereby moving the cycle upward; in fact, it has led to only slight motions in the cycle, but the recession phase still remains and is hardened by industries increasing the rolls of the unemployed as they reduce production costs to increase their competitive positions.

The business cycle can also be considered as a consequence of managerial decisions based on liquidity positions, formed through revenues from investment gains and from commercial transactions. With high liquidity, firms are likely to take more risks in developing existing markets and opening new ones. High liquidity is a result of good profitable turnover, which reflects consumer liquidity directed toward consumption as aggregate decisions are made to transfer disposable income to consumer income. When the conditions of closed-ended production cycles meet with managerial decisions based on liquidity, they bring about dynamics unique to their own special circumstances. This is why no two business cycles are alike, and why both aspects must be treated by managerial and government policies.

Managerial policy with respect to both open and closed systems is based on the subjective and objective utilities of their programs. Objective utility is of prime importance because this is the probabilistic interpretation and understanding of the validity of the information pertaining to the programs, and on this basis the subjective utilities are formulated by which the decision makers and consumers order their personal utility preferences and choose to enact programs and purchase the resultant goods and services, respectively. From the managerial position these programs have their influences on the economy. As they get under way, using resources and plant facilities that could have been used for alternative programs, their dynamics are generated and incorporated into the objective and subjective utility schedules of other decision makers, both managers and consumers.

Basically, the business cycle moves in response to the expansion and contraction of innovation and imitation, primarily to those projects that are open-ended. The decision to act on these projects or to refrain from acting depends on the firm's objective utility positions, the objective ratings given to the proposed projects as best as they can be ascertained, and managers' subjective utility preferences for the proposed projects that influence their decisions to act or not to act on these projects.

The contemporary business cycle is thus a combination of product cycles and liquidity positions of the many firms in a society. With respect to the paradox of industrialization, when the utilities of production are low, the recession phase of the cycle persists, for because of the intense domestic and foreign competition, the commitment of funds to the low profit potential of continued imitation or innovation is not forthcoming. When liquidity is already committed to the extent considered feasible by managers, further investment in existing or new projects is unlikely. Moreover, to reduce costs and thereby increase profits given the current market conditions, the policy of unemployment is undertaken. This is a short-term policy, however, because aggregate consumption depends on the Say-like condition of aggregate employment. Given the time lag for this policy to be felt on the macro scale, eventually aggregate demand declines and the requirements of the welfare systems in these societies are increased.

Consider now how the cumulative effects of the various firms' product cycles bring about the aggregate business cycle while they influence industries and the economy in toto. For example, the firm F in time t_n has high liquidity, and its production is competitive and imitatively oriented. Imitation is the production of products whose markets have already been established. The products in question differ from those already existing, but are geared for those consumers who demonstrate either pioneer or sheeplike behavior — to use Marris's terms — and who are willing to try close substitutes for those products they have been consuming. The cycle's dynamics will be suppressed for the moment in order to isolate the firm as a working unit to show how it generates dynamics. Since F's markets are imitative, its supply and demand functions are fairly stable (the condition for the heuristic law of markets).[7] All fluctuations that do occur are minor, requiring no serious managerial attention.

In a situation of stability and high liquidity, managerial decision making becomes oriented toward innovation. Innovation is the introduction of new products and hence the opening of new markets in competition for aggregate consumer liquidity; innovation can also be the introduction of a form of a product that already exists, but is so radical that it is construed to be a new product. In the first instance the markets have to be formed through research and advertising; in the second instance the markets already exist, but the product is not a close competitor in the imitative sense, but a unique aspect of the existing competing product that generates dynamics of imitative competition. The computer was certainly an innovative product and has generated close competition among the computer companies. Various components for this already-established and expanding market are also innovative, and this is demonstrated by the close competitors they too generate in the competitive situation.

For both forms of innovation, entering the markets after sufficient advertising to generate pioneering consumption of the product in time t_{n+m} (m being the time of marketing) generates the interest of the managers in other firms who have recognized a positive consumer response in the targeted groups. As sales increase and the consuming public continues to respond, **F** has initiated a market situation that draws imitators and stimulates new growth. **F**'s profits will then be reduced according to the extent of competition; eventually a point will be reached in this particular product cycle where **F**'s growth will decline and a level of stability will set in once again. The same occurs with the products of the competing firms until market saturation allows for no further profitable competitive entry. It must be noted, however, that **F**'s technological base and those of its competitors are broadened as a result of the product and the consequent competition.

This process in itself, however, is insufficient to generate the dynamics of the aggregate cycle. The point here is that competition is directed to the new successful product and those of the firm's competitors, which means that it is drawn from other uses such as the consumption of other products. Money for consumption may also be taken from savings, in which case the liquidity positions of these institutions and their funds available for loans and investments are reduced accordingly. The money drawn from other consumption patterns may result in the phasing out of those competing products in firms whose profits are marginal, thereby increasing their liquidity as a result of eliminating the product, and perhaps their proclivity toward innovation and the dynamics that successful innovation generates.

Still, these dynamics in themselves are inadequate to generate the aggregate business cycle, for the recirculation of money brings about a decline in one sector while raising the growth level of that sector that receives the money. Shifts in consumption patterns are not causes of cyclical motion as such unless these shifts are very large. Innovation and imitation are effective only when they reach their initial target groups — these being the consumers who allocate their liquidity according to their liquidity preferences developed by their acquired and accumulated tastes and interests — and, under conditions of success, spread to groups not originally targeted in the marketing processes. Thus the fact that innovation and imitation bring about shifts in consumer spending is not sufficient to generate cyclical economic movement when they are undertaken on a small or moderate scale.

However, the cycle is generated by the cumulative effects of innovation and imitation due to the establishment of consumer purchasing patterns for the duration. Again, when the liquidity positions of the majority of firms are high, this is due to the preference for liquidity brought about through the phasing out of products with low utilities and the costs saved from production expenditures. Fixed capital expenditures are written off in taxes so that short-term payments are cancelled out by the long-term return on costs. The point is that high liquidity results from the decline of the firms' involvement in economic activity — the special case that is the exception being when the paradox of industrialization takes hold and market saturation is nearly total — which leads to an increased gearing ratio and provides the basis for accumulating liquidity, especially through investments, at a sufficient level to underwrite other innovative and imitative undertakings that management had been unable or unwilling to undertake previously. Thus for the economy in the aggregate the trade-off between liquidity and production, with the preference being to hold liquidity instead of investing in production, means that for conditions other than aggregate market near saturation, as is our present situation, economic activity has declined to the low through of the dynamic cycle's movement.

This trade-off is of short duration, however, because holding liquidity over time instead of channeling it into production means that plant facilities and labor are not being used and that the liquidity held will not yield a profit. This liquidity allows for the initiation of products that have not previously been acted upon but through market research are determined to provide consumer utility when marketed, given the right conditions. During this phase production has declined generally and prices are high because consumer goods and services are in short supply compared with the earlier cyclical phase; that many firms have opted for liquidity instead of production indicates that their products have reached the stable stage in their particular product cycles and that revenues have been reduced because of competition. This results in scarcities sufficient to drive consumer prices upward, even though consumption has declined because of the declining employment level due to the firms' policies of increasing liquidity by reducing employment costs to compensate for revenues lost from competition and the decision to cease production. High prices, together with unemployment, bring about a psychological socioeconomic condition in which innovation is engaged in reluctantly and consumers alter their purchasing patterns, mainly by restricting consumption.

To resume economic activity, the trade-off has to be reversed. Innovation as a trade-off for holding liquidity must get under way, leading to an increase in employment and the establishment of new purchasing patterns. The underwriting of this socioeconomic climate is the task of the government and must include both industry and labor. These three components comprise the welfare utility function, which will be discussed shortly. This, in turn, leads to the revival of local secondary and auxiliary businesses and the establishment of new ones to service the branches of industry, thereby increasing the general level of employment and hence consumption on the local scale, where the target groups and their spin-off consumers are located. The consequences of innovative and subsequent imitative production are therefore the revival of the economy, the reemployment of workers and the increase in their purchasing power, and the shifting of consumer patterns so that those products unable to retain their utilities in the reviving economy are phased out, thereby providing producers with greater liquidity to enter other innovative or imitative markets. The result is the ultimate widening and deepening of the economic infrastructure and its consequent expansion of technologies. Hence new innovation and the following imitation on a large scale move the cycle upward, and recovery is under way.

This process continues until full employment is reached — full employment being defined by industrial demand for employment and by the government — and most of the aggregate industrial capacity is utilized. As innovation continues, followed by imitation, purchasing patterns are fairly established for new products, but not necessarily for brand names. Demand fluctuates as bargains are offered and as competition improves quality. Some competitive product brands are phased out because of competition and because of opting for liquidity or investments. When employment is near capacity in this phase, and when imitation is slowing down because of the reduction of innovative products that brings the opening of fewer new markets, the cycle's motion continues upward, though at a decreasing rate. This is the prosperity phase, and in it are the dynamics of the impending downward movement.

As this phase of the cycle slows down, entropy sets in until the upward movement ceases and the cycle turns downward toward recession. Without sufficient aggregate innovation, imitation declines, but for a while near-full employment provides sufficient consumer liquidity to maintain a fairly steady consumption level. Competition increases in rigor as firms maintaining their imitative output vie with each other for consumers; products of low competitive utility are phased out, which results in unemployment and eventually reduces aggregate purchasing power. This sets in motion the phasing out of other products as purchasing power continues to decline while the existing competition maintains its full rigor. The period of prosperity has passed its peak, and the cycle turns downward toward recession and, if the trend is not checked, ultimately to depression.

Our current situation reflects this standard position, but with one unique difference. Depressions have been ruled out since the Great Depression by government commitment, guaranteeing that such a situation will never again occur. Financial institutions such as banks are underwritten by goverenments, and a watchdog role is exerted in the world's stock exchanges to eliminate unauthorized speculation that can bring about crises. Indeed, as the October 19, 1987, stock-market collapse demonstrated, conditions that reflect the Great Depression are dealt with by governments. Neoclassical depressions are part of the past era and, because of government intervention, will never occur again. Our situation is unique in the sense that technologies are more advanced and diversified than previously, and also that while industries are following the procedures stated in the preceding argument — reducing employment to reduce production costs for greater competitive ability, phasing out products of low profitability and opting for liquidity, and seeking to maintain their full competitive rigor — the developing and emerging economies are experiencing recession as a result of that in the postindustrial economies and must nevertheless turn to the postindustrial economies for assistance, aid, and markets. This situation will be explored further in part III, chapters 10 and 11 of this work, but it suffices to say that the general dynamics of the business cycle are as stated here.

For example, all contemporary recessions are marked by increasing numbers of unemployed persons, increasing bankruptcies among the secondary and auxiliary businesses, and the weakening of the big industries to the point that the threat of takeovers is realistic. Inflation is high as prices are raised to protect profit levels as much as competitively possible to compensate for the reduced production levels resulting from increased unemployment and the phasing out of low-utility goods and services. Fixed costs remain, however, and must be paid out of the increased liquidity; but with cuts in production and declining revenues, the liquidity levels also decline. Innovation during this phase has all but ceased, and imitation is maintained only for those products that are profitable given the circumstances of high prices and high unemployment. This process of recession is continuing and is dynamic, with the cycle moving downward until it reaches its lowest plateau. In the theory of the contemporary business cycle a time lapse is required for the cycle to begin its upward movement. But unlike neoclassical economic theory and more in accordance with Keynes, this requires assistance from the government and receives it through policies of interest-rate regulation and taxation benefits. When the cycle's upward motion begins, the economy is not of the same composition as in its previous cyclical completion, but is altered due to the new technologies and its product composition. Its secondary and auxiliary businesses are different, and as the cycle moves upward they are oriented toward promoting and servicing the products of the time. Moreover, the processes of distribution have been altered as new businesses replace those that, as a result of bankruptcies and mergers, no longer remain. The big firms differ in the sense that their technologies have been altered to accomodate the new production lines and the competition that will develop. Target groups for new products are different, and so are the compositions of the different socioeconomic groups because of the cycle and the consequences of the recession. The economic infrastructure has been broadened by the new products and by the technologies incorporated in business to produce them.

The point made by Keynes and accepted by every macroeconomist ever since, that the downward swing should be minimized and the upward swing extended, is certainly the goal of industry and government. But as our current recession illustrates, neo-Keynesian policies are insufficient to move the cycle upward. It was demonstrated during the Great Depression, in accordance with neoclassical reasoning, that if the cycle is left on its own, it will eventually move upward. Our world, however, is in an important historical state of change in which the emerging and developing countries rely on the postindustrial countries, which, in turn, are experiencing their own economic difficulties. There is no time for the "natural" motion of the cycle, nor can government policies that are based on past theories but are ineffectual now be given much more credit for performance when they have not succeeded in accomplishing their objective of restoring growth.

It is in industry's best interests to minimize the downward swing, as this allows it to maintain its liquidity and its trade-off between liquidity and production for innovative and imitative projects. It further allows for shortened periods of declining demand and increased periods of stable and rising demand so that innovative and imitative projects can be analyzed more carefully and the decisions can be taken with less immediate economic pressure. Industry also has available its labor force, which will not migrate geographically — a point especially important for the emerging and developing economies — or seek employment elsewhere if the low phase is of short duration, because labor will soon be employed again. This is the goal of the world's governments for the obvious political reasons: to maintain their offices and the goodwill of their voters and supporters; to maintain the support of industry and prevent destructive social unrest; to maintain strong socioeconomic infrastructures in light of foreign competition; and to maintain strong postures in light of the political tendencies of unification and neonationalism that have developed in the wake of the Soviet Union's demise. For these reasons the welfare utility function has been formulated.

THE STATIC FORMULATION OF THE WELFARE UTILITY FUNCTION

AT this stage the welfare utility function will be treated statically so that its components can be analyzed. In the next section it will be placed in its dynamic setting with respect to the business cycle. If W stands for the welfare utility function, $W_t = U(I, G, L)_t$, with the enclosed letters standing for industry, government, and labor, respectively. As these are generalized terms, they can be broken down into components. Industry, for example, contains the subsets of all industrial firms, secondary businesses, and their auxiliaries. Government contains the subsets of all governmental activity bearing on the economy, such as defense, taxation, and welfare payments of all kinds.[8] Labor is organized labor in all branches of industry and government, viewed in terms of its wage-bargaining positions and strike actions as they affect the economy. Labor's position, although unique as a force in itself, is nevertheless somewhat ambiguous, because it depends on both the strength of industry and the commitment of government to maintain a strong economy. This holds true both for the postindustrial societies and for the emerging and developing economies, as our current situation demonstrates.

In general, the utility of W_t is determined in the same manner as that of the information system S_t; that is, the utility of W at any time t is $0 < W_t < 1$. For each of W's components there are subsets, so that the component I of industry and business, for example, is composed of subsets for the various industries such as the automobile industry, the steel industry, the computer industry, and so on. For each of these subsets there are further subsets, such as the various automobile manufacturers (including those foreign manufacturers that have plants in the domestic market), the various steel companies, the various computer companies, and so on. The utility position of the individual firm within each of these subsets shows its competitive ability within its specific markets. This, of course, depends on the firm's information system and the responses from investors and consumers that this system evokes. Moreover, consideration of a specific industry may determine that while one or more firms may not be competing effectively, other firms competing in the same market may be doing very well and thus show high profits. The total of these firms at time t gives their respective utility positions, so that if some of these firms have low utility while the majority have high utility, then for these firms, say F_1 in the complex of firms composing I, utility tends to 1.

The low utility ratings for some firms may be due to several reasons. For example, there may be a reduction in their efforts to market the competing product as their managers rechannel their resources into developing other products, either innovatively or in imitation; or these may be conflict within the firm at the decision-making level as managers seek to liquidate their own positions and look for employment elsewhere. Another reason may be opting for liquidity instead of maintaining strong production in order to achieve a strong position to fend off corporate raiders. If the utility ratings of all or the majority of the firms are low, while those of a few are high, this is an indication that the market itself is changing, in the sense that the cycle is bringing consumers to act with greater restraint in their purchasing. Hence for all the businesses and firms in the economy symbolized by the letter I for industry, and at time t, $0 < I < 1$.

For the government G the situation is similar. There is a difficulty, however, because while the domain of business activity is fairly clear-cut, because firms act within their markets, the impact of government activity is not as well defined.[9] Governments can order from businesses products that may or may not be necessary for the smooth functioning of governmental activity, and while businesses may profit from these orders, they may be a wasteful bureaucratic expenditure on the government's part.[10] Another big spending objective has been defense, although the thawing of the Cold War has reduced this expense considerably among the postindustrial societies; nevertheless, among the emerging economies, where stability has not yet been achieved, and among several of the developing economies, such as Israel, the defense portion of the national budget is extremely high, requiring these countries to turn to the postindustrial countries for aid and assistance; this, in turn, is calculated in the postindustrial economies' budgets as foreign assistance, and perhaps as part of defense expenditures, according to the requirements of the accounting procedures. However, now more than ever, defense expenditures among the postindustrial economies may be wasteful due to the end of the Cold War, while the firms benefiting from these expenditures may achieve very high profits.

The area of government activity where this is not a difficulty is the building of infrastructure to enhance long-run economic activity. Such projects as building dams and roadways and investing in state and regional education are examples of this activity. While these projects require contracting of businesses for their realization, their utilities can be determined with respect to the economic growth they provide, even though this may be over the very long run. Measuring G within the W_t equation is thus somewhat problematic, but because the government is a powerful factor in the economy, its position with respect to utility must be considered. Because the government's various economic functions are subsets of its overall activity, assessing the utility of each activity within the upper and lower boundaries at time t provides the overall utility of G. Hence $0 < G < 1$ for time t, and G provides the general utility of the government's economic policies, including those in such areas as health and welfare, for that time.

Labor's situation tends to be very clear-cut. For labor no distinction exists between the government or industry as employer; they are both employers, and labor has to reckon with them and they with labor. This holds for governments, including local and regional governments as subsets of national governments, whose employees are not allowed by law to engage in work action against the governing bodies, such as the armed forces and police and fire departments; these are workers who have well-defined jobs and who, in their roles as wage earners, are supported by organizations that enter into collective bargaining on their behalf. It is understood that they are deprived of work sanctions and strike actions, and they must have good contracts to prevent discrimination and provide benefits that will continue to make their jobs attractive and encourage others to join them.

For organized labor in the free markets, however, it is clear that regardless of the stage of economic development, the labor-industry dichotomy still exists. Workers want high pay for their efforts, and business managers want their employees to work long hours with low pay. The utility of labor's actions must be considered in light of this dichotomy. Bargaining for higher wages in an industrial sector weakened by international competition is not likely to yield the wages desired by the unions nor to be within an acceptable wage-scale range and therefore tends toward entropy as a policy. Similarly, bargaining for higher wages when the economy is in recession is not very effective, because so many jobs are threatened as firms eliminate production lines and employees and opt for liquidity.

Programs sponsored by unions and management alike, allowing for retraining of workers threatened by redundancy and unemployment and providing for their reassignment to profitable divisions within the firm, are certainly steps in the direction of keeping able workers off the dole. Like all other labor and business actions, however, these too must be evaluated in every instance for their utility and entropy. For some of these programs it might be demonstrated that while the intentions are sound and the idealism motivating them is very healthy, the programs are of very low utility and must therefore be abandoned. Other programs might be of high utility, thereby providing the incentive to expand and diversify them, but these actions must be subject to utility evaluations in their own right.

The welfare utility function thus contains the three forces in the economy. When each of these forces has utility tending to the upper limit, then the economic welfare is operating at a high utility; when their utilities are low, then so is the general welfare of the economy; and when these utilities are mixed, then the economy's welfare moves with those utility ratings that are dominant.

The welfare of the individual in the economy is derived from the economic situations of these sectors and the manner in which they interact with one another. The individual is a resident in a society, and these sectors are the society's economic forces from which the goods and services are produced, from which the socioeconomic infrastructure is derived and generated, and in which employment is sought and maintained as best as possible, given the unique economic conditions at any one time.

The individual can compute his or her utility preference functions with respect to income earned, the goods and services available for consumption, the option for liquidity, the labor opportunities and possibilities, and, for those able to vote, voting for that person or party whose election platform tends to coincide with the individual's utility preferences. Ultimately, in the industrial sector, the contemporary individual's utility function with respect to the goods and services available determines, when taken in the aggregate, which firms will survive and which will not, which firms will continue their production lines and which will alter them, and which firms will maintain their labor composition, which will hire more workers, and which will fire or temporarily lay off workers. Through the vote the consumer can determine the type of government he or she wants, and through consumption he or she can determine the direction that industry takes, the composition of the labor force, and the economic policies of businesses that governments must consider in their operations as an economic-sector force.

THE DYNAMIC FORMULATION OF THE WELFARE UTILITY FUNCTION

Now that the welfare utility function has been stated with respect to a moment in time, it must be considered in a dynamic setting. Its components of industry, government, and labor can be understood only over time, for only over time can their subsets be analyzed and their utilities and entropies be understood. This is important for each economy, no matter what its stage of development is, for it enables its citizens and the industrial, political, and labor leaders to analyze the direction their economies are taking with respect to growth; it is also important because it reflects the political systems' positions with respect to growth and therefore allows for reconsideration of policies when necessary. For example, the postindustrial economies in the current phase of recession can redirect their priorities with respect to innovation and imitation and can generate new economic dynamics that will begin moving the cycle upward. The developing economies, dependent on the postindustrial economies, can rearrange their marketing priorities both for domestic consumption and for exporting to the postindustrial and emerging economies. In turn, the emerging economies can move into the directions of growth suitable to their current economic abilities and their projected future potentials.

Moreover, the static moment in time captured by the subscript t cannot explain the dynamics of the welfare utility function. For example, in explaining the industry component, it was said that some firms may have low productive utility because they have opted for liquidity or because changes in production procedures for new product lines have weakened the firms' productive capacities. Because utility is measured with respect to the markets, and because these operations bring the firms into a weakened market position, the static W_t cannot provide the explanations for the low utilities, and attempts to explain this situation merely move W from being bound by the static t to a dynamic $t + n$ ($n \geq 1$).

The same holds for the government and labor components. Capturing them in a single moment in time provides no explanation of their utilities. The government, for example, may undertake to provide economic infrastructure in the regional area of the country where growth is lagging behind that in the other areas; in time t how can this policy be evaluated? Or how are government investments in the industrial sector of such a region to be analyzed when the investments are for infrastructure and education to provide employment and income in that region? Labor policies also cannot be understood in the moment of time captured by t. A strike action, for example, may seem to be counterproductive when it is viewed in the moment with respect to the industries threatened by the action; the longer-term view may clarify the situation that protectionism is evoked to a certain extent and that the goal is that the industry's labor sector be less threatened by cheaper foreign products. Or it may seem advantageous for labor to resist new and efficient technologies that threaten the employment situation as it exists in certain industries. Capturing this resistance in the moment t gives no reasons for labor's strategy.

The welfare utility function, to be viable, must therefore be dynamic, moving with the changes in the economy and offering opportunities to evaluate these changes with respect to utility and entropy. A computer firm, for example, may embark on a new line and seek to capture the markets of its competitors. In a static situation this may seem to be good marketing of an innovative product; over time, however, this project may place a drain on resources when it meets expected sales neither from the customers loyal to the firm nor from those consumers that the firm sought to attract from its competitors. The timing of introducing an innovative product has to be evaluated with respect to the general market dynamics, and this is far from a static situation.

Government investment in infrastructure in a depressed region may be sound planning, but only over time can this be assessed. The region may respond to the injection of money in the form of wages and the purchasing of goods and services locally, so that the government's objective is attained, or it may continue to rely on its traditional attitudes and approaches in its industry and labor position so that in spite of the initial stimulation due to the injected liquidity, the region reverts to its previous level of economic activity, and in the long run there is no significant difference in its economic situation.

Because the welfare utility function is a measuring function of the utilities of the industrial, governmental, and labor sectors over time, it also takes into account the fact that the economy is not an entity in which these sectors operate independently of one another, but that these sectors are intricately related in the dynamics of economic growth and development. This function does, however, measure the utilities of each of these sectors as they operate with the inclusion of the other sectors within them. The purpose is not to isolate these sectors, but to assess their utilities in their dynamic settings over time.

The concept "over time" refers to the time period of cyclical fluctuation, because the utilities of the sectors depend on the cycle's position. For example, during prosperity, just when the cycle's upward motion is increasing at a decreasing rate, innovation may not yield the firm's expected profits. Saturation is setting in, and in spite of the optimistic situation, profits in the industry to which the firm belongs are declining, albeit slowly. Innovation in a similar market will then yield declining profits in spite of the expectation of higher profits, and the firm's utility thus declines with respect to the innovative project. This is measured by the specific industry's welfare utility function and may have a bearing on the industrial sector, depending on the industry's weight in the economy.

Government projects during recession, for example, tend to alleviate the difficult conditions because, in Keynesian terms, the increased money in the form of wages and investments stimulates demand, and this generates restocking of inventories, bringing about increased employment; it also stimulates innovation as the element of risk is reduced due to the increased liquidity. These projects during the recession phase have high utility, and their influences on industry and labor are noticeable and positive for economic growth.

With respect to labor, sanctions and strikes may be of low utility for a specific industry or firm within the industry because of the impact that foreign competition has on that industry. For example, the electronics industry may be experiencing demand due to the increase in aggregate liquidity because of the cycle's movement toward recovery and because of the increased innovation that the cycle's upward movement brings. But because innovation generates imitation and because there is an international imitation effect in which foreign companies seek out the newest in successful domestic products and attempt to manufacture imitative substitutes at lower prices even when tariffs are considered, labor unrest will not be beneficial to that section of organized labor engaged in industrial action, be it in the form of sanctions or strikes.

Because $W_{t + n} = U(I, G, L)_{t + n}$, and because the utilities of these components depend mainly on the business cycle's position at the time of measurement, the welfare utility function is, to the same extent, dependent on the cycle's position. This dependence is as weak or as strong as that of the component during the measuring period and indicates the utilities as a result of this dependence. Moreover, as the measurement takes into consideration the time factor, circumstances that are relevant during one part of that time may not be as significant during another part. Hence this utility measure does not account for the real events that have occurred during that time; it merely assesses the sector's utility over that time period.

In general, then, the welfare utility function $W \approx 1/C_p$, where C_p is the cycle at its phase during the measurement, and the approximation sign indicates that a strict equation does not exist because of variations in the subsectors due to responses that are not general but specific. For example, a single firm during the recession phase may generate demand because of its innovation and may also bring imitation into the dynamics. But the industry in which the firm is included may have a very low utility rating due to the recession. Thus, because $W_{t + n} = U(I, G, L)_{t+n}$, $U(I, G, L) \approx 1/C_p$. Attaching $t + n$ to the cycle's phase p allows for both the cycle's phase and the time element to be considered. If the time element for a given imitation is one year, and during that very time the cycle has moved from recovery to prosperity, then because $p = t + n$, this time period can be substituted by the cycle's phase, in this case by recovery.

The advantage of substituting the cycle's phase for the time period is that this substitution allows for the isolation of each sector for observation and, indeed, the isolation of the components of each sector for further scrutiny, evaluating their performances in their general compositions and for their specific utilities. For example, consider the **L** sector during recovery. Partial derivation allows for **L**'s isolation from the other sectors and their components, and the corresponding partial derivative of $C_{recovery}$ allows for **L**'s position during recovery to be evaluated. Hence $0 < \partial l < 1/ \partial \mathbf{C_{rec}}$. Moreover, this allows evaluation of a specific labor organization in **L**, so that for **L, l** $_\varepsilon$ **L** can be substituted. This also provides for the evaluation of the labor situation in a single firm within the labor structure so that (**l** $_\varepsilon$ **F**)   **L** can also be evaluated.

Another advantage of this approach is that the cycle's phase, say prosperity, can be further broken down. Prosperity, for example, may be a very long-term process, but the **L** is being considered for only the first two months (or whatever time period is considered necessary for evaluation. The approximation welfare utility function takes the form $\mathbf{W_t} \approx 1/\mathbf{L_{Ct}}$ **(2 months)**, from which can be derived the utility position $0 < \partial$ **L** $< \mathbf{l_t}$ **(2 months)**.

Moreover, as seen with **L**, this equation can take into account two of the three sectors — **L**, for example, relating to a firm **F** as **l** — so that from time **a** to **c**, for, say, labor and industry, the situation takes the form $\mathbf{W_t L} \approx 1/\mathbf{C_{p(L, I)}}$ **ta-c**, allowing $0 < (\partial$ **L** ∂ **I**$) < 1$ to be evaluated. Another advantage of the welfare utility function is that it provides for the breaking down of each of these sectors into their components and subcomponents for still further evaluation. Because Σ **(F** $_\varepsilon$ **i)** $_\varepsilon$ **I and** Σ **(gp** $_\varepsilon$ **g)** $_\varepsilon$ **G, gp** being a specific government policy, and because Σ **(lp** $_\varepsilon$ **l)** $_\varepsilon$ **L, lp** being a specific labor policy, with the "sigma" sign being a summation of these policies and being the inclusion sign, each breaking down is readily accessible.

For example, consider a specific firm in an industry for which utility has been sought over the past three months. The firm in question, $\mathbf{F_1}$, can be placed in this equation in the following manner: Because $\mathbf{W_t} \approx 1/\mathbf{C_p}$, and Σ **(F** **I)**   **l**, and because $\mathbf{F_1}$ is one of the subcomponents of **I**, this summation can be substituted for **I** in the approximation equation. Because $\mathbf{F_1}$ is one of **I**'s subcomponents, the equation can be written $\mathbf{W_{F_1}} \approx 1/\mathbf{C_t}$ **(3 months)**, for which the derivative is stated $0 < |\Sigma$(**F** $_\varepsilon$ **i)** $_\varepsilon$ **I** < 1, and because $\mathbf{F_1}$ is a component of the summation, it can be placed within the utility evaluation separate from other firms and industries. Isolating the **L** or **I** sectors, or any other two sectors, also provides no difficulty. Substituting the specific industry (or firm) and the specific labor policy for the generalized **I** and **L** notation yields the results. This can show the influences of industry on labor and/or labor on industry, as the case may be, by way of isomorphic relationships of each's utilities on the other, as was discussed earlier in Chapter 5. The reason why only two sectors at most can be treated at a time is that if all three sectors were to be treated at the same time, this would give the general **W** approximation, and no sector isolation could be undertaken. It must be understood that so far the discussion has pertained to the utility measurements over time past up to a point in time, from the past to the present. This itself involves a dynamism because the measurement takes into account the changes over the signified time, while the point of the present is somewhat difficult to capture without its isolation from the dynamics surrounding it. If the present includes today and the next seven days, this is a very small segment of time, but it is far from static. Other firms, other labor issues, and other government policies are likely to come up and be implemented during this time period, but the greatest dynamic lies, again, with the "engine" of economic activity, the single firm in an industry, where programs of innovation and imitation are devised, planned, and acted upon. This is the case no matter what the economy's stage in economic growth and development is.

The present, in this sense, is a sufficiently small amount of time that it is not affected by cyclical fluctuations in most situations; the qualified "most" in this case allows for events not really expected in the general run of economic events, such as the October 19, 1987, market crash, which, while not cyclical in nature, was certainly an extremely disturbing event. Such events, unpredictable and unexpected, cannot be ruled out, and their effects will certainly be made known in the very short time period of a few days allowed by the concept of the present in the welfare approximation. In general, then, the use of the past in relation to the present or whatever cutoff point is chosen for analyzing the welfare utility position refers to a period of time during which, while there may have been changes in the economy, there have been no radical deviations from the path on which the economy has been running. This includes events that are expected to occur such as the policy speech of a president or prime minister reporting on the conditions of the country and perhaps proposing tax and monetary reforms or replacement of a finance minister or secretary of the treasury due to previously known clashes of opinions or because of indicated plans of retirement.

The question still remains: If the past and present as defined here can be treated in this manner, what about the future? Cannot the future utility of a project be stated, and cannot the future utility of a firm and its extension, the industry to which it belongs, be predicted? This raises the issue of expectation discussed earlier in chapter 5. While a firm's project can be assessed with respect to internal utility in the sense that one can determine that there are no contradictions in the project's formulation and that the resources and technologies are available for its execution as planned, its overt utility can be assessed only with regard to its actual market performance. Hence, if the consumer response is within the range acceptable according to the program, then utility approaches 1; if the deviation is outside the allowed boundaries, then the project becomes entropic and should be treated in the appropriate manner of either altering it or rejecting it if the costs of alteration are too high or if the resources and technologies involved are considered to be better used elsewhere. Thus, while the firm is included in the industry, the future of the industry cannot be predicted by the influence of the firm's policy on the industry. Utility is assessed according to performance, and the individual firm's performance is no indication of the industry's abilities in its markets.

But cannot the industry's utility itself be predicted, even in the short run? If we had the power of prophecy the answer would be an unqualified yes. But even in the somewhat arbitrary time span of the short run too many difficulties exist. For example, assuming that the short run is delineated by industries undertaking either innovative or imitative projects, and that sales are going as expected, in this situation there are no market disturbances and stability exists. This short-run stability can certainly be disrupted by labor actions or by a change in government policies that were not accounted for in the industry's calculations, or by risks that are always involved even though they may not be apparent or in the offing. Utility in industry can be estimated, based on current conditions and projected expectations, but we cannot do more than this.

In this sense industry is in the most volatile of positions. Whatever the stage of growth a country may be in, its industrial sector is the driving force of its economic activity and sets the pace of innovation and imitation; industry exerts control over labor and government through market operations. By this is meant that industry employs labor and generates the economic conditions that form the basis on which government can act in either a corresponding or contrary manner, depending on the economic geopolitical situation as understood by the governing officials.

While industry generates the conditions for economic growth, it nevertheless has very little control over them. For example, with respect to innovation, labor, realizing that a profit is to be made above the current profit level, may consider this as grounds for demanding a new contract, in as much as the terms of the current contract can be interpreted as being altered or even void. There may be a contractual clause that prevents these difficulties, but labor may introduce sanctions that reduce industry's earning power, thereby setting back the innovative process and resulting in losses as market saturation sets in for industry's other products.

Government policies may also hinder industry's operations. While such policies as taxation and investments in various regions targeted for assistance may be subjects for public debate, such policies as devaluations or the unexpected replacement of officials, with the consequent effects on the stock exchange and the uncertainty in the markets that these events often cause, may result in the postponement of innovative or imitative projects or, depending on the seriousness of these polciies and how extensive they are for industry's short- and medium-range planning, may bring about major revisions in industry's operations.

Of course, not all responses are negative. For example, labor may propose the adoption of profit-sharing programs, with the consequence of being more flexible with respect to management and stimulating work rather than evoking sanctions or strikes. This may also result in workers undergoing retraining where necessary to learn to operate the new technologies being introduced as well as those technologies that will result from spin-off processes, thereby upgrading their competitive positions with respect to the rest of the total work force.

In the area of trade, especially where competition is great, devaluations may be positive if they increase the medium- and long-run competitive pricing positions of domestic industry with respect to foreign competition; this is especially true for the emerging and developing economies where the beggar-thy-neighbor stimulus is marginal. Reducing the domestic currency's value makes it that much more expensive for foreigners to maintain their present purchasing patterns, and they will tend to opt for the cheaper-priced products of the domestic country's currency. Levelling tariffs against the devalued goods and services removes the devaluation advantage, and especially for the postindustrial economies this could set off a trade war, because such actions are reciprocal, in that tariffs are set up against those countries that have reacted in this manner. These countries can also devalue, eliminating any advantages gained from this action. Devaluation must be undertaken from the viewpoint that while such actions may be necessary, retaliation may not take place. Other countries may consider it politically expedient to maintain a relatively higher-valued currency for such internal considerations as pride in the national currency — especially during election time — or in response to industrial pressure to prevent devaluations because a devaluation in kind tends to weaken a strong industrial base that produces innovative and imitative products at competitive international prices. Governments may hesitate to devalue because of the potential of labor unrest to gain higher wages to offset the higher prices that may follow, but in countries with strong industrial bases this unrest can be prevented by industry offering discount rates for goods and services as a price to pay for labor tranquility.

Replacing officials — especially in the emerging and developing countries — may not necessarily be to industry's disadvantage, if the reason for so doing is that the new officials are more sympathetic to the problems of competition, the relation between environmental protection and economic growth, and the effects of foreign trade on domestic industrial development. While this last point is especially significant for the emerging and developing countries, the paradox of industrialization is such that it also pertains to the postindustrial countries that are competing with each other for imitative products in the same domestic and foreign markets. In all cases the replacement of officials will bring about slight tremors because of the uncertainty that this causes, but these tremors will soon subside if the replacements are pro-industry and seek to promote it, bringing industry into regions in which it is lacking or of small quantity but where feasibility studies show that it can be beneficial to these regions and profitable to management.

Government policy toward labor can be positive, especially during downward movements of the business cycle, when unemployment begins to set in. Financial relief in the form of unemployment benefits, the encouragement of early retirement, thereby allowing younger people with greater obligations to move higher on the pay scale and in jobs, and provisions for job retraining under various government and union schemes are measures that benefit labor. Furthermore, when government supports industry, more jobs are provided and guaranteed. Support comes through tax relief, both to industry and labor, and by way of orders from industry, which must be supplemented by industry from its various subsectors that supply services, basic materials, and components. This requires employment, and government ordering from industry, whether for civilian or military purposes, benefits both industry and labor. Government support can also come indirectly by way of research at academic institutions supported by grants, the benefits of which are then incorporated into industry through the processes of innovation and imitation as the research yields technologies that are acquired by industry and worked by labor, providing labor with the acquisition of greater skills that are developed and kept up with the advances in technologies and their industrial applications. The significance of this in international trade, especially among the postindustrial economies, cannot be minimized, especially when the competition is for the same markets and the products over time tend to be imitative — another consequence of the international imitation effect.

The question to be considered now is whether in our changing world, with the rise of the emerging and developing countries and the seeming stagnation among the postindustrial countries, some degree of planning can exist in the industrial, governmental, and labor sectors as clarified by the welfare utility function. The welfare utility function is able to describe utility and entropy for the past and present as defined earlier. What, however, can be said about planning for the future and this approximation equation? While the future is unknowable, are there some aspects of the future that we can predict and to which we can apply our technologies and exert some control over our activity as a result? The answer is in the affirmative, for while economic activity deals with the problems of everyday commerce and of growth and development in the macro sense, the very processes of this activity — planning and developing projects, bargaining for higher wages and offering modern and more efficient work techniques as a result, and doing more than trying to determine what the government's next steps are to be by seeking to find protection against them and avoid them if they are detrimental and exploiting them as best as possible if they are positive occur within the phases of the business cycle, and this cycle can be understood and addressed.

THE WELFARE UTILITY FUNCTION AND THE BUSINESS CYCLE: FURTHER COMMENTS

The word "cycle" comes from the Greek *kyklos,* meaning ring or circle. Just as a circle is never-ending, since the Industrial Revolution the term "cycle" has been applied to the recurring (non-Ricardian) phases of business activity. According to classical and neoclassical economic thought, the cycle has four phases: prosperity, recession, depression, and recovery. The Great Depression of 1929, however, changed this approach and indeed brought into critical light the assumptions of classical and neoclassical thinking that resulted in the Keynesian revolution. The period just prior to the Great Depression was one of prosperity in which the greater bulk of wealth was not made in the field of production, but through speculation in the buying and selling of stocks and properties. While this aspect of economic activity is important for growth and development, Keynes pointed out a fact that had been overlooked, that the true wealth of a nation is its productive capacity and ability to market its goods and services.

The Great Depression hit so suddenly that the cycle bypassed the recession phase, moving down violently from the paper prosperity to the deep depression phase that held the world for ten years until World War II. The consequence of this depression was the pledge on the part of all postindustrial economic leaders that such a depression would be ruled out entirely from the business cycle, that Keynesian policy would be used to prevent depressions. Recessions, however, cannot be ruled out by government policy, because, by definition, a recession is a lowered position of prosperity, and recovery depends on the extent of the recession.

Nevertheless, the cycle in its three phases is repetitive, moving from prosperity to recession, from recession to recovery, and from recovery back to prosperity. But no two cycles are the same, because each cycle contains its own special conditions. For example, our current recession is certainly unique and differs from every previous recession phase. Our levels of technology in the postindustrial economies, in every branch of research and application, are of greater sophistication than ever; yet our economies are deep in the recession, although governments are taking measures to move the cycle upward. It seems that competition among the postindustrial economies has brought these economies into the recession, in which heavy industries lay off workers as their financial positions with respect to profits and liquidity worsen. Despite the recession, we possess the greatest technological potential that can be absorbed by industry and worked by the most highly skilled labor force in the history of industrialization. Moreover, the amount of goods and services available and the standard and quality of these goods and services are certainly the highest in the history of industrial output. This is the case because of the applications of science to industry and research in the many forms of technology in industrial output, stimulated by competition through the processes of innovation and imitation. Our current recession exists not because of market saturation in the contemporary sense of the lack of purchases because of the declining utility of additional purchases and therefore the opting for consumer liquidity to the extent that production is hindered. Such a mass turning toward consumer liquidity would be for investments, and the money from investments would be made available to industry and businesses for production. Our unique situation of the contemporary paradox of industrialization will be examined and resolved in part III, chapter 9 after more concepts are developed with respect to the business cycle. It must be said here, however, that because of our high state of technology and high standards of goods and services, the paradox of industrialization as we know it may be the cyclical pattern of the future, in which case, so will be its solution.

What must be understood here is that when the business cycle does begin its upward motion, the economy will not be of the same composition as its previous cyclical completion. It will be altered due to its product composition, and its secondary businesses that survived the recession and that have entered the markets will be oriented toward promoting the new products. The process of distribution has been altered as new businesses replace those that as a result of mergers and bankruptcies no longer remain. The big firms are different because their technologies have been altered to cope with the different conditions of socioeconomic groups in both the domestic and international economies that have formed as a result of the cycle and the consequences of recession. The economic infrastructure has been broadened by the new products, and the technologies have been incorporated to produce them. Moreover, while emerging and developing economies may undergo their own business cycles, restricted to their economies only, the cycles of the postindustrial economies are so intense that they generate similar phases in the emerging and developing economies, regardless of their own economic situations. This is especially the case now in the changing world political situation, when the emerging and developing economies are in need of assistance in the forms of aid and trade, and the postindustrial economies are deep in the recession of the paradox of industrialization. In general, business cycles result in the forming of somewhat different socioeconomic income groups because of those who benefited and those who lost as a result of the cycle's motion. The broadened economic infrastructure contains products that hitherto were nonexistent and has technologies developed during the cycle's movement, while those products and technologies that were no longer relevant were phased out through the disequilibrium dynamics of innovation and imitation. Except for those products that were produced during the cycle's movement, the new products that have since become established in the markets during the processes of innovation and imitation must also face the dynamics of the cycle to follow.

The dynamics of the cycle to follow are based on the previous cycle, and in this sense only there is continuity. During the recession phase innovation can only be constructed on the infrastructure already established, using mainly the technologies and resources that already exist. In this phase the newness comes with the ideas incorporated into projects, setting the tone, as it were, for the cycle's upward movement through the process of imitation if innovation is successful. This alone accounts for the similar aspects of the very long-trend business cycles. Because each cycle is unique because of the infrastructures and technologies developed within its movement, the long-term cycle research now in vogue only demonstrates that there is continuity of history as manifested in economic development from preindustrialization through our contemporary era. Moreover, the uniqueness of each business cycle is further derived from the historical era in which it occurs. For example, during the Industrial Revolution depressions were part of the business cycle, and during depressions economic activity was slowed to the extent that inventories had to be nearly depleted before retooling and reordering could begin. The neoclassical description of the cycle was therefore fairly accurate and accepted by most economic thinkers. This situation also accounted for the neoclassical confidence in full employment, because as soon as the dynamics of recovery set in, employment was reinstated. Depressions were temporary, part of the necessary business cycle, and resulted in clearing the markets for the next round of production. This situation also accounted for the durability of Say's law, for the markets were cleared through the various phases of the business cycle, so that those goods not consumed during prosperity would be sold during depression when their prices were sufficiently low to make their purchases worthwhile.

Of course, this situation required consumer liquidity, for consumption had to be maintained during depressions, and inventories had to be cleared to provide for retooling and restocking. The Great Depression that ended the era of the Industrial Revolution not only demonstrated the errors of neoclassical thinking, but also ended consumer liquidity on a basis sufficient to maintain the cycle's momentum. Historical continuity in the process of economic growth and development does exist, but as the termination of the Industrial Revolution illustrated, this continuity is era based. Industrialization continues, not only in the emerging and developing countries, but in the postindustrial countries as well, with the latter being oriented to high technologies provided by our contemporary era of knowledge. Moreover, the cycle is no longer four-phased, but three-phased, because depressions have been ruled out by governments willing to take all measures available to prevent another depression of the depth and extent of that of 1929. While an era builds on the contributions of its historical predecessors, it nevertheless has its own unique contributions that define it. Business cycles occuring in our era have as their trademark, as it were, the technologies unique to our era incorporated into the economic processes that generate the cycle as well as those that are developed and incorporated into the processes of innovation and imitation that move the cycle along. Moreover, each era has its unique circumstances, and our present paradox of industrialization is certainly unique to our time. Despite our highly skilled labor forces, our advanced technologies, and our abilities at marketing and distribution, our heavy industries are in deep recession even though competition is rigorous and dynamic. Therefore the continuity in long-term cycles that does exist is not that of economic forces prevailing over specific industries and markets throughout historical eras; graphs that plot such cycles merely show apparent consumer consistencies over time, and not some metahistorical-cum-economic force moving through the socioeconomic processes of development and growth.

Thus our contemporary cycle is three-phased, with prosperity, recession, and recovery completing its motion. Moreover, this cycle is appropriate for the emerging and developing countries engaged in market economics — a qualification that will be discussed further in part 3, Chapters 10 and 11. The cycle is not to be considered mechanistic in any sense because the timing of its phases and their dynamics and extent cannot be foreseen. The only aspect of certainty in the cycle is the recurring nature of its three phases. The questions pertaining to the length and extent of each phase have to be considered during the phase; there are no prophets in economics, just economists working with given situations trying to understand how things will develop over time.

The welfare utility function can be applied to the cycle in its phases to enable predictions to be made about the short- and medium-run future, given the conditions and the cyclic phase during which the predictions are made. It must be clear, however, that as predictions, they are subject to unreliability and uncertainty. While they are useful within the context of planning and considering further operations in the current markets, they are certainly invalid as accurate bases for decision making. Hence the dynamics of the open-ended information system allow for changes to be made within the firms' operations within their respective markets.

The situation here is one of the business cycle undergoing its phases and of the general economic activity of industrial, governmental, and labor decision making, as well as other events that occur and affect the economy's behavior within its phases. In this sense the welfare utility function is oriented to the past, allowing measurements of utility as these events have occurred over time past. This time is delineated according to the current conditions as interpreted by decision makers. However, with respect to the business cycle, the welfare utility function is future oriented, because it is on the basis of the cycle's past phase that short-and medium-run decisions should be considered. For example, entering into an innovative project during recession, when unemployment is high and liquidity is diminished due to consumers' declining purchases and reduced savings to offset lower wages, might not make good sense unless the target groups will consume, no matter how extensive the recession, and both resources and labor are available and guaranteed in this period of great uncertainty. In other words, not only must the targeted markets be present, but the means for developing the project and distributing it to these markets must also be available; this is so especially during recessions.

But if it were not for sufficient innovation, the cycle's recession phase would never move up into recovery. This requires innovation on a serious scale, involving financial institutions, the accumulation of natural and productive resources, and the assembling of labor, much of which was hitherto unemployed and receiving government assistance. During this phase innovation would not be undertaken on any significant scale if the decision makers of industry did not consider innovation viable. During recession a cutoff point is reached, allowing industry to take risks with the understanding that both labor and government are ready for the cycle to begin moving upward. Thus, for the recession phase, the welfare utility function takes the form $W_r \approx 1/C_r$; in which r represents the recession phase, and the approximation sign signifies that dynamics are existing even during the recession. While for time tr $0 < (I, G, L) < 1$ and $(I, G, L)_{tr} \rightarrow 0$, the cutoff point is reached at time t_{r+n} ($n \geq 1$), so that at, say, time $tr + 2$ innovation is being considered and even undertaken to the extent that it brings in its wake significant imitation.

This results in a shift in the welfare utility function so that $W_r \approx 1/C_{r+2}$, as the recession phase has not yet moved up, but its cyclical response is making its impact on economic activity. As innovation and subsequent imitation increase, bringing more people into the disequilibrium economic activity of shifting markets, and as new markets are being developed, there by generating employment and increased consumption, the cycle moves into its recovery phase. Moreover, industry begins to undertake trading liquidity for short-term investments and/or imitation, in which case a major attempt is made to enter a market, with the intention of withdrawal if short-term profits are unrealized. Governments, during this phase, seek to invest in regions requiring government assistance, but only in projects that are viable as determined by feasibility studies. Labor is regaining its position in both industry and government, and while it remains quiet because of the emergence from recession, it is beginning to realize its strength in the revitalized dynamics of recovery. Hence from time $r + 2$ the cycle has moved into recovery so that $W_{rec} \approx 1/C_{rec}$, with all the dynamics of this phase performing accordingly. Thus $0 < (I, G, L) < 1$, but there is no tendency toward the entropy of recession or the utility of prosperity; the situation pulls both ways in the sense that while the economic climate is favorable for innovation and imitation, and indeed such activities are taking place, at W_{rec} a major commitment has not yet been made to the dynamics of innovation and imitation. The economy has moved into recovery, but the cycle is still hampered by the inertia of recession. Innovation and imitation have to continue and intensify if recovery is to be stabilized as the cycle's phase, for if industry should hesitate, the gains thus achieved would be lost in the slowdown that would result. When the conservativism of the recession phase yields to profit motivation from successful innovation and imitation, the recovery phase will stabilize and begin moving the cycle up still further toward prosperity. As innovation gains momentum and the conservativism of the recession fades, industry increases its pace of developing new projects and entering into new markets. If these new markets are successful, they bring in competitors, and profits are channeled into innovative projects. Government investment in regions considered needy increases, bringing industry into these areas. Labor becomes more daring because its position is more secure because of the increasing demand by industry for employment. Labor action usually begins during this period of the cycle's phase, but it is still subdued, with sanctions and strikes occurring mainly in those firms that are in a weakened bargaining position because of the upsurge of consumer demand for their products and the need for workers to fulfill their orders, even though there has been increased technology in production as a trade-off with employment.

During this period of the cycle's phase government officials are reconsidering the tax structure. In the recession taxes were high and were used to reduce consumption, while industry was cutting back on production as innovation slowed down and imitation declined drastically due to market saturation and the risks that imitation then held. These high taxes were held over from the final prosperity phase in which inflation was gaining momentum and taxation was used to reduce aggregate liquidity. High taxes and inflation are two important factors in the cycle's turning downward and will be discussed shortly.

The point of note now, however, is that there exists a time lag between the cycle's period within its phase and the taxation rates levied by governments to absorb or release liquidity. This is necessary because taxation is employed as a corrective procedure to regulate the cycle, and the cycle's period within its phases have to be studied and understood. As these periods become settled within the phases, each period carries its own dynamics, which the tax authorities have to comprehend in order to devise programs to either accommodate the period within its phase or to counteract it, as the situation requires. This has to be accomplished without affecting the phases motions so they will not be halted. There must be a time lag, therefore, so that the period's special conditions can be understood and programs can be formulated to deal with them. The difficulty with taxation is that once these programs are implemented, the period will most likely have shifted to another period along the phase; as the dynamics of the period work themselves out, the tax programs of the period are rigid and restrict the period in realizing its full dynamics. For example, when innovation occurs in a specific industrial branch and its spin-off moves into another, as in the case of biogenetic engineering in medicine and agriculture, taxing these sectors removes both liquidity and, to some degree, incentives that are necessary for further research and the applications of the results of research into industry. However, taxation cannot be flexible, showing favoritism to one branch at the expense of another. Because taxes are formulated to pertain to specific conditions over time, and because these conditions are far from static but are subject to the dynamics of the time, tax policies are always inadequate, as their effectiveness with respect to their designed purpose is always hindered by the time lag.

The point to be considered now is that tax incentives to industry for investing in new or impoverished regions, while encouraging, do not allow for sufficient protection for the risks involved during this period of the recovery phase. While industry's investment in these regions in the form of plant location and liquidity in the banking system may stimulate economic activity, in which construction is an important initial factor, supplies of the necessary resources must be available to allow for production, and adequate infrastructure must exist for acquiring the resources and distributing the finished product — points of concern especially for the emerging and developing economies. In this situation, while the risks are real, an optimism prevails due to the cycle's moving upward, and governments rely on this optimism to encourage firms to move into these areas.

This optimism is based on increasing innovative and imitative projects that are successful with respect to profits. Greater employment provides greater liquidity, and this, together with the profit motive, stimulates innovation and imitation. Consumption increases with increased consumer liquidity, but savings also increase, sharpening the demarcation between consumption and disposable liquidity, largely absent during recession as aggregate liquidity was diminished and savings were reduced considerably to maintain living standards. The demarcation between disposable liquidity and consumption enters at the second period of the recovery phase and is sharpened further as recovery continues. This demarcation also contributes to the general optimism because it enables both individuals and firms to expand consumption and enter into innovation and imitation, respectively.

During this period of the recovery phase $W_{rec+2} \approx 1/C_{rec+2}$, $0 < (I, G, L) < 1$ and $(I, G, L) \to 1$. The recovery phase is gaining in momentum as more firms enter the dynamics of production and through innovation and imitation open and develop new markets and expand the existing markets when this is profitable. Employment is increasing, and government officials are examining industrial activity to determine ways to maintain the increasing momentum of growth and expansion.

The recovery phase moves into the prosperity phase after there have been sufficient periods in the recovery phase to bring innovation and imitation into a situation in which all firms are engaged in these activities.

This is important, because as the cycle moves from recovery to the early period of prosperity, most of the country's citizens are gainfully employed. It must also be noted, however, that during this period governments begin to withdraw from active intervention in the form of infrastructure building and tax incentives in the postindustrial economies, while these measures will still prevail to a lesser extent in the emerging and developing economies. In the postindustrial economy it is assumed during this period that industry is no longer in need of support, while support in the developing economies, will be maintained or weakened according to government oficials' understanding of their countries' problems and needs. Nevertheless, during this period sales are up, profits are good, and employment and consumption, as the consequences of innovation and imitation, are at levels that reinforce production and the opening of additional new markets.

However, the opening of new markets during this period relies on the liquidity available to the targeted groups, and most likely this liquidity is committed to either savings or investments and to established consumption patterns. For innovation to be successful during this period of prosperity, therefore, consumers have to be taken away from established markets. This results in strenuous competition that takes the forms of price reductions, in those firms that have either lost customers or seek new customers, and higher-quality products to attract new customers; this is achieved by trading off liquidity for production in order to enter new or established markets, thus leaving the previous markets for marginal producers. Aggressive advertising also has to be used as perhaps the final and most effective weapon in competition — advertising that is directed toward the primary consumer group and yet can generate sales among secondary groups.

During this period of the prosperity phase $W_p \approx 1/C_p$, and $(I, G, L) \rightarrow 1$. At this time taxes are low, reflecting the previous phase of recovery when they were reduced to stimulate business activity and to provide greater liquidity for consumption. Low tax levels also assist in prosperity, because for a time they allow for increasing consumption and production to support it. Labor is either quiet and working, or discontented and expressing this discontent in sanctions or strikes, which may affect certain industrial sectors but have no major bearing on the economy itself. During this period the economy has become buoyant and is resilient in the face of labor unrest because it has liquidity to back it when labor takes action.

However, during the next period of this phase signs of decline begin to set in. Innovation increases at a decreasing rate as consumer liquidity is accounted for in the purchasing patterns of imitation, and the risk of innovation is commensurate with the available opportunities for profit taking. Imitation also increases at a decreasing rate as market saturation begins to set in, reducing the opportunities for profit taking. Labor's restiveness begins to subside as labor leaders recognize the decline in industrial activity and realize that it is not opportune to continue conflicts during this period. The government understands that business activity is slowing while consumers still enjoy high levels of liquidity. Inflation results as consumer demand remains high, but because market near saturation is setting in and competition is rigorous, prices are raised to maintain profit levels.

In the following period higher taxes are levied to reduce or curtail inflation. This also adds to the price increases as these taxes are passed on to the consumers. Innovation ceases almost entirely, and imitation declines considerably, functioning only in those marginal markets where room still exists for market entry. Prices continue to rise, and because of higher taxation and the lack of new production, consumption begins to decline.

During this period labor's situation is uneasy. Employment begins to decline because of declining consumption, and increasing taxation on both industry and consumers reduces still further the motivation for risk taking and new market ventures. Signs are beginning to appear that higher unemployment is in the offing, making labor quiet industrially but somewhat restive because of the realization that the cycle will begin moving downward. Most workers seek to maintain their jobs, but others seek employment elsewhere, in other regions and, for the developing and emerging economies, in the postindustrial economies, accounting for the migration of talented people to countries where the opportunities are greater. This is somewhat difficult because consumer liquidity has declined and government support for the outlying regions has been withdrawn, bringing about a decline in potential employment. Labor finds little relief for its restiveness; those workers able to hold on to their jobs are well off, while those who cannot have difficulties in finding employment elsewhere and turn to the dole. The cycle has peaked and begins moving downward toward recession. $W_{p+3} \approx 1/C_{p+3}$, $0 < (I, G, L) < 1$, and the next time period $p+4$ equals the first period of the recession, in which $(I, G, L) \rightarrow 0$.

THE WELFARE UTILITY FUNCTION AND DYNAMIC DISEQUILIBRIUM

The theory of economic growth and development formulated in this work is based on the broader concept of the modern economy in dynamic disequilibrium. This concept of the modern economy is relevant here because the emerging, developing, and postindustrial economies are so related in our contemporary era and social time that regardless of the state of economic growth and development, all economies undergo business cycles in the manner of dynamic disequilibrium. In those emerging and developing countries that rely on economic planning boards to regulate the markets, the tendency is away from this type of regulation and toward market economic planning and distribution, with the government taking a passive but regulative role when the need arises. One reason for this movement toward the market economy is to achieve wealth on a national level in which all citizens can participate. National wealth is based on personal wealth, and under government planning boards the ability to acquire wealth through initiative and labor is restricted and the authority of the planning board is all-pervasive. Another reason, however, is the need to prevent the dissolution of countries, such as the decline of the Soviet Union and the bloodshed in Yugoslavia, as people seek wealth, national identity, and personal values.

Hence the world's economies are in a state of continuous dynamic disequilibrium in which new markets are initiated, existing markets expand through imitation, and other markets, having reached the condition that further expansion through imitation is unprofitable are eventually phased out and the resources are used for other production lines.

Hence on the micro scale of the modern economy, regardless of its stage of development, there are firms employing vast amounts of labor force to perform the tasks of economic activity, and there are also individual consumers engaging in producing and exchanging a tremendous assortment of commodities. The theoretical and practical dynamics of such economies are those of markets expanding and contracting and of new products being manufactured, while others already marketed attract close competitors, and still others are being phased out because of too much competition and too little profits, as well as decisions taken to enter other new markets. Firms do not seek stability in their marketing plans; their managers consider the dynamics of the markets and how to exploit them in the long run, even while their short-run products are on the markets. Thus on the micro level the emerging and developing economies share the same situations as their postindustrial counterparts. All three economies are undergoing disequilibrium changes, fluctuating between innovation and imitation, opting for liquidity when the managers of firms consider this to their firms' advantage, and at the same time moving with the business cycle according to its phases.

On the macro level, both in theory and in practice, disequilibrium holds when the industrial sector, the government in its capacity as economic participant, and labor are unified into a dynamic force of economic activity. The relationship between the micro and macro levels in the economy involves the micro components of specific firms, government policies, and specific labor policies with respect to the firms and to government policies — the (Fp ε i) ε I, the (gp ε g) ε G, and the (lp ε l) ε L that is, the policies of government on specific subsectors of the firm, the government program, and labor policy in a specific region and field of employment, and I, G, and L as the components of the macro economy, so that if restriction on foreign trade is removed, there is a good working model for the contemporary economy regardless of its stage of growth and development, with its micro components functioning in dynamic disequilibrium and moving along with the business cycle. Statically, it was stated that $W_t = U(I, G, L)_t$, and that as $(F \mathrel{\mathcal{E}} i) \mathrel{\mathcal{E}} I$, $(gp \mathrel{\mathcal{E}} g) \mathrel{\mathcal{E}} G$, and $(lp \mathrel{\mathcal{E}} l) \mathrel{\mathcal{E}} L$, to determine the utilities of these components either the sectors themselves can be evaluated, or their specific components can be evaluated and then assembled into their respective sectors, which is a more tedious but more accurate process.

When one examines the sector, only a general picture can be obtained. Industry as a whole may be found to be dynamic upon examination, but specific firms within each industrial subsector may be inefficient. It may be significant to examine these and to determine how their situations can be improved, so that they may opt for liquidity, innovation or imitation, as the case may be. Firms not doing well are usually in markets in which saturation is approaching. Their utilities are declining because they have been exploited almost to the limit in all the variations of production that their managers have been able to construct. Further alterations in these markets will thus lead to marginal sales at best, and at worst to no positive changes in revenues. This is significant, because either those firms with declining revenues have entered the markets too late to exploit their viabilities, or their prices are too high due either to inefficient production, the need for higher profits with respect to market conditions, internal difficulties among the managers and their staffs, or perhaps inadequate promotion of their products with respect to advertising, packaging, or both. Thus, when the markets are approaching near saturation and the utility positions of most of the markets are high, those firms with low utility positions can either reconstruct their production programs, opt for liquidity, or channel their resources into projects where, upon evaluation, the markets appear more favorable. If the liquidity option is taken, there are the problems of phasing out production lines; if the reconstruction option is taken, there are the problems of reprograming, given the loss of competitive time and the dynamics of the current markets that may render such programing entropic as the markets' declining situation brings other firms into the same decision situation. These decisions are taken on the basis of utility considerations, including the cycle's phase and period.

The cycle's phase and period are of great significance because of the general conditions. For example, because government policy depends on the cycle, when the cycle is in the period of peak recovery, the welfare programs enacted during the recession and realized in their utilities during the early recovery period tend to be entropic, because their reasons for being applied have been diminished with the reviving economy. When the cycle is moving from prosperity into recession, the government's policies on welfare become entropic with the cycle's downward swing if they are not revised to cope with the impending difficulties.

Similarly in the case of labor, strike actions and sanctions possess utility when the cycle moves into peak recovery and into prosperity, because the markets provide the firms with revenues that labor can bargain to have channeled into higher wages and better working conditions, if they are not already designated for innovative and imitative projects. Hence for labor timing is important; as workers produce, they know when projects are new, and whether they are innovative or imitative. They also know when the general economy is healthy and whether the cycle is moving upward, as this can be judged by the ratio between employed and unemployed workers. These are considerations that must be evaluated before sanctions or strike actions are undertaken. If they are ignored or misinterpreted, the sanctions or strikes are likely to be counterproductive — entropic — because the economy will be unable to meet the workers' demands and there will be wasted hours of work that could go into strengthening the economy, making their demands more feasible during better economic conditions.

To accomplish economic growth and development, both industry and labor should act affirmatively with the cycle's movement. During the end of recession and the beginning of recovery firms begin engaging in innovation and imitation, reemploying greater work forces to get industries going and manufacturing again. The government, however, should move somewhat countercyclically, so that when industries begin recovering through innovation and imitation, the government should realize the time factor necessary to ease off from its policies of welfare support according to the conditions as they develop regarding unemployment and industrial expansion. This counterbalancing assists in maintaining the economy in disequilibrium because of the government's withdrawing of funds that are no longer of utility, as they are not based on productivity and sales but on welfare. This allows for inflation to remain low during this phase because money in circulation is related primarily to productivity and sales, so that wages and revenues from sales can be channeled into consumption and the utility option without unnecessary distortions from excess and unproductive money affecting prices. Liquidity derived from revenues can be rechanneled into production and/or savings for future production, or into maintenance of the liquidity option, with inflation in the postindustrial economies resulting only when the cycle peaks out at prosperity. For the emerging and developing countries inflation is very often brought about by government decisions concerning the areas and sectors on which direct control is exerted; in these cases prices rise as officials see fit to increase them, reducing the real value of their currencies and resulting in a strong black market for hard currencies that is very often under government control. This aspect of economic development for the emerging and developing countries will be discussed in part III, Chapter 10 of this work. It suffices here to say that inflation and the disturbance of unproductive money in an economy, whatever its stage of development, are certainly unnecessary during the prosperity phase. Preference for the dole to being employed and adding to production, or consuming without considering the possibilities of saving because of the difficult straits of being on welfare, merely add to the diseconomies brought about by government intervention and are almost entirely unnecessary during the latter period of recovery and the early period of prosperity, but are necessary when inflation occurs as the peak of the prosperity phase approaches and innovation and imitation decline.

The welfare utility function's micro components are the industrial sector, government economic policies, and organized labor operating in their individual programs, projects, and markets. The micro components of the industrial sector are the innovative and imitative projects, opting for utility as it affects firms' performances, and the firms' expansions into foreign markets. The government's micro components are those policies such as regional development, the building of infrastructure, and the support of specific industries that can be evaluated in the same manner as all other utility systems, either open or closed. This last point is especially pertinent for the emerging and developing countries when industry protection in light of trade is a real issue. Moreover, included in this classification is the government's activity with respect to economic relations with other countries, a point significant when aid and trade are concerned. The micro components of labor are those relations that organized labor has with each firm and include the decisions taken for labor harmony or sanctions or strikes as the labor officials understand their situations. The advantage of micro utility for these micro components is that it provides a basis for analysis prior to the initiation of policy and action. Consistency in mapping of the operational language onto the area language allows for sound reasoning, and the isomorphism restricts the degree of ambiguity in the languages until entropy sets in. Once these information systems are established, they provide the basis for alteration, expansion, and maneuvering according to managements' perceptions and understanding, government economic decision makers' considerations with respect to the business cycle and the economies' needs, and labor organizers' understanding of their situation and options within the economy.

From the micro components, the macro sectors are constructed. From the sum of activities of firms in a single industrial subsector and the sum of subsectors into the general industry, the I component is constructed. From the specific types of government economic policy summed into a single subsector to the more general policies and finally to the fiscal and monetary policies overriding the lower-level decision making, government economic policy can be summed into the G component. For labor, from the specific management-labor contracts and conflicts when the contract time expires, the sectorial labor relations, the general labor attitude, and policy considerations with respect to the business cycle, the L component is constructed.

These constructions can be made from the general to the specific as well. In the general industrial sector, for example, by stating what the industrial subsector consists of and then breaking them down into their individual firms from **I**, **F** can be derived. The same holds for government policy. Beginning with the general monetary and fiscal policies, one can derive specific policies with respect to regional policies, and these can be analyzed still further. The situation for labor is a little more complex because in addition to the overall labor policy established by the union leaders, the unions also act according to the conditions within each firm. While the guidelines for such actions must be broadly stated at the union level, specific actions of a local branch do not necessarily follow the broad guidelines, and this may lead to clashes with the major unions — especially in the emerging and developing countries — and often to the denial of national support for the disturbing local branch.

Because the welfare utility function depends on the cycle and because the economy fluctuates in a condition of dynamic disequilibrium, in which markets expand and close and innovation and imitation open up new markets and bring about near saturation in existing markets, resulting in shifts in market orientation, the discussion of this function would be incomplete if it did not include the individual in the economy. While the firm is the generator of economic activity, the target groups of each specific firm's projects are composed of contemporary individuals, and it is to the individual that the firm ultimately seeks to program its project by appealing to the individual and attracting his or her consumer loyalty. The government's economic policies must gain the contemporary individual's support, for if dissatisfaction is too great or if government programs become entropic and fall short of their objectives, the consumers as citizens will register their negative opinions where they count most — either at the polls or on the streets. Labor's situation is somewhat different, because of closing down firms that are not union workplaces and preventing nonunion workers from suffering. Moreover, the paradox of industrialization and the high technologies available to industry have somewhat altered labor's position, requiring skilled workers to develop still further skills to work the high technologies in all their stages. The issue of the nonunion shop has certainly become marginal due to the inroads in economic decision making gained by union officials and the requirements of industry and society during our contemporary era and its social-time paradox of industrialism; nonunion shops are marginal in production and have an impact only locally. Moreover, unions require skilled workers for contemporary technological advances, and during periods of recession, when unemployment is high, unions can provide courses for their members to train them in the skills to use the new technologies in the production processes.

The relationship between individual utility functions and the welfare utility function, therefore is evident in the following: Individual utility functions are formulated on the basis of information that the individual places in an isomorphic relation to his or her needs and wants. This strict relationship is due to the expectations to be derived from the reality of consumption and preference. Such utility functions are attempts to impose on a seemingly chaotic reality of vast consumer products an order derived from individual tastes, needs, and wants. With respect to firms, governmental agencies responsible for economic policies, and labor organizations responsible for their workers, these functions pose little or no difficulty. The leaders in each of these sectors and subsectors, including the micro level of the firm, the specific government agency dealing with a certain branch of the economy, and the specific labor branch of the local union in a firm, are managers, and their decisions are made with respect to their positions in their organizations, based on their individual perceptions and understanding and tempered by the perceptions and understanding of those with whom they work.

Often these information systems clash and are thus subject to entropy, the extent of which depends on how well these systems perform when they are in conflict. The managers of a firm may have to consider the responses of their workers when new products are placed into operation. Workers have to consider their strategies with respect to management's situation in the firm's competitive position. Moreover, both business and labor leaders have to consider the effects of government economic policies on their operations, because these considerations influence their relationships with one another as well as with the government.

When this information is considered important, therefore, it is included in the system. The system is open-ended if it is not closed for a specific project over a very short period of defined time, and this open-endedness allows alterations and responses to alterations to be generated within the system by the influences of the marketplace. Changes are made within the system either because of management's intentional alterations in the operational and/or area languages to cope with the reality for which the system was formulated, or because reality imposes changes within the system for which changes have to be made in one or both languages. This process is dynamic, related both to the business cycle and to the requirements of competition, and continues until the alterations outweigh the original system and entropy is too intense, or until the system is abandoned for other projects. This holds for the firms' information systems, the government agencies, and labor management, and the systems of each of these must take into account not only their competitors — for the government agencies this also includes foreign trade — but also the information systems of the others.

The decisions of each of these sectors is dependent on both the currenty situation and the dynamics of the cycle. Innovation and imitation, for example, will definitely slow down when the cycle approaches the peak of prosperity. Government decisions tend to be countercyclical in order to eliminate as much as possible the difficulties of unemployment and the problems of financing welfare projects when the cycle declines, and to prevent too much liquidity and inflation when the cycle rises. Labor realizes during the peak of prosperity and the cycle's movement toward recession, as well as in the obvious situation of recession itself, that it has to refrain as much as possible from taking sanctions or striking, and that the best time for these actions is when the cycle moves into recovery.

The contemporary individual as a consumer, outside the framework of employment and managerial decision making, does not have information systems formulated with respect to rigor, as do the managers of business, government, and labor. Consider, for example, the contemporary individual as a manager in a government agency dealing with a specific aspect of economic policy. This individual constructs his or her information system using operational and area languages to attempt to define the problem situation and form a working relationship that will provide the conditions for effective use of the system, which is constructed for expansion and alteration as the circumstances prescribe.

Consider this same contemporary individual as a consumer. This person has tastes, preferences, and income limitations on his or her allocations for consumption and is open to try new products regardless of these tastes and preferences — this last condition being necessary in our expanding markets. In one very important sense this individual shares with all other consumers the property that his or her consumption is influenced to a great extent by the business cycle's phase. When the cycle is in its depths of recession, goods and services are somewhat limited in quantity, and their prices are high. The result is a combination of stagnation and inflation, or "stagflation," as it has been termed. Business managers then share with government and labor managers and all employees in the economy the situation that consumption is limited to a relatively small amount of goods and services at prices that are fairly high. The consumer, no matter what his or her employment status may be, is then restricted by this condition. This restriction is one of degree and requires that each consumer budget his or her purchases according to the liquidity possessed with respect to alternative purchases.

When the business cycle begins to rise, the opportunities for consumption increase as competition forces prices down. This process continues throughout the various periods of recovery and into the prosperity phase until innovation declines significantly and imitation follows suit shortly after, plunging the cycle into recession once again, only with a broader-based socioeconomic infrastructure, so that the next movement to recovery will bring a greater variety of domestic and imported goods and services due to new innovation and imitation and the new technologies on which these processes are based. The completion of each cycle enriches the economy that much more, an important consideration for the emerging and developing economies.

From this it can be stated that consumer's utilities are cyclically oriented, so that if we set UC for consumers' utilities, it can be stated that $UC \approx 1/C_p$ with the subscript **p** standing for the period in the cycle's phase. The subscript **p** could also be substituted for **t** for time, but it is important to note the cycle's period in its phase when discussing consumers' utilities, as this indicates the general purchasing patterns from the available goods and services with respect to income.

It will be remembered from the section of Chapter 6 of this work on the theory of value and liquidity that income **Y** is separated into y_c and y_d, with y_c being income in circulation and y_d being disposable income. Income in circulation is income for consumption, as it is through consumption that money is placed into the economy in exchange for goods and services. Disposable income can also be placed into circulation through consumption, but it can also be saved and invested if this done rationally, to earn returns greater than the cost of living index. Hence disposable income can be used for consumption or investments as the consumers see fit. The point is that while income **Y** holds for the entire economy — **M** = y_c+y_d — y_c and y_d hold for the contemporary consumer, so that his or her money supply is equal to personal income for consumption as well as the disposable income that exists after the usual consumption is completed, and that can be directed toward further consumption or savings or investment, as the consumer desires.

Just as consumption is dependent on the cycle's phases and its periods, so are individual savings and investments, for they influence the direction to be taken with regard to disposable income as well as consumption. This is important because on the basis of the cycle's phases and periods, investments are made and savings are put aside. Of course, investments and savings have the element of risk not associated with the business cycle, and this is manifested in the expectation of the returns from programs in which the money is placed. This is based on the utility of the investment or saving and is associated with the expected rate of interest, so that **E/U(idnr/cdn)**, with **i** being the interest, **dn** being the deferred number of time units, **r** being the rate of return which differs from the interest rate because interest is fixed, while the rate of return is compounded on the basis of the interest rate and the amount of money involved for the time units, and **c** being the currency in which the savings or investments are made. Because velocity of money is equal to the utility of money, and because **M** = **Y**, the velocity of money invested or saved is equal to its utility as savings and investments. But because this utility cannot be evaluated with a high degree of certainty due to the disequilibrium dynamics of shifting markets and the demand for loans as a consequence, the utility has to be of an expected value, in which the interest rate depends on the expected percentage of the savings or investments, and the money value of the return is determined by the conditions of the markets, both domestic and foreign. The exception to this is guaranteed returns at a fixed rate over time such as those offered by banks and savings institutions, with interest rates changing after the fixed time period expires.

By considering $UC_p \approx 1/C_p$, the individual consumer's utility function can be further explained. Because $UC \equiv \Sigma\ UC_i^n$, $uc_i\ \mathcal{E}\ UC$, and therefore $uc_{ip} \approx 1/C_p$. Once the individual consumer utility position is isolated, it can be analyzed further: $uc = m(y_c + y_d)$, that is, individual consumer utility is a money function of consumption income and disposable income. As y_c is the main component in this function, from it most if not all consumption is made. Hence it is used for the purchase of goods and services having the set elements $\{1, 2, ..., n\}$ for time t. At time $t+1$ there is no guarantee that these elements of consumption will be identical to those of time t, but as people tend to be creatures of habit except for pioneers, the deviations will usually not be too profound; this, of course, depends on the impact of innovation and imitation, on the consumer and his or her peer groups, and on the impacts that the new products have on the general consumption patterns. Imitation can inlfuence purchasing patterns by way of lower prices and/or better packaging and even good effective advertising, or by being a better product for the same price, as in the case of two different automobiles, one offering more options and having a longer warranty than the other.

This argument is based on the assumption that each consumer knows what is best for him or her. For this reason consumer tastes differ as much as do the consumers themselves, and this renders any attempt to quantify over the individual consumer impossible. Tastes are as fickle as the weather; while general patterns can be established, individual details escape the pattern. On this basis innovation and imitation are undertaken to influence the consumer to change the direction — in the case of imitation, perhaps slightly — of his or her purchasing patterns. This does not mean that general statements cannot be made about the consumer, statements that are valid for consumers in the emerging and developing economies as well as in the more established postindustrial economies. For example, consumers' purchasing patterns are influenced directly by the business cycle's phase and period. On the basis of this reasoning, substitution in consumption takes hold. For example, when inflation is high due to the peak of prosperity or the beginning of recession, the consumer will seek substitutes of lower-priced goods for the higher-priced ones. Substitution is not limited to inflation, however, because it also forms the basis of imitation as firms compete for consumer liquidity.

Still another generalization is that as the cycle moves up in recovery, less of consumers' incomes will be directed toward consumption because of price declines due to competition. This enables greater consumption at fixed rates of income allotted for consumption, thereby releasing disposable income for savings and investments. There is no necessity for this to occur throughout the cycle's upward movement, but the tendency is for savings programs to be acted upon during this upward swing. For this reason fixed rates of return are popular savings incentives because they allow for hedges against uncertainty, even though the interest and rates of return are far lower than risk-taking investment rates.

Another certainty exists concerning the consumer as a member of a consuming group. The term "group" is used loosely here in the sense that it does not refer to organizations or organized behavior set by others to be followed. It does mean that certain standards of living and modes of consumption experienced by peoples on different income levels establish the targets at which commercials are directed, packaging is oriented, and innovation and imitation vie for consumers' liquidity, according to the stage of development and the ability to compete internationally. Nor are the groups rigid, for while they are targets for sales, they or their consumers may prefer to venture into purchasing patterns allowed by their income levels that bring them into other such group classifications. Hence expensive available wines can be enjoyed by those who have the money and by those who decide to splurge and cut back on consumption later. This mobility is not always upward, but can be downward as well, as in the case of wealthy people who prefer a common brand of cigarette.

The determining condition establishing the grouping to which a consumer belongs is the group's social orientation to the consumer's status and position within the economy. Whatever the stage of development is, a banker has a higher status economically than a street cleaner, and the banker's consumption patterns are based on the salary he or she receives, allowing for greater consumption compared that of the street cleaner. The contemporary individual in the economy decides to which group he or she belongs by his or her aspirations, but the grouping is also determined by the common property of the salary range. This determinant is socially oriented and quantifiable, while inner feelings, expressed openly through aspirations, are strictly personal and hence nonquantifiable.

What is quantifiable, however, is the contemporary individual's total consumption, and this is expressed by the **uc** function over the time period considered. But because consumption varies with the business cycle's phase and period, for each consumer, $\mathbf{uc_t} = \mathbf{m} = (\mathbf{y_c} + \mathbf{y_d})_t = \mathbf{m} \approx 1/\mathbf{C_{pt}}$. Hence the consumer's utility function approximates the welfare utility function, which in turn approximates the economy's position with respect to the cycle's phase and period. This is so intuitively, for in times of recession and unemployment the consumer cuts back on consumption, and during recovery and prosperity, when the economy is active in innovation and imitation, the consumer increases and expands consumption. That this is so logically has been derived from the argument.

As both the contemporary individual's utility function and the general welfare utility function are approximations of the cycle's phase and period, it can be seen that economic growth and development involve both the individual as consumer and the economy's organizations — business, governmental, and labor — in which they work. Their work generates income, part of which is directed toward salaries and generates liquidity for consumption, savings, and investments. But while this is so, business, government, and labor each have a specific role in the processes of economic growth and development.

As the generators of economic activity, businesses initiate programs of innovation and imitation, producing goods and services for both domestic and foreign consumption. Moreover, as a result of business activity, when cyclical conditions allow, businesses respond to the cycle's dynamics through innovation and imitation.

While businesses generate economic activity, the government's role through monetary regulation, fiscal policies, and supporting the development of infrastructure is to counter the cycle in its extremes and to ensure a smooth transition from recovery to prosperity. This requires that the government prevents the cycle from moving too fast during recovery, allowing firms to maintain the pressures of competition and production while keeping aggregate prices fairly stable even though there is revitalized and increased demand due to the increased liquidity obtained through employment. For example, if the psychology of recession is one of caution that prevails even though recovery is progressing, then the liquidity option for firms will be stronger than otherwise. While profits are gained through successful innovation and imitation, the liquidity option acts as a form of security, even though this is unrealistic during recovery because fixed costs are reducing unproductive liquidity and aggregate demand is increasing. Other firms will shed the recession psychology and act on production, and as aggregate demand increases, supply may not follow the pace. The result may be inflation, and the government must take steps to hold this inflation in check.

During recovery increased taxation is not a policy to be undertaken, for this restricts spending only marginally, but mostly reduces the personal income allocated for savings and investments — monies necessary to maintain the liquidity flow of businesses. Levels of consumption are largely maintained, applying increasing pressure on limited supplies and increasing inflation that much further. Because the problem is psychological, so is the solution. Governments should invest in social infrastructure while maintaining current tax levels, thereby stimulating a more positive economic picture that encourages the liquidity option to be lessened so that production can be increased, and the full dynamics of disequilibrium, through changing production orientation by innovation and imitation, can be realized.

Labor in the emerging, developing, and postindustrial economies has the tradition of imposing sanctions and striking to gain workers' rights, and when various government legislation has been enacted in the emerging and developing economies to impress the postindustrial economies with their social concern and to maintain a basic income to provide socioeconomic stability during growth and development, allowing for the purchases of both domestic and foreign goods and services, labor's policies are fair when they correspond to this legislation. There is another aspect of labor that must be considered, however, and this involves the changing approaches of labor to the changing industries, certainly relevant in the emerging and developing economies. The traditional industries that evolved as a result of the Industrial Revolution, such as the steel, oil, and automobile industries, still exist; however, in our contemporary era new industries have developed, those not requiring the traditional blue collars and hard hats, but demanding skills at extremely high levels of perfection. These are the computer industries and biotechnological industries involving genetic engineering, industries that are highly competitive, especially among the postindustrial societies, both domestically and in foreign markets.

Because of its historical hard-fought struggles and the concessions gained from business, both historically in the postindustrial economies and currently in the developing and emerging economies, labor has tended toward conservatism, requiring stringent procedures, such as long periods of apprenticeship and a long waiting time before such apprenticeships can be obtained, as well as restricted mobility of workers within plants, to maintain labor's own position of authority and bargaining power with businesses. While this conservatism is understandable in light of the history of labor's struggles, it has little bearing on our contemporary situation. Contrary to popular opinion, technology does not have to be specialized in orientation. As it becomes advanced and increasingly sophisticated, technology requires the conceptuatlizations of mathematical and physical disciplines, among others. The point is that the traditional concept of the blue-collar worker, hard hatted and assembly-line oriented, is being replaced by workers who are acquiring higher degrees in education and further sophistication in their labor. Competition among the emerging, developing, and postindustrial economies requires the latest state-of-the-art production techniques and the skills necessary for working with these tools. Moreover, innovation and imitation impose on labor the necessity to maintain its competitive edge in order to remain employed and to be productive. Labor unions, therefore, cannot impede progress in productivity by resting on traditions, but must make efforts to ensure that their members are kept abreast of the latest in technological developments and their applications in the industrial structures of their respective countries, regardless of their stages of development.

The demands of industrialization vary from one cycle to another, leaving the economy that much more enriched as the cycle is completed. This places demands on the labor force for retraining and further education to prepare for the next cyclical upswing. This pertains not only to the uses of robotics in operating the assembly lines and to the workers programing them, but also to those workers, technologically oriented, who construct the robots to relate to the production processes for those products being manufactured. The consequence is that industry requires the replacement of blue-collar and hard-hatted workers by college-educated workers who are developing new materials for industry. They are members of unions, and when circumstances of the business cycle bring them into the ranks of the unemployed, for the betterment of the economy they should still receive further training to allow them to advance in their careers when industries require their services once again.

Another service that labor unions can provide their members, one especially important in the emerging and developing economies, is the educating of those workers who, for whatever reasons, were unable to complete their formal education. This will allow these workers to become competitive with their fellow workers, providing them with the opportunity to move up the wage scale and improve their personal positions, perhaps to the point of entering the more demanding technological levels of employment. Not only will these people benefit, but industry will also benefit by having a higher level of skilled workers employable, so that projects requiring advanced technologies can be introduced into the production process with little difficulty and need for worker adjustments. What happens to those workers on the lower end of the wage scale, whose jobs are associated with menial labor? One of the advantages of technology should be to remove the drudgery of labor and replace it with the challenges of work, with the consequence that the dynamics generated by the information gained from the technologies in their applications being incorporated into the information systems of other types of work. The very fact that some work remains laborious is a remnant of the earlier economic era, and through rational planning and retraining by labor organizations, such work should be abolished.

As firms innovate and imitate, they require new technologies and different approaches to work in order for their projects to be economically viable. Labor has more to do than merely adjust accordingly, seeking retraining whenever possible; the unions should become dynamic in the introduction and expansion of retraining programs, perhaps even developing their own contributions to technology that can be provided to, and used by, the firms. Even in the emerging and developing countries this type of cooperation will make the firms more profitable and improve labor's earning position as a consequence, perhaps to the extent that this type of cooperation can be used in the wage-bargaining process. If business management is not forthcoming, however, leaving labor's contributions either unrewarded or insufficiently remunerated, as determined in the wage-bargaining process, then there is still the possibility of recourse to sanctions and strikes, perhaps with the backing of the general public in extreme situations. Moreover, this policy will provide higher levels of technology that can be translated into greater productive efficiency, freeing resources for other projects and allowing for the liquidity option when this is considered necessary.

Still another advantage to technological education in its manifestations in work is that more widely available technologies can prolong the cycle's recovery and prosperity phases by their transformation into innovative and imitative projects. The duration of innovation and imitation and the economic expansion that they allow maintain the cycle's motion upward. Markets may reach near saturation, but as long as technology provides for the opening of new markets or for firms to shift into markets that are still competitive, the cycle's upward motion can be maintained. Technology tends to release resources for other purposes, so that the greater the technologies, the greater the resources available for new projects. Labor can retrain its members, keeping them skilled in the latest technologies, especially during cyclical decline and unemployment, so that when the cycle begins moving upward again, labor's contribution will not only be in the execution of work plans, but perhaps also in increasing the efficiency of executing these plans through the introduction of technologies that are then approved by the firm's management and incorporated into the working project. The time has come for business management and labor to retreat from their traditional roles as antagonists and to begin working together for their mutual benefit and that of the consumers. This is certainly important in the emerging and developing economies where resources tend to be scarce, and also in the postindustrial economies more rigorously involved in the contemporary paradox of industrialization.

Because the welfare utility function depends on the business cycle, and because the economy fluctuates in a condition of dynamic disequilibrium in which markets expand and close, innovation opens up new markets that are developed through imitation, and the imitation dynamic brings about market near saturation over time, policies conducted by the economy's three sectors can be evaluated still further. It must be understood that these sectors are ultimately answerable to their constitutents, for without the support of the main body of constituents in the country these sectors will not remain in their present form, as the popular protest in the Soviet Union demonstrated. Emerging economies are the most unstable, and government leaders, industrialists, and labor leaders must work together to implement their system of political and economic development for the benefit of their citizens, or else political and perhaps military upheaval will alter the regime and the system. Developing economies have achieved their status because of their economic stability and their orderly procedure for economic and political change, so that discontent is usually expressed at the polls rather than on the streets. The postindustrial economies have achieved a high degree of socioeconomic stability and sophistication, and because government, business, and labor leaders are certainly aware of this, they tend to develop their policies to suit their constituents, so that political discontent is expressed by the ballot, economic dissatisfaction is manifested in consumer alternatives, and discontent with labor organizations moves workers to join other such organizations, thereby reducing the influence of those labor organizations unable to satisfy their constituents.

The welfare utility function is subject to partial differentiation to determine the effectiveness of the sectors' performance. Such a partial differentiation on G, for example, isolates it from the equation and allows it to be examined more closely. $G_t = < g_1, g_2, \ldots, g_n >_t$, the set of government policies, and in any time t its economic programs can be evaluated. If these programs emphasize the maintenance of a strong welfare system because the cycle is deep in its recession phase, the welfare system will be maintained even though the industrial and labor sectors begin to move up as recovery sets in. This is because recovery in its early periods does not abolish the necessity of the welfare system, and during prosperity, while some welfare programs may be phased out, the basic infrastructure remains to be strengthened when prosperity begins to slow down and the early signs of recession begin to appear once again.

During recession, if $g_{rehabilitation}$, $g_{education}$, and $g_{future\ employment}$ are elements in the G economic policy, then as they increase in efficiency due to their better working ability and the upward movement of the cycle from the deepest recession to the recession phases that are moving toward recovery, the elements of $g_{unemployment\ insurance}$, $g_{welfare\ payments}$, $g_{subsidizing\ industries}$, and $g_{investing\ in\ low\ utility\ regions}$ can be reduced and phased out as efficient programs become entrenched for the duration of the recession and early recovery, and as industry and labor once again begin to participate in the processes of economic growth and development. Rehabilitation can be maintained, directed toward abolishing poverty through inner-city programs and financial incentives for businesses. This can ease the burden of unemployment insurance by providing employment to people in their areas of residence, and welfare payments can be reduced by taking the chronically unemployed and giving them the opportunity for employment in these businesses. In the emerging and developing economies this often requires some basic education so that the skills for conducting a successful business can be learned, and perhaps the required education and the business experience can be coordinated. People with qualifications can then find employment in small businesses and industries outside their residential areas, providing labor mobility in those communities where poverty had previously held them fixed and immobile, with little or no hope for improvement. Because G moves with the cycle, its economic program will be intensified as the cycle moves downward and will ease during the final period of recession and into recovery.

Because $W_t = U(I, G, L)_t$, and because government policies bear on industry and labor, the improvement of the economic situation due to rehabilitation, education, and future employment results in changes in industries' and labor organizations' planning and strategies. First, people enter the mainstream of economic activity in the sense of being contemporary individuals, that is, consumers and producers with consumer utility functions that have to be considered by industry. As employees they also contribute to the economy but compete for positions as well, a situation that has to be considered by labor. Moreover, their membership provides greater strength to the labor unions, even in emerging economies where labor unions are lacking in bargaining power, and their dues strengthen the unions' coffers. Because these people have come up from poverty, they can be assets as individuals in the labor movement and as employees in industry, since they know the feelings of economic impotency in the system that had kept them in poverty. These feelings can often be channeled and directed by these very people into increased work motivation and labor activity.

While the government is the underwriter of the economy, industry must also take part in improving the economic situation and must employ those who were in poverty but have met industry's qualifications. There is no altruism here, because such an attitude has no place where profits and losses are involved. It is for industry's benefit, and for this reason it should be done. For example, by investing in deprived areas where profits can be made, industries provide the stimulus for secondary and auxiliary businesses to develop there; because this requires infrastructure, the government will assist in providing the infrastructure within its realm of activity, and the resultant employment will generate demand, competition, and profits. Of course, only those areas with intrinsic or potential cost advantages and/or those provided by the government should be considered; the goodwill gained from such ventures must be a consequence of the economic considerations and is a positive spin-off when it is accrued. The main point is that when more people are employed, there is greater liquidity, resulting in greater demand and increased sales and profits. Moreover, when more skilled workers are employed, job competition will maintain the high levels of these skills. Labor organizations can participate in maintaining worker efficiency and the improvement of the levels of skill in labor when unemployment results from the downturn of the cycle.

Finally, because the welfare utility function is inferred from the aggregate of individual utility functions, and because the contemporary individual's utility function is derived from the welfare utility function, with both functions being derivable from the business cycle and its periods and phases, both these utility functions are far from stable. They are in a state of dynamic disequilibrium, just as is the economy. Tastes are influenced by the types of products, but these products are also influenced by tastes as determined by market research and actual sales. Product compositions fluctuate because of innovation and imitation, and tastes respond accordingly, as manifested in demand. Thus the contemporary individual's utility function is dynamic and is in disequilibrium.

Because governments formulate policies to cope with the changing world, their institutions are maintained until they are no longer adequate to deal with the changing economic realities, or until they are no longer politically viable for the leadership, a situation that exists in the emerging and to a lesser extent in the developing economies. Some agencies within finance ministries may thus be either closed down or restructured to allow for greater efficiency in performing their economic functions. Also, other branches may be added, such as the value-added tax authorities to the tax department, so that greater financial control can be exerted through greater specification and functional specialization. Thus government policies are altered when the economic situation deviates too far from that which its economic agencies are currently set up to handle. It is therefore the case that emerging, developing, and postindustrial economies operating in the atmosphere of dynamic disequilibrium exert their influences on the government agencies responsible for overseeing them and alert them accordingly.

What about labor? Even in the emerging and developing economies the concept of organized labor is based on the traditions that evolved in the postindustrial economies. In all three stages of economic growth and development labor has to consider its position in each economy and see how it can contribute to its progress. The battles on the streets to confront the scabs and strikebreakers have largely been won, and organized labor must now come to terms with itself to consider its somewhat archaic system of quotas, apprenticeship, and seniority ranked above talent. For the benefit of productivity, the older workers should not be turned out, but should be retrained where necessary to allow industry and government to develop new concepts for effective domestic and international competition. Labor should certainly not neglect its past, for it is a past of great struggle for a worthy cause. But the past holds no promise, and the present and future must be dealt with. The conflict between business and labor has been significantly weakened, and the real conflict now is of business and labor versus poverty to maintain the processes of development and growth.

Because **L** is a component of the welfare utility function, it relates to the cycle and the influences of business and government policies. The point that must be considered is the quality of labor that is available and the skills of those entering the labor market. In the early stages of recovery industry relies not only on new technologies, but also on those from past business cycles that still have utility and that industry expects the labor force to be able to work with. If the labor force is not able to work with these technologies, then, as is the case with emerging economies, the cycle's upward motion is slowed that much more because retraining is required for labor to use these technologies. This also results in higher prices because time is translated into money and passed on to the consumers at every stage of the production process, which is another reason for value-added tax, as it also diminishes purchasing power and allows greater de facto government control on production, even though such control is direct interference in the economy. However, this slowing of the cycle's upward motion can be greatly reduced or eliminated altogether if workers, using funds at their disposal and perhaps subsidized by government agencies, are reeducated in state-of-the-art technologies relevant to their domestic output and international competition. A certain consequence of this is that the cycle will move upward more swiftly and expand the industrial base and hence the employment situation that much more broadly and productively.

We live in a world united economically to a large extent, and the economic events of one country or region have direct effects on the rest of the world. The dissolution of the Soviet empire has led to the formation of nation-states seeking economic viability and turning to the postindustrial countries for assistance, while these economies and those of the emerging and developing countries throughout the world are in recession. When Federal Reserve Bank of the United States raises or lowers interest rates, the economies of the rest of the world are affected. When the Organization of Petroleum Exporting Countries agrees on cartel prices for crude oil, the effects reverberate throughout the world. Moreover, these policies affect the business cycle and economic well-being, as the high prices in the 1970s demonstrated all to clearly. There is an international disequilibrium effect associated with these policies, one in part responsible for the paradox of industrialization. This paradox and its consequences in our current social time are the subjects of the final part of this work.

NOTES

1. Michael Guillen, "The Cloudy Crystal Ball," in *Bridges to Infinity* (Los Angeles: Jeremy P. Tarcher, 1983), p. 137. Italics in the original text.

2. See Werner Heisenberg, *The Physical Principles of the Quantum Theory* trans. Carl Eckart and F.C. Hoyt (New York: Dover, 1949). If gravity results from the interaction of force fields, these fields are generated by the wave motion of particles. According to Heisenberg, we can determine a particle's position or its momentum, but not both, for observation of the particle will exert an influence and alter one or both of these factors. A force-field theory of gravity depends on particles to generate the force field; to understand how these particles operate, they must be analyzed, thereby exerting an unavoidable influence on them due to the action of observation. Moreover, whatever theory is used for explaining gravity, it must be tested, and because testing requires observation, no matter how sophisticated, such influences on the quanta cannot be avoided. The difficulty of this situation seems insurmountable and certainly provides a challenge for innovative physicists.

3. See Arthur C. Pigou, ed., *Memorials of Alfred Marshall* (London: Macmillan, 1925).

4. See Joseph A. Schumpeter, *The Theory of Economic Development,* trans. Redvers Opie (New York: Oxford University Press, 1969); Wesley C. Mitchell, *Business Cycles: The Problem and Its Setting* (New York: National Bureau of Economic Research, 1927); Vilfredo Pareto, *Manual of Political Economy,* trans. Ann S. Schwier and Alfred Page (New York: Augustus M. Kelley, 1971); and Eugin E. Slutsky, "On the Theory of the Budget of the Consumer," in *Readings in Price Theory* (London: Allen and Unwin for the American Economic Association, 1953). See also the discussion of Pareto's and Slutsky's theories in David Z. Rich, *The Economics of Welfare: A Contemporary Analysis* (New York: Praeger, 1989), pp. 19, 24-26.

5. See also Alvin H. Hansen, "Cost Function and Full Employment," *American Economic Review 37* (1947): 100-122; and O.H. Brownlee, *Economic Policy for Economic Growth and Stability* (Washington, D.C.: Government Printing Office, 1958), pp. 575-582.

6. The policy of increasing the money stock is based on the Keynesian velocity theory $M = VD$, so that if M increases, V and D will increase, and if M decreases, V and D will respond in the same direction.

7. In David Z. Rich, *Contemporary Economics: A Unifying Approach* (New York: Praeger, 1986), the heuristic law of markets was formulated as a replacement for Say's law. The heuristic law depends on five stages of management activity: first, innovative or entrepreneurial activity or imitative activity; second, the planning and consideration of various proposals for manufacturing the accepted product; third, the commitment of resources and the analysis of the feedback that this resource allocation provides, including the diversion of resources from other projects if necessary; fourth, the managerial assessment of the product's internal development in production and the economies of scale and plant utility; and fifth, the external evaluation of the product in markets it pioneers, or if it is imitative, in the markets in which it competes. The heuristic law of markets is a managerial imperative based on the profit motive, requiring production to meet actual and

potential demand that it generates through the stages of managerial activity. This law of markets thus states that consumption should be related to production in the aggregate for the firm's total output. Hence general managerial activity is within the domain of the heuristic law of markets, thereby relegating the product cycle to second place within the overall planning and production procedures. See Rich, *Contemporary Economics,* pp. 96-108.

8. Even matters of defense can be directly related to welfare, because the decision to establish a defense-based industry in a certain region can boost business in that region when the plan is implemented, thereby reducing unemployment and generating regional growth.

9. An exception to this occurs when governments use businesses for political purposes, a practice not uncommon in many of the emerging and developing economies, as in the cases of oil in the OPEC countries and gold and oil in Russia.

10. Providing financial incentives for firms to move into new regions — a practice common in the emerging and developing countries, but also used in the postindustrial economies and sometimes implemented to encourage foreign investment and plant location — is a form of taxation against the other firms, and while this is often considered necessary by government officials, it is certainly discriminatory.

Part III

THE CONTEMPORARY CHALLENGES TO ECONOMIC GROWTH AND DEVELOPMENT

Chapter 9

THE PARADOX OF INDUSTRIALIZATION

The more global and mobile the rich countries' money becomes, and the cheaper the transport, the greater their power over static resources. The world markets offer distant communities the choice between rapidly adjusting to their own pace of change or being left off the economic map.

Anthony Sampson
*The Midas Touch*₁

IDENTITY AND TECHNOLOGY IN EMERGING AND DEVELOPING ECONOMIES

The more mobile and global the postindustrial countries' currencies have become, the greater the proportions of these currencies that are held by the emerging and developing countries to underwrite their own economies and to be used in foreign trade. It is not the case that the world markets offer the emerging and developing countries the choice of rapidly adjusting to change or being left off the economic map. They are the trading partners of countries of their own class, countries of their development status, as well as recipients of aid and assistance in the technological fields and trading partners of the postindustrial countries. However, movement from the emerging and developing stages to the postindustrial stage is not continuous, but requires major adjustments in the political, social, and economic concepts under which the emerging and developing countries operate. This point will be discussed in Chapter 11, but now it suffices to state that because of the expansion of trade and the relatively low cost and rapid speed of transport, the world has definitely become integrated, and the multinational corporations both contribute to and profit from this integration. Those countries that, in Sampson's phrase, are left off the map are those very countries that are not even in the emerging stage of growth and development, and the reason for this is political.

Moreover, our social time has presented us with a new awareness of the challenges of economic growth and development. The dissolution of the Soviet empire has resulted in the formation of nation-states, somewhat in the concept of nineteenth-century geopolitics, but certainly unique in the sense that war is no longer used for conquest but in the search for new national identity. Those countries that are searching for this new identity, one that will allow them to take their places among the countries of the world, and that are conducting this search without war, possess the status of emerging economies even though they may have a fairly well developed infrastructure for growth. Their difficulty is that they lack the technologies of the postindustrial countries, and their competitive abilities are therefore limited. They are not developing because they lack a fairly well defined concept of identity and national purpose. Those countries that are engaged in internal military conflict, however, are not even in the emerging stage of growth, because their resources, both static natural and intellectual are not being used for economic purposes, but for engaging in battle internally to seek the identities that will allow them to begin the very rudimentary processes of economic growth and international commerce to ensure development.

The postindustrial economies can assist here, but they will do so only when political stability and direction have been achieved in the emerging countries. The postindustrial economies have the unique problem of maintaining their own growth and development, expanding their own economic bases and infrastructures, and working within their business cycles to maintain maximum growth and minimum poverty. The postindustrial economies export, but they require markets that provide stability for sales, which is one reason why some developing economies have multinational corporations because of their political stability, viable markets, and labor potential, and why multinationals seek out emerging economies that also have these properties.

Whether the emerging and developing economies can keep up the economic pace with the postindustrial economies is certainly debatable. While some Eastern European countries that were part of the Soviet bloc are manufacturing products such as automobiles that are also manufactured in the postindustrial economies and indeed are part of these economies' heavy industrial base, this does not qualify them for inclusion in any sense in postindustrial status. It is not the copying of products that is important here; it is the potential for innovation and profitable imitation that designates an economy as being postindustrial. Competing successfully for markets that have already been established and exploited successfully may be necessary for the emerging and developing economies in establishing their own industrial bases; their comparatively low wages and production costs make their finished products highly competitive internationally, and their revenues are plowed back into expanding production and infrastructure. The education gained from such production is necessary for industrialization and for advancing in the stage-of-growth process. But this form of competition releases resources in the postindustrial economies for research in technologies for innovation and imitation, and many of the consequences of this research are used to improve the standard industrial products such as computers and automobiles. The advanced technologies are incorporated into the industrial bases of the emerging and developing economies, but only after time lags suitable for each economy to absorb these technologies. By that time the postindustrial economies have engaged in further research to be incorporated into the production processes of the economies according to the phases and periods of their business cycles.

DEFICIT SPENDING VERSUS INVENTORY DEPLETION

The concept of deficit spending that prevailed in the 1980s in the world's economies illustrates a previous time in our contemporary era. This was the period of the oil crisis's aftermath and the rise of the business cycle after the recession in the 1970s, a period of big spending on credit and of loans to emerging countries. Businesses relied on low interest and easy credit, but the period was not without its warnings, such as the October 1987 stock-market crash. Moreover, this was a period of deficit budgeting on the part of governments that was based on potential and actual national wealth and resources, but was certainly unrealized within the concept of the accounting balance sheet of credits and debits.

The concept of balancing the budget, however, is not without its difficulties. Governments cannot be run like businesses, for while businesses establish markets and engage in innovation and imitation, governments must provide infrastructure, regulate the money supply, provide fiscal policies, and regulate the business cycle. Businesses can run a deficit profitably only if they can afford the interest on debts and can use the interest payments to reduce taxes paid to the government; governments have no such obligations as taxes. Governments are, however, obligated to their citizens to use the resources at their disposal with utility, and this obligation was cast aside in the 1980s due to expediency. This expediency is not without cost, and this cost is manifested in the realm of foreign obligations and international debt. This debt has interest owed to foreign governments, and for the postindustrial countries this debt and interest are paid in hard convertible currencies held in foreign countries' coffers.

This is not to be confused with mercantilism and the favorable-balance-of-trade approach measured in terms of the amount of hard currencies. Mercantilism, as an economic system, was overthrown by the writings of Adam Smith and the classical economists who followed him. The issue here is far more serious. Because hard convertible currencies are used in international transactions, those countries with the greater foreign currency holdings are those countries with the greater foreign purchasing power.

The postindustrial countries gain such purchasing power by exporting to countries that can afford to pay for the products. Because all countries rely on exports in varying degrees, and because all exports are paid for in hard currencies, in the 1980s a situation existed that now has serious consequences, this being the choice to spend more than was earned through production and sales, and to repay the deficit with low interest. This was conducted by many businesses through the placing of inventories on a lower status than money, that is, by opting for the liquidity position over production. As the utility of liquidity is in consumption, the goods and services consumed were becoming more import oriented at the expense of domestic production and exporting.

This situation and the underwriting of questionable loans to foreign countries that have not been able to repay them and have sought rescheduling on terms favorable to them demonstrated the folly of both industry and government. However, the collapse of the Soviet empire brought about a new social time, and with it, the realization that the liquidity option is viable only when there are competitive inventories to support it. This realization became glaringly apparent in the paradox of industrialization, as foreign competition takes place only for imitative products.

This realization has also led to the rise of neonationalism. In the drive to promote the purchase of domestic products over foreign products, "protect our jobs" and "place our country first" are offered as slogans to rally people to the call of patriotism in light of successful foreign competition. While patriotic stirrings are useful to promote pride in a country, its history, and its values, they have little effect in the realm of economics, where foreign currencies go to those countries that earn them and liquidity is channeled into regions that provide the highest return, even at the expense of production.

Moreover, an appeal to patriotism is of little utility in a world now divided into nation-states based on economics and seeking viability in their status as emerging and developing countries. Not only do these countries require the aid and markets of the postindustrial economies for commerce and foreign currencies, but their leaders realize that the neonationalism to which they are willing to commit themselves for the sake of trade is counterproductive and a serious cause of potential conflict in light of the recession and the paradox of industrialization.

Still, patriotism has its purpose here if it is properly channeled. The liquidity option has already been explained in Chapter 6 of this work. If it is temporary and is acted upon as a result of the business cycle, then it has a significant role in the economic process; if it is acted upon as a choice for businesses at the expense of maintaining inventories, then it is noncyclically oriented and has no role in the economies' growth and development. With respect to the paradox of industrialization, the way to regain lost foreign markets and reduce foreign competition in domestic markets is to maintain inventories at a high level of quality and servicing and to maintain prices that are competitive. This is not a beggar-thy-neighbor policy of reducing foreign competition by higher tariffs and quotas; it is a way to increase competition by providing the consumers with greater options through imitative products at competitive prices. Countries such as Japan, with import quotas and high tariffs, will certainly ease these restrictions as less of their products will be sold internationally due to their restrictive practices.

What can be said for deficit spending? Cutting the budget deficit is certainly necessary for lowering national debt, but politicians oppose cuts in their jurisdictions. While everyone agrees that deficit spending needs to be reduced and perhaps eliminated, those in power oppose such cuts where the cuts affect them. The real issue, therefore, is not reducing deficit spending, but increasing the utility of the monies spent. This requires careful planning and the consideration of alternatives for placing government funds, both in the short run and the long run. Such projects as health and education cannot be cut, but the monies can be examined and better ways for using these funds can be constructed. Development infrastructure cannot be cut, but alternative methods, cost-effective with respect to utility, can be formulated and acted upon. This is the G component of the welfare utility function, and its efficient applications can certainly assist industry and labor in their planning and actions.

Because of our current global recession due to the paradox of industrialization, businesses have opted for production in place of the liquidity function as a means of earning profits; production for viable imitation is being restored. But the paradox of industrialization is due to rigorous imitation in domestic and international markets, resulting in the international disequilibrium effect, in which international markets reach near saturation and are phased out as competition reduces profits significantly. To restore economic growth and development, the emphasis must be on innovation, but because research into high technology is also competitive and costly, this is a slow process.

Nevertheless, as the postindustrial economies absorb the technologies into the production processes, and as these technologies are employed in the developing and then the emerging economies after the appropriate time lags necessary for their incorporations, the international disequilibrium effect develops, in which imitation spreads through the world's economies for these competing products, requiring the shifting of resources for their production. This necessitates the phasing out of products that yield less profits and the rechanneling of resources, including liquidity, into the new production lines. The time lag is significant here because from the postindustrial economies to those that are developing, competition is fairly rapid as the developing economies' industries seek to gain both domestic and foreign markets for these competing products. The emerging economies lack sufficient infrastructure and resource-use sophistication to join in the competition at the same rapidity as do the developing economies. They therefore serve as bases for multinational corporations and/or import these products and begin their competitive manufacture only when sufficient productive capacity and skills exist for effective competition.

There is disequilibrium here due to the resource shift into the new competitive products. Moreover, this shift occurs in products that are only barely profitable or that are breaking even with respect to aggregate costs. The long-run advantage of such imitation — the international imitation effect — is that it generates disequilibrium in the emerging and developing economies, thereby placing them within the context of the business cycle and the broadening of the economic base that the cycle provides. This is especially important for the emerging countries, because when they share in the dynamics of the business cycle, they have broken out of stagnation and total reliance on other countries for assistance and have begun the development of their own markets and the banking system that provides the financing for the formation of industry. When labor is working in industries that are being developed, labor organizations are formed, patterned on those in the developing and postindustrial countries but suitable for the emerging countries' own unique circumstances. Once this is achieved, the welfare utility function sets in, as its components are in place and operating. When the business cycle is moving in its phases and periods, and when government, industry, and labor function according to their unique perspectives, the emerging economies have the internal disequilibrium dynamics, brought about by the international disequilibrium effect and generated by the international imitation effect, to get the economy in motion and to enter the stage of the developing economies. The decisions taken for economic growth and development, and the economic direction countries choose to take, are not purely economic decisions, for governments are political in nature, and industry and labor are also political in the sense that they have to conform to the laws of the countries and understand their loopholes so that even the exceptional actions are legal according to the country's statutes and in the opinion of the citizens alike.

Of course, when both domestic and international markets reach near saturation, the paradox of industrialization sets in. In this situation the business cycle turns downward into recession in the postindustrial economies, as innovation has almost ceased and imitation is rarely profitable. Businesses in the postindustrial economies seek to maintain their market positions, offering competition in the form of better products at competitive prices, providing better conditions of purchase, and offering better servicing than their competitors. The developing countries are also affected as their markets reach near saturation and their export markets either stabilize or are closed due to the better competitive terms offered by the postindustrial economies. The emerging economies are the worst off because their markets are effectively closed and their growth, which requires domestic output and the establishment of trade, is now dependent on the goodwill of the postindustrial countries for assistance and outright aid. These are the consequences of the current recession, which is a manifestation of the paradox of industrialization.

NOTE

1. Anthony Sampson, *The Midas Touch* (New York: Truman Talley Books Plume, 1991), p. 229.

Chapter 10

THE INTERNATIONAL UTILITY FUNCTION

While a country's domestic economy is evaluated according to the welfare utility function, its trading ability — the ability to manufacture and deliver to foreign markets at competitive prices — is determined by its international utility function.[1] When currencies were fixed, prices of imported goods and services were determined by the domestic economy's ability to reap the highest profits in light of competition from domestic alternatives. However, because exchange rates are now fluctuating, domestic prices for imported goods and services have to account for differences in domestic markets in light of domestic competition. Of course, in the emerging and to some extent in the developing economies domestic competition for goods and services is lacking, except in the case of those imitative products that can be sold cheaper in the postindustrial economies than those economies' own manufactured competitors. This, of course, is a manifestation of the paradox of industrialization and results in market near saturation, with prices and servicing being the factors that encourage the greater sales.

A country's exchange rate is determined by its balance-of-payments situation with respect to other countries. As the United States has a balance-of-payments deficit with respect to its trading partners of postindustrial status — united Germany and Japan being examples — its currency value is not as strong as it could be, but a lower relative currency value provides an incentive for other countries to export to the United States, as its goods and services tend to be highly competitive, both in quality and price.

A country's trading position is thus determined with respect to its international utility function $\bar{I}$, a utility function of a country's currency value and its welfare utility function. Hence $\bar{I} = U(c, W)_t$. The status of c, a country's foreign currency, depends on the supply of that currency in foreign markets and the demand for that currency as a hedge against other currencies. Internationally, currencies are in somewhat of an ambiguous situation in the sense that they are the money of countries and hence part of the countries' welfare utility functions, as well as separate commodities that are traded, bought, and sold, somewhat like other commodities on foreign markets.

For example, because inflation is the overabundance of a country's currency with respect to the country's domestic and foreign products and services, it is viewed with respect to the purchasing power of that country's currency, where the price of a basket of representative goods and services is compared over differing time periods. If that basket costs more, then there is inflation at the percentage rise of the basket's price. While the currency is devalued in its domestic market, foreign demand for that currency may be high, and hence its price may be higher than those of other currencies because their countries may have higher inflation rates, or because a country's inherent political and economic stability may make its currency strong on foreign markets, and/or because the dynamics of speculation involve the currency, bringing many buyers into the market for the currency and driving its price upward. The ambiguity of c due to its being part of the country's economy and a commodity in itself for foreign trade nevertheless requires that it be treated separately within the $\bar{I}$ equation, for the very reason that its influence is incorporated within the $\mathbf{W}$ component for domestic dynamics and because of its significance as a commodity for foreign trade. Even those currencies of the emerging and developing economies that are not hard in value are traded, exchanged for the hard currencies to conduct foreign transactions; hence their values also fluctuate according to the strength of their economies and the inernational demand for their currencies.

While the $\mathbf{W}$ component of $\bar{I}$ is an approximation equation and depends on a country's cyclical phase and period, $\bar{I}$ itself is an equation that holds at time $\mathbf{t}$ for all foreign transactions in which the country is engaged at that time. When contracts are signed for international commercial agreements, unless otherwise stipulated to allow for flexibility over time for exchange rates, the transactions are conducted at the exchange-rate ratios for the currencies of the countries involved at the time of signing. A contract of long duration may stipulate that transactions are to be paid at the exchange rate at the time each transaction is undertaken, or there may be some leniency in this, depending on the financial positions of the exporter and importer; but this depends on the specific terms of trade.

Because $\bar{I}$ represents a country's position with respect to trade, it must portray two conditions. One is the country's ability to export, and this depends on its $\mathbf{W}$ components for any specific time period. For example, when a country is in recession, its exporting ability is diminished because of reduced employment and hence its comparatively low output. Even in the postindustrial countries with a high capital/labor ratio, recessions reduce demand for industrial output, resulting in unemployment and disused capital equipment. The postindustrial countries' currencies may be stable in spite of recession, but this is because the developing and emerging countries may be experiencing recession and their currencies may lack the potential economic backing, thereby placing heavy demand on the postindustrial countries' currencies. As floatings are not wild in this situation because most, if not all, countries are in recession, demand for the postindustrial countries' currencies will make them stable instead of rising. Moreover, these countries' central banks will sell if there are deviations in the stability, making exports profitable, as the trading currency will most likely be in the postindustrial countries' coin.

During recovery, as employment increases, so do demand and output. Foreign markets are sought, but success in securing them depends on the periods of their recovery phase, indicated by their international utility functions. For prosperity, the same condition holds: Exporting depends on the targeted markets' abilities to absorb the products, and this depends on their cyclical phases and periods. However, for a country in recovery or prosperity, demand for foreign goods and services increases accordingly, providing incentives for foreign countries to increase output, at least for the domestic markets of the importing countries. This, then, provides for the country's ability to import. When the recovery and prosperity phases occur, demand increases for domestic and foreign products; the increase may at first be slight, but as employment increases, so does the demand for imported products. This provides incentive for importing and results in further employment for those businesses engaged in importing, thereby providing further stimulation to the domestic economy and ultimately to the exporting countries.

Hence, in general, trade is both internal and external in orientation. An economy's ability to conduct trade, both as exporter and importer, depends on the status of its international utility function. Because $0 < \bar{I}_t < 1$, when $\bar{I}_t \to 0$, this means that $W_t \approx 1/C_{recession}$ and that the economy is sluggish with respect to trade, both importing and exporting. The c component usually reflects this condition, but due to speculation the currency may be at a high float, thereby increasing its demand. This may also affect $\bar{I}$ adversely, because a high currency and sluggish economy may reduce demand for that economy's exports because of the high exchange rate involved in possible transactions. But the tendency is that the currency's value reflects the economy's condition, so that when the economy is in recession, the currency's value is comparatively low.

Moreover, keeping the value of the currency relatively low may be intentional, because this may stimulate demand for the country's exports, thereby assisting the cycle in its upward movement. The extent of demand, of course, depends on the importing countries' financial ability to pay. The dynamics of innovation and imitation enter here, because through innovation new markets are established, and through imitation competitive alternatives are offered.

While innovation is primarily domestically oriented, it is also directed to foreign markets. The success of both domestic and foreign innovation depends largely on the firms' open-ended information systems, whether they are of utility or entropy as the innovative products become marketable.

During recession opting for production instead of hedging production with the liquidity option has a greater risk of failure, and careful planning and advertising are required. A stable or low currency exchange rate makes competition more profitable in foreign markets, especially when innovation is involved. Again, this depends on the cyclical phases and periods of the countries; entering into new markets, however, is never without risks, and these risks must be taken into account by the flexibility of the firms' information systems, thereby providing a basis for maneuverability in situations where expectations and reality are in conflict.

With respect to differing cyclical phases and/or periods, there is an international imitation effect, based on the success of a product in its country of origin. Success is determined by two factors. One factor, of course, is the profits from sales of the product, so that the greater the profits, the greater the product's success in its markets. The word "markets" is intentionally plural, because when a product is planned and its targeted groups are projected, only a certain amount of profits can be earned from these consumers. Success comes when the product is purchased not only by these selected consumers, but also by other groups, perhaps of different social and income classes. The greater the consumer exposure, the greater the consumption and the higher the profits. The markets will have thus expanded, incorporating a greater consumer awareness and willingness to devote the necessary liquidity to consumption.

While this aspect of success increases profits, the other factor, imitation that follows successful innovation, tends to reduce them. While substitutes are always close, there are always differences that distinguish them. The innovative product competing successfully for consumer liquidity in markets it originally initiated thus maintains a respectable profit rate. However, a successful product in the domestic markets leads to market near saturation over time as imitators reduce the profit rate for each competing firm with respect to this product. To protect profits, firms will seek to export the product, so that domestic saturation will not have such an effect on business. Successful communications are important in the form of advertising, which often requires portraying the product in its original domestic setting. A short time lag usually exists after market research and advertising are conducted before the product is introduced in the foreign markets; if the product is successful according to the criterion of consumer liquidity being allocated for the product, the international imitation effect takes hold as the importing countries enter into imitation.

The international imitation effect also operates when the firms in one country, possessing the necessary infrastructure and perhaps the appropriate competitive products, enter other countries' markets with these products on an imitative footing. In this situation the important consideration is not which country innovated the product, but how well the exporting countries can compete through imitation.

The international imitation effect contrasts with the international demonstration effect, the latter being the effect, to quote Charles P. Kindleberger, "under which underdeveloped countries have learned about the existence of goods in developed nations which lighten their burdens, satisfy their physical appetites, and titillate their innate sense of self-expression or exhibition."[2] These are several reasons for contrast between these approaches. One reason is that the international imitation effect holds for postindustrial or developed economies, the developing economies, and the emerging or underdeveloped economies. Imitative exports, or exports resulting in imitation, require adequate sophistication and supporting infrastructure in the importing countries. While sophistication concerning consumer orientation may be present, in the emerging countries infrastructure may be a serious problem. Exporters are aware of this and export to countries in which their products can be distributed with relative ease. In the emerging countries the governmental and economic leaders adopt the conditions of the developing economies to allow for the necessary imports. The markets are oriented for the absorption of these products, for if this were not the case, exporters would ignore them and importers would realize no demand for them. Moreover, whether imitation originates in the exporting country's domestic markets and the products are then imported by other countries as innovations, to be imitated by the importing countries' industries, or the imitative products are imported to compete with similar domestic products has no influence on the dynamics of the markets once the products are absorbed. A product that is imitative but enters a country as innovative will generate greater imitation if it is successful; a product exported to compete with similar products will increase competition within the market through further imitation. In the first instance the product will generate competition; in the second it will increase it. In both instances competition is stimulated to the benefit of those consumers directing their liquidity into purchasing the product.

The international demonstration effect refers to the emerging and developing economies. For imports the demonstration effect is valid, but its validity is limited. It fails to explain, for example, how domestic markets are generated as a response to imports; nor does it explain how the costs of these imports are to be paid. The international imitation effect pertains to postindustrial economies as well and relates to imports from the economies in all three stages of growth. Moreover, it explains the domestic market development as imitation of successful foreign and domestic products. Payments for imports are therefore supplied by monies earned through imitations and innovations they also export. The demonstration effect prevails in those countries whose economies are hindered from growth because of natural constraints such as drought and insufficient techniques for soil treatment and agriculture, and man-made restrictions such as politics and war. In countries with relative political stability and the willingness to acquire and apply technologies for development, these restrictions are nonexistent, and while imports from the postindustrial countries generate demand, this demand is soon met by domestic industries manufacturing close imitative substitutes. The demonstration effect is thus a limit case of the imitation effect, especially since multinational corporations and customs unions are bringing the world's economies closer together, making imitation that much easier and innovation more likely to be exported.

The international imitation effect can be derived from the $\bar{I}$ equation. Because the equation represents a country's importing and exporting abilities and capabilities, $\bar{I}$'s **W** component describes the economy with respect to its business cycle. During recovery employment rises, increasing aggregate liquidity. Industry expands production and exports are planned. Moreover, imports are increased due to increasing general consumer demand. This sets off the imitation effect when exports are successful and firms opt for production instead of liquidity. Those firms not engaged in innovation will be active in imitation, and part of the imitation in the economy will be directed toward competition with foreign products that have demonstrated their success in the domestic markets. The imitation effect is therefore included in the category of imitation within the economy and provides a source for market dynamics in the same way that these dynamics are provided for by domestic imitation. In general terms, a country's $\bar{I} \to 1$ if its firms have high utilities in their foreign markets. If its firms' successes are mixed with respect to their goals as stated in their information systems, $\bar{I}$ shows no particular tendency. Logically, if the firms fail to achieve their goals, then $\bar{I} \to 0$, which is a situation that exists only when the country's government is unable to provide the necessary political stability for internal development and growth, thereby affecting its firms' abilities to export. Countries that are emerging in their political and economic growth and development, subject to power struggles and coups, are in this situation, and it is resolved only when political stability allows the country to establish its business cycle and move into the contemporary economic era of dynamic disequilibrium.

The two aspects of trade for a country are, therefore, governmental and industrial, the latter being private and each being dependent on labor for productivity. The dynamics of each of these aspects depend on the value of the trading countries' currencies at the time the transactions are agreed upon. For the importing country, a lower currency value for the exporting country means that domestic sales prices can be adjusted to bring about high profits, depending on the percentage of tariffs levied on the products. For the exporting country, a lower currency value means that in general, less of the domestic products will be purchased; the exceptions are when demand for the product is held constant or rises because of appeal, or when the products are raw materials and the price is less of a concern than the possession of the materials themselves, with the high costs passed on to the consumers. Countries trading in weak foreign currencies will conduct their transactions in hard currencies, the values of which depend on the trading countries' currencies. Again, the high costs — this time, the high costs of trading — will be passed on to the consumers, but the sales prices will be maintained competitively with respect to other imitative products.

Thus it is necessary to consider a specific country's trade situation with respect to its firms and its government's international commercial transactions. This requires the analysis of the country's international currency value, because these two factors present its international utility function and the willingness of other countries to engage with it in trade.

Given $\bar{I}_t = U(c, W)_t$, c can be removed from this functional equation by partial differentiation. The c variable is the country's money, which is domestically composed of money for consumption and money for savings and investments. The utility of money in the domestic market depends on the business cycle's position, and in the domestic markets money is measured in value with the cycle's movements, as was discussed in Chapter 8.

In international commerce, however, money takes on a different significance by becoming a relative measure for both the exporting and importing countries' transactions. For example, the U.S. economy may be moving deeper into recession according to the projections of the nation's indicators, but trading with another postindustrial country having its own recession may make the dollar a stronger currency in the transaction, in which case fewer purchases will be made from the U.S. firms than would have been made had the currency values been reversed, subject to the reservations on purchases stated earlier. Thus money has three commercial uses: for consumption, which entails the purchase of domestic goods and services and those imported; for savings and investments; and as a measure of foreign transactions, in which their values are determined with respect to the currencies involved. The trading process — bartering is not a consideration here — depends on the goods and services being traded, on the demand that they generate, and on the values of the trading partners' currencies with respect to each other and to the other currencies in circulation in foreign trading. A country's currency is demanded, that is, it is hard and highly negotiable, if its utility approaches 1. This to some extent reflects the country's internal economy, although this is relative. For example, while a postindustrial economy is in recession, with all the internal diseconomies this involves, its currency is still stronger internationally than the currencies of the developing and emerging countries and may be in greater demand than other postindustrial countries' currencies. This is an expression of the relative cyclical positions of the various trading countries, as well as their political stability and their potential as well as actual abilities to produce and market effectively their goods and services in the domestic and foreign markets.

Hence, while a country's political leaders can set the exchange rate for their national currency at whatever level they choose, the actual trading will be conducted within the value of that currency set by international demand, or in a hard currency agreed upon by the trading partners. In emerging and developing countries where hard currencies are often obtained on the black market and a premium is paid for hedging against the uncertain future, banks try to purchase foreign currencies legally and lend them, for a premium, to traders. The extent of the black markets is a manifestation of the lack of confidence people have in their own currency, which reflects in turn their lack of confidence in their finance ministers and perhaps in their entire government. This is expressed within the country's business cycles in the value of money during the cycle' phases and periods. Taxes are raised, subsidies are abolished, and the ratio of businesses in financial difficulties or even closing to those solvent and those opening usually greater than ever, and sometimes very high as a reflection of the lack of confidence in the government as the overall financial manager of the economy. A country's currency is of utility when its political and economic systems are sound and its economic potential is great, so opting for hard currencies in an economy is an expression on the part of the citizenry that confidence is seriously lacking in both the political leadership's efficient managing of the economy and in domestic industries' abilities to cope with their own markets domestically and internationally. Competition here refers to innovation and imitation in both domestic and international markets. Countries in situations in which innovations and imitations are far from frequent and countries that rely on imports for a large portion of their supplies often undergo devaluations to reduce the purchasing of foreign products and encourage exports of domestic products on the basis of a better currency ratio for exporters. In these situations not only are devaluations frequent, they are also ineffective in encouraging exports. A country's currency is only one component of the $\bar{I}_t$ equation, even though it reflects the country's value internationally. Without effective management of the W_t component, devaluations are merely short-run measures lacking significance. They result in inflation at levels higher than the devaluation because of spiraling prices and labor sanctions and strikes as workers seek to protect their wages. The consequence is that while prices rise, wage increases follow, and aggregate consumption remains fairly stable. The increased export currency ratio brought about by devaluation therefore has no real effect on international trade, because the economy's structural problems, found in W_t, have not been corrected, so that W_t's inefficiency in the dynamics of the economic cycle remains. A policy for changing

W_t, that is, changing government economic policies, changing industry, and changing labor's attitudes, requires great acumen and energy on the part of the country's leaders, but these are too often sapped by political infighting and the concern for each politician's, industrial leader's, and labor leader's individual welfare that results. Instead of going to the source of the problem, the W component, devaluations are easier to implement, because they lower the price of the country's currency and provide political propaganda showing the concern of the government in boosting exports. If the source of the problem is not addressed, it will not be long before devaluation is undertaken again and the same reasons given to a public that will continue to sell and buy on the black market.

In contrast to devaluations initiated by governments, there are market devaluations as well as revaluations, depending on the domestic and international demand for the country's currency. This also relates to W_t, to the government's ability to act in response to the cycle, to the country's industrial output as well as its potential for innovation and imitation, and to labor's interests in maintaining a skilled and up-to-date work force and responsible behavior during the phases of recession and recovery. Currency fluctuations depend on buying and selling of foreign currencies to profit from exchange-rate flexibility as currencies move in value between points established by agreement among the trading countries. If a hard currency becomes overvalued, rising with respect to other hard currencies at rates that may possibly hinder foreign trade, central banks intervene and sell off as much of their holdings of that currency as their directorates consider feasible according to their banks' holdings. They then use the money from the sales to purchase their own and/or other hard currencies in order to raise their values with respect to the overvalued currency. Hence in this situation currencies fluctuate in value as do other commodities because of demand for them. Their demand, however, is based on their economies' abilities to remain dynamic, maintaining the innovative and imitative processes and expanding the domestic economies and their international commerce. Indeed, an economy's ability to maintain innovation and imitation through its recovery and prosperity phases and to expand its foreign markets determines its currency's value; it is this ability that creates demand for its currency, making it hard.

Soft currencies, therefore, reflect economies that are unable to maintain successful innovation and imitation, conditions that are exclusively found in the emerging and developing economies. These currencies are soft because they are not used in international transactions, as they reflect their economies' inability to maintain the dynamic processes necessary for growth and development, and therefore the reliance of these economies on the postindustrial economies for assistance and aid. Hence their foreign transactions are conducted in hard currencies, their imports exceed their exports, and the major part of their cash exports go to countries of similar economic positions, while their imports are primarily from countries with hard currencies.

Thus, although c and W are related components of the economy, because they pertain to different aspects of the economy, they are treated separately in the $\bar{I}_t$ equation. W_t is internal, is cyclically based, and refers to the economy's ability to develop and grow as a result of cyclical movement. It relies on the utilities of government policies, on the utilities of firms' information systems and their realizations, and on labor's activities on behalf of its members. It also relates to the value of money and its purchasing power as well as the interest on savings and investments that can be obtained during the cycle's phases and periods. The c component relates the economy to others in the international markets, and if it is hard, it is also traded internationally, in which case its value fluctuates with respect to other hard currencies and other alternatives available for foreign consumption. How does an economy's international utility function relate to international commerce? Because $\bar{I}_t = U(c, W)_t$, because W represents the economy's ability to innovate, imitate, and produce, and because the foreign value of its currency is assessed with respect to its productive ability, an economy's ability to import and export depends on its I, that is, its ability to absorb imports and generate exports. This ability is manifested in the two types of markets that compose an economy, those for international commerce as imports and exports, and those for products produced domestically. The latter are targeted originally for domestic consumption, but if they are viable, they will be extended into export markets. Thus, as the economy's currency value and its ability to produce determine its international utility function, c and W can also be written as **Markets$_{domestic}$** and **Markets$_{foreign}$**, so that $\bar{I}_t = U(M_d, M_f)_t$. Factoring out the foreign markets for their consideration weakens I_t's relationship to these markets, because they are as dynamic as the economies engaging in international trade, and because c's value shifts according to its demand and the demand for alternative purchases. Therefore, while both M_d and M_f provide an equation for $\bar{I}$, with only M_f considered, $\bar{I}_t \approx (\Sigma\ M_f)_t$, with the sigma sign summing both import and export markets. The approximation sign with respect to the time signature demonstrates the fluidity of trade. It captures agreements being formulated but not yet finalized; it portrays currencies' values in fluctuation according to demand for them; and because both imports and exports are the result of W_t's ability, it demonstrates the innovations and imitations of exports and imports and the possible market dynamics they may generate with respect to the firms' information systems and with respect to trade.

The utility of foreign-market summation can be assessed with respect to the upper and lower boundaries. If there is a greater amount of domestic money spent in toto on imported goods and services than the foreign markets spend on that country's exports, then that country is in a general balance-of-payments deficit, because more of its national income is diverted to imported goods and services than to those exported. This, however, is a very limited view, shedding little light on a country's export-import balances. For example, in considering a country's position, both the government and private firms have to be viewed. The government's actions are not conducted from commercial considerations alone, because the government is a political organization and not one motivated by profits. Government-contracted deficits are therefore not based on the motivation of enterprise; there are no innovations or imitations exported by governments, only surpluses in production purchased from firms for political leverage both domestically and internationally. Consider the example of grains. The government purchases surplus grains from private farmers and stores them to be resold to farmers and to commercial processing companies for marketing, thereby preventing the type of gluts that prevailed during the Great Depression, as well as preventing shortages in times of diminished agricultural output. These grains are also used as exports to countries in times of need and famine, for example, to Russia and the former Eastern bloc countries and to Ethiopia, the Sudan, and Somalia in times of serious food shortages that are catastrophic. Payment may be demanded in hard currency or in international goodwill, depending on the government officials' view of the grain shipments. The problem of long-term government loans to the emerging and developing countries and their need to reschedule repayment on these loans also has to be considered for the balance-of-payments position. In this case there is more than an accounting problem involved; the problem is that of the receiving countries' utilities in the applications of the liquidity. This is a manifestation of these economies' relationships to their domestic and international situations with respect to innovation, imitation, and the dynamics of their cycles.

The utility of government economic policies is determined by the achievement of the objectives stated in the information system of each policy. Because the profit motive is excluded, social and/or political objectives are the aims of these policies. Hence with respect to these policies the balance of payments for goods and services exported is not the real issue, because governments rely on private firms engaging in foreign commerce to make up whatever financial losses are thus accrued.

Private firms, by the very nature of their ownership, cannot allow themselves the luxury of trading without making profits, for if they did, they would soon find themselves without liquidity and, being insolvent, would go bankrupt. Their trade is motivated by profits, and the utilities of their business ventures are determined with respect to the expected and actual profits gained from each venture. Hence engaging in foreign trade requires some degree of comprehension of the markets being entered. This is easier now than in previous eras because of the influence of the postindustrial countries after World War II and the domination of the world's markets by these countries. A degree of "commonness" was established, enabling the export of soft drinks, clothing, and eventually products of high technologies such as automobiles and computers.

Exporters have acquired the acumen of the developing markets in which the cultures of the importing countries are preserved, while using cultural appeal to promote sales of their products. The prestige of British products, the durability and quality of U.S. exports, and the flair and the taste of French products are important selling points for these countries' exports. Moreover, they are exploited by the domestic importers who market and sell these products in their own countries.

Exposure to these cultures because of increased travel and the impact of World War II and the Cold War that followed has helped in the promotion of exports. Additional help in the export markets has certainly been gained by the thaw of the Cold War. The Eastern bloc countries that were allied to the Soviet Union have become exposed to the Western-oriented postindustrial markets, importing and exporting as much as the hard currencies and market absorption allow.

Market absorption depends on the cycle's position. In those emerging and developing countries whose markets were once dominated by their ruling political parties, there were no business cycles in the sense of the cycle in contemporary economics. There were, however, bottlenecks in planning and production due to the absence of signals from the markets as to which products needed to be increased in quantity, which needed to be reduced in output, and which distribution points were in need of increased and reduced supplies. Hence there were long lines of consumers who often found empty shelves when their turn came. The diminution of state authority in the economic realm and the increasing emphasis on private enterprise and the profit motive mean that these economies will enter the contemporary dynamics of the business cycle in disequilibrium, with the profit motive stimulating innovation and imitation.

While developing countries tend to impose high tariffs in order to protect their industries, government-to-government grants and favored-country trading are incentives to lower these tariffs, thereby stimulating production for export. Export production cannot have the same market exposure as domestic production, so that these incentives stimulate production increases across the board that are motivated by profits and therefore generate economic efficiency in production. The products have to be of high quality so that they will sell in the imported markets. Because efficiency and quality are necessary in competitive production, applying these rules results in innovation as new products are planned and produced to gain consumer liquidity. As economic liberalism continues to operate in the Eastern European countries and the other emerging and developing countries, their business cycles become established as a result of their producing. The consequences are industrial expansion, increased domestic and international competition, and seeking to place the economies of these countries more in line with the postindustrial economies. The economic goal of these countries' leaders is that their international utility functions will eventually be considered within the same frame of reference as those of the postindustrial economies, and thus that their currencies will change from soft — unwanted in international trading — to medium and respected in trade among countries in their own growth and development stage.

A country's trading position depends on the policies of its government and the commercial success of its firms. Although the government functions from political considerations, there is still an economic cost for its actions. Humanitarian shipments of foodstuffs to disaster areas in the various needy regions of the world require logistics and payments within the countries receiving the shipments, a cost that must be considered when one is calculating a country's balance-of-payments position. Extensive aid, financial and material, also has costs. Financial aid could be used internally to reconstruct those areas of the domestic economy that are in need; material aid could be applied to the domestic economy in the form of regulating supplies to either stimulate the markets or to cool them down, whichever is needed. While firms, on the other hand, seek profits in exports, they may not always be successful according to the requirements stated in their information systems. Indeed, it may even be to their advantage to take losses to reduce their taxes, but this calculation requires the decision of the firms' directorates.

A country may be in a surplus balance with respect to some countries and at a deficit with others when aggregate accounting is considered. When countries are trading, they are in functional relationships with each other, and these relationships are manifested in the elements of the countries' international utility functions. For example, because industry, government, and labor are elements of the welfare utility function, and because W_t is a component of $\bar{I}_t$, the elements of this function generate economic activity and provide international value to the country's currency. This function's utility is measured within the upper and lower limits of 0 and 1 and determines whether or not the country is performing well or badly in the aggregate with respect to trade. This measurement includes the government's economic policies, which may be conducted at a strict accounting loss, but which may pay off in political dividends. However, because $\bar{I}_t$ is strictly an economic concept, financial gains and losses are the only relevant consideration here. Industry may be exporting and importing at gains or losses, but determining which industries and subsectors are at a surplus and which are operating at a deficit requires the analysis of each industry, its subsectors, and individual firms. Labor is the contributor to the manufacturing process, executing the plans established within the various information systems. Sanctions and strikes hinder firms' abilities to export, to meet existing agreements, and to open new markets; such policies by labor also affect a country's $\bar{I}_t$ position.

Therefore, to state that a country's international utility function is between the upper and lower limits is, in itself, insufficient. A country's trade position has significance only with respect to its trading partners, because their $\bar{I}_t$s are interrelated with that country's. The significance and importance of international trade are such that countries with political hostilities over many centuries are now forming into common markets, customs unions that allow for the free movement of goods and services and people across national borders, without tariffs and other restrictions. While most of a country's business is conducted within its borders — the W of $\bar{I}_t$ — an important part of commerce is international, prompted in part by the domestic market situation and at all times by the profit motive. Even in customs unions each member country has a balance-of-trade position with the others and with trading partners outside the union, based on its share of importing and exporting. However, customs unions act as single countries with respect to the aggregate international utility function generated by their combined economic activity.[3]

World trade is conducted on the basis of countries' international utility positions, and each country is considered with respect to its $\bar{I}_t$ when its firms and government leaders engage in trade. The firms' utility positions with respect to trade can be projected in their information systems, and these positions can be adjusted when trading takes place in accordance with the situations in the foreign markets and the domestic ability to meet the assigned deadlines for manufacturing and shipping. The government's utility function, assessed in terms of these goals, is often of longer duration before the information can be received; it is also less controllable, because various political influences tend to enter the situation, affecting the government information system's expectations.

Hence there is flexibility in trading, depending on the international utility positions of the partners involved. Cyclical fluctuations among the postindustrial countries tend to move in the same phases, although they differ in the periods, because of interlocking economic and political relationships. This tendency is not as strong among the emerging and developing countries because of the unique circumstances each of these countries has with regard to its own history and sociopolitical dynamics. Thus, when a developing country is in recession, the reduction of commerce will continue to exert a downward influence on its economic activity. This can be offset to some extent by diversifying trade ties whenever possible, and this requires alert directorates among the country's firms, seeking out new markets for exports and imports if the country can afford them, while maintaining levels of commerce acceptable to the information systems of each of the partners.

In general, then, because a country's $\bar{I}_t$ position is measured within the boundaries of utility and entropy, this measurement has to be understood within the relationship to the country's trading partners. Suppose that country C at time t trades with ten partners. Some of these partners will be in debt to C, while others will be in surplus. The concepts of debt and surplus are both financial accounting concept, in which the country holding more hard currency as a result of the transaction is in surplus over the country will less hard currency. However, there is more than the accounting of debt and surplus in hard currencies. A country's economic strength is based on its productive abilities, and while greater or less hard currency may be important in the calculations of governments when they consider their countries' trading positions, the very processes of trade stimulate the economy by mobilizing resources and the dynamics of innovation and imitation. Hence the time signature is significant, for if a country is in debt to its trading partners, this will stimulate its firms and managers to move into innovation and imitation, to build new markets, and perhaps to eliminate the debt position. Moreover, countries in surplus will have larger resources of hard currencies at their disposal to make their trading that much easier, and this advantage should be used to maintain their position.

A country with a trade debt has imported greater goods and services than it has exported. There has to be consumption of these goods and services; otherwise there has been a misreading of the cycle's position with respect to the exporting firms' calculations and the importing firms' awareness of their country's economic circumstances. In either situation, when the products are consumed, this stimulates the domestic market into imitation to reduce on eliminate the foreign influence and perhaps to establish export markets similar to those in the partner countries. The international imitation effect takes hold, and the production processes become integrated into the business cycle.

Countries that are debtors can move into the position of surplus by the very dynamics that hold for the domestic markets — by innovation, by imitation, and by products that carry the cultural identities of their countries, with imitation referring to those products that are sold successfully domestically gaining profits internationally. While the notions of surplus and debt reflect countries' currency positions, they can also stimulate greater production, especially for international commerce. The summation of the $\bar{I}_t$s for the trading countries therefore reflects their internal dynamics with respect to their business cycles and the values of their currencies in the international markets. The importance of world trade was understood sufficiently by the drafters of the International Monetary Fund, the General Agreement on Tariffs and Trade, and the World Bank, and given the contemporary economic and political situation, trade is certainly of the greatest importance now. The manner in which countries implement their dynamics to generate trade depends on the acumen of their economic and political leaders, acting with respect to their business cycles and the values of their currencies, that is, their international utility functions.

NOTES

1. The branch of economics that deals with international trade is perhaps the most complicated aspect of economic theory, for it contains micro and macro elements and the dynamics of countries as trading partners and must therefore include tariffs and exchange rates that can be fixed, freely fluctuating, or fluctuating between points. The argument for the international utility function was formulated in David Z. Rich, *The Economics of International Trade: An Independent View* (New York: Quorum Books, 1992).

2. Charles P. Kindleberger, *International Economics* (Homewood, Ill.: Richard D. Irwin, 1963 3rd ed.), p. 132. With respect to the demonstration effect, Kindleberger referred to Ragnar Nurkse, but did not provide a source. See Ragnar Nurkse, *International Currency Experience* (Geneva: League of Nations, 1944); see also Nurske, *Equilibrium and Growth in the World Economy* (Cambridge, Mass.: Harvard University Press, 1961).

3. Now that the European Common Market has come into existence, customs *unions are being analyzed by international trade economists. See Rich, The Economics of International Trade,* chap. 10, "Circa 1992: Customs Unions," pp. 166-173.

Chapter 11

ECONOMIC GROWTH AND DEVELOPMENT: POLITICAL CONSIDERATIONS

Had political economy sought to follow a right method, it should certainly in a first part of the science, corresponding to the present conception of economics — as a mere natural science of economic intercourse — have started out with the present economic condition of the world, with all the wealth of phenomena it presents, and *its manifestations when left to itself.*

Karl Rodbertus,
"Overproduction and Crises"[1]

PRESENT AND FUTURE ORIENTATIONS

Limiting economic discourse to the microeconomic realm of the firm allows the discipline of economic thinking to be considered as a mere natural science of economic intercourse. The formulation of an information system, the development of the product from its inception to its marketing, and the evaluation of the product's success in terms of sales and profits and losses are all aspects of economic interaction with society. Even when innovation and imitation are considered by the firm, the mere natural science of economic-intercourse position can be maintained. But when the ramifications of innovation and imitation are calculated with respect to the market development and disequilibrium dynamics that such economic intercourse generates, both for the domestic economy and for international trading, the limiting concept of economic intercourse has to be replaced by the broader view of political economy.

Keynes and his followers realized that the natural sphere of economic activity had become far too complicated to be left to total free enterprise without some form of government regulation. Even prior to the Great Depression governments were not totally excluded from the realm of private enterprise. As the holder of the land, the printer of the national currency, and the decision maker for the nation's foreign affairs, government influence on the economy was noted. But when government was maintained in its somewhat passive role, it was unable to perform its function of government; the realm of economics and its influence on politics had become far too involved for this passive attitude. Moreover, when such a severe depression was affecting the entire industrialized world, passivity was ineffective. The political economy that began with Adam Smith and the early classical thinkers was revived again by Keynes and his followers. The economic condition of the world, with all the wealth of phenomena it presents in all of its manifestations, could not be left to itself, and government activity had become necessary to maintain the dynamics of growth and development.

The question that has to be considered in our present social time of our contemporary era of knowledge is just what type of government activity has to be used to maintain the economy as dynamic and to make sure that stagnation and inflation will become part of past history. This question is especially pertinent in our social time because of the political and economic events that are now occurring. We are in the midst of the paradox of industrialization, which has our postindustrial economies in recession; we are in the midst of a new economic situation in which many peoples have shed their old ways and seek economic independence yet lack political direction; we are witnessing the rise of peoples in economies that are emerging from an uncertain past, yet they too lack the political direction necessary to move them into the stage of developing economies. This question is raised in light of our global political paradox, in which the arsenals of nuclear weapons with the power of destroying all of humankind are being phased out, in which Russia and the United States are expanding their arms treaties to reduce the threat of global destruction, and in which small nations are destroying their countries as the fires of ethnic nationalism light up the passions of racism and isolationism, with the consequences being senseless starvation, bitter and durable hatred, and "ethnic cleansing," a euphemism for attempted genocide.

With the promise of our era, however, we can stem the destruction. We can heal a part of the human nationalistic wounds and repair some of the damage. We have an opportunity that has never existed before in human history, the opportunity to rid humanity of starvation and to form a lasting peace based on economic diversity and international economic competition. However, economics is unable in itself to achieve this; there must be political direction that provides the basis for this activity. While we have reduced greatly the threat of global war, we have provided ourselves with the opportunity to consider our national histories, and we must therefore not forget our past while we view our dynamic and changing situations to determine the directions we should take. Our postindustrial societies have achieved great technological progress in the arts and sciences and in medicine and education; yet our developing and emerging societies are reminiscent of the early years of industrialization, sharing our technologies, but still behind in the ability to produce and export.

For world stability the gap between the postindustrial societies and the developing and emerging societies has to be narrowed, but this cannot be done by slowing the dynamics of the postindustrial societies. They possess the great technologies, and in spite of the paradox of industrialization they continue their technological advances that will be used by industry in the production processes.

Still, within the postindustrial societies the homeless, the uneducated, and the unemployed, affected by the recession brought about by our paradox of industrialization, must become involved in the socioeconomic processes of economic activity and development in order to maintain the dynamics of growth. Otherwise they will continue to be a burden on the welfare of their countries. We have the knowledge and the technological capabilities to achieve this.

Hence the postindustrial, developing, and emerging economies are confronted not only with the issues of disequilibrium in developing their markets and in engaging in foreign trade, but also with the political issue of direction and orientation in our era of knowledge. In general, governments have to govern according to their peoples' national characteristics, and these are formed by their common histories. In the postindustrial societies these histories were formed in the preindustrialized eras, but they were forged into their present historical and national forms during the Industrial Revolution. This era provided the basis for their manufacturing, transforming these countries into economically productive countries with strong industrial bases. The strength of the Industrial Revolution was such that even after the devastation of World War II those countries that suffered from the destruction had sufficient dynamism that they were able to enter our era of knowledge as strong manufacturing economies with stable political systems. The developing economies formed after the war inherited the technologies of the postindustrial societies and managed to adapt them to suit the historical temperament of their peoples. However, the emerging countries show the greatest political instability, and their leaders are often placed in the situation of counterrevolutions and internal strife. Those emerging countries that have achieved stability in the foundation of their economic cycles and the transfer of power in an orderly fashion that is maintained both with respect to ceremony and the procedure of this transfer have made the commitment to move into the stage of the developing economies and eventually to the postindustrial stage. They have committed themselves to future orientation and thus to the full dynamics of our contemporary era of knowledge. Whether they achieve this status over time will depend on both internal conditions, as manifested in how well they are carrying out this movement into the postindustrial stage, and how well they are able to maintain their integrities in light of their geopolitical situations. Countries in Africa, for example, may seek to develop their natural and industrial resources to establish industry and a labor force, and to use the government authority in its economic capacity to underwrite the economy and to regulate cyclical fluctuations. These very same countries may also border on unstable emerging countries that from time to time foster expansionist tendencies and therefore may wage war. The skirmishes that have occurred between Egypt and Libya, both emerging economies, are examples of this.

The situations of future and present orientation are therefore political as much as they are economic. The postindustrial economies are future oriented by virtue of their having achieved high technologies and sophistication in the production and marketing processes. Their economies are fully developed with respect to the business cycle. They have a strong labor force to work with and, when necessary, to counteract the industrial sector, and a watchful government sector that seeks to regulate the business cycle. They are future oriented in the sense that they are committed to the development of knowledge and to the application of knowledge in the advancement of technologies that improve industrial output and maintain the dynamics of growth through internal development and international commerce.

Present orientation refers to those emerging and developing economies that are industrializing, but because of their needs are heavily dependent on assistance, aid, and trade from the postindustrial economies. The future-oriented societies set the standards in the arts and sciences and in industry and technology; this is certainly recognized by the present-oriented societies as they seek the postindustrial future-oriented societies' knowledge, aid, and assistance in both the economic and political spheres. Granting the involvement of the future-oriented societies, especially now, when the newly formed independent countries are trying to establish their identities, the present-oriented societies present a real challenge for the world. They provide experimental grounds for new societies as they benefit from their own unique pasts and from the contributions made by the future-oriented societies. Moreover, the people in these countries can take shortcuts in development and growth by using the advantage of our contemporary era of knowledge. These are the pivot countries; as they change their customs and life-styles that do not fit with such development and growth, and as they discard the realpolitik of the earlier social time, the direction they take determines their opportunities for real economic and political development. They can no longer move from one big-power bloc to another to suit their own ends, because the big-power-bloc competition is no longer viable; the life-style of the Soviet Union is no longer an option, and China is undergoing its own social and economic development, accompanied by temporary but real thaws in its politically authoritarian restrictions on freedom and enterprise.

Moreover, with industrial development to ensure their independence, and with the support of the postindustrial economies in the establishment and deepening of their industrial-labor bases, the developing present-oriented countries are technologically mature enough to take advantage of the contributions of the postindustrial societies, adapting them to their cultures and incorporating them into their societies as the basis of imitation and perhaps as a guide to innovation. These developing countries have both the stability and the economic potential to enter fully into the dynamics of our contemporary era and its social time and to build new societies that neither deny their pasts nor belittle their mixed cultural heritages, but that will allow the development and growth of their talents and skills in industry, the sciences, and the arts.

The political, industrial, and labor leaders must therefore be aware that their mandates depend on how they handle the pressing problems of poverty, illiteracy, disease, industrialization, and political direction. They must maintain their concern for industrialization, improving its status for both internal and foreign competition. Their objective in the long run is to move into postindustrial status, and their leaders cannot wait for the slow process of industrialization. They must provide the social and financial conditions for innovation and imitation and regulate the business cycle so that these dynamics will continue and the movement into the postindustrial status will be achieved.

PAST ORIENTATION

The future- and present-oriented countries provide the great promise for economic growth and cultural development. The future-oriented countries have already established themselves economically and in the arts and sciences, and the present-oriented countries have the promise and the capability to achieve postindustrial status. The past-oriented societies, however, are the source of political instability in the world. The future-oriented and present-oriented countries employ their cultural diversification in the processes of political stability and economic growth and development. The past-oriented societies exploit their cultural unity and negate diversification in order to maintain their existence. In these societies their past orientation is the conceptualization of both their present and future development. They rely on fundamentalism and carry this to the extremes of exclusion, so that situations such as those in Somalia and Yugoslavia, where cultures are in conflict and manifest this conflict in war and even genocide, plagues on civilization and its accomplishments throughout its historical eras, prevail over cultural diversity and accommodation. Resources are involved in the processes of destruction and starvation, senseless waste, and a blight on the human spirit.

The past-oriented countries base their social, political, and economic practices on the teachings of those who founded and developed their specific cultures, to the exclusion of all other influences. Because of their preoccupation with the past, not only have their industries suffered — such as they are — but their education systems are not of this era and its social time, as education requires the diversity of opinions and the dynamics of knowledge that can be translated into industrial output for competition and the accumulation of wealth.

So long as the past orientation is maintained, wealth is a goal that will remain elusive for these countries. Their citizens lack freedom of thought and inquiry, and their resources are directed into maintaining their past orientation at the expense of nurturing the inner dynamics necessary for prosperity and national wealth. Like the emerging and developing countries, they seek the technologies and assistance of the postindustrial societies, but because they lack the necessary ability to separate their devotion to their past from their needs and the ability to handle these technologies within their own countries, the emphasis is on financial assistance in the form of aid. Trade is not conducted at a significant level, for there is little of their production that is exchangeable in the international markets. The emphasis is therefore on aid and often on military assistance, either by mercenaries or by countries intervening in these past-oriented countries' affairs. These countries are now the source of great global instability. Their past orientation takes the place of their present, and in Yugoslavia, where the strong central government broke down and ethnic regions asserted their political independence, civil war — not ideological in its cause, but strictly ethnic — resulted, so that the pasts of the peoples involved are also their present, and fundamentalism has replaced sensible reasoning. War rages with tremendous loss of life; economic activity in any meaningful sense has ceased. In Somalia this past orientation is manifested in the existence of war camps, each struggling for domination over the other. The consequence is a parched land unfit for crops or livestock because of the constant power struggles and the destruction of life that has resulted. Thirst and starvation have plagued this area, and relief has been offered on a humanitarian basis, only to be harassed by the warring factions. Postindustrial and developing, and emerging countries, on the initiative of the United States, have sent in military forces to ensure that humanitarian aid is not confiscated by the warring sides that are trying to assert their power and authority in that country.

Cuba is another such country. The Castro regime maintains a dictatorial system, resulting in an inefficient and crumbling economy. Cuba's two major crops, sugar and tobacco, are exported, but the revenues gained from these exports are far from sufficient to sustain economic activity. Its other industries are producing only for the domestic economy, and the level of output is seriously threatened by the shortages of raw materials and marketing outlets. Its sponsor country, the Soviet Union, has disintegrated, and Russia is withdrawing its financial and political support for the island country. Cuba's citizens seek ways of escaping from the country to seek political refuge in the United States, while the Cuban organizations in Florida hostile to the Castro regime train clandestinely in the Everglades, preparing for the invasion that will topple the regime. Even though they are constrained by the U.S. government, they maintain that they will return and perhaps sit in the seats of power when Castro is gone. The country is in economic depression brought about not by a business-cycle downturn but by the conditions that evolved in Cuba, partly because of the withdrawl of financial suport from the defunct Eastern bloc, but mostly because of the lack of political acumen in Castro's regime. Cuba's past orientation has not allowed the country to take its place in the scheme of genuine economic development and growth, and until it sheds its past orientation, steeped in impractical communism, its situation will only worsen, as is the case in Yugoslavia, Somalia, the Sudan, and other countries that remain in the past as a substitution for the present and future orientations of those countries whose political, industrial, and labor leaders are actively participating in the processes of economic growth and development.

The days of neocolonialism have ended for these past-oriented countries. They will no longer be a source for big-power-bloc political and military action except in the sense of preventing destruction, as in the cases of Somalia and Yugoslavia, where apparently only military intervention can resolve the issues. The political boundaries of these countries are no longer the subject of interest to the postindustrial societies and hence remain the concern only of the peoples involved. But their presence is a source of disturbance, of global chaos, and, to a smaller extent, of economic instability. Since the beginning of our social time with the breakup of the Soviet Union, there has been a new realization that strategic location has changed in its meaning. Whereas previously countries were strategically located according to big-power interests, now every country is strategically located because of its effect on the stability of the world political situation. Situations such as exist in Yugoslavia and Somalia cannot be allowed to continue because they pose a broader threat to the new nationalism that is a rising because of the independence of countries that broke away from their previous relationships. For example, the peaceful dissolution of the Czechoslovakian peoples into their respective nations of Czechs and Slovaks may not become the rule, and the economic viability of such a separation may be brought into question — a situation that could lead to attempts at resolution through war. Warring nations throughout Europe, Africa, and Indochina may spark another world conflict or perhaps attempts at world domination and control by the postindustrial countries as they in turn seek world stability in order to carry on the processes of growth and development. Resources have to be obtained and trade routes protected in conflict situations, and military presence is one way of achieving these objectives when all other methods have failed. This may initiate a rivalry among the postindustrial countries that could set off another global conflict.

Perhaps the only way to remove this potential conflict is to convince the peoples of the past-oriented countries that economic prosperity cannot be obtained through such breaking apart and through relying on the past for their present and future situations. This can be done by bringing these countries into the dynamics of economic activity by encouraging their leaders to resolve their differences peacefully through the understanding that only through viable economies can power be held and maintained, that viable economies can exist only where there is a business cycle, and that the cycle can become part of the economy only when strong governmental, industrial, and labor leadership prevails. This means that the welfare utility function has to set in, and this will eventually lead to a currency that has internal value that will provide a basis for international commerce.

The key to moving the past-oriented nations, closed as they are and always in conflict among themselves and/or with their neighbors, lies in the resolution of the political conflict and the subsequent formation of a government, for only a government concerned with its citizens' welfare can provide political and economic stability by working within the dynamics of the business cycle in disequilibrium to maintain a viable welfare utility function and economic growth and development. If such a government cannot be formed by these countries themselves, the only alternative is one of imposition. The only countries of sufficient economic strength and military power are those whose future orientation has maintained their postindustrial status. Because these countries have political systems with representation, the imposition when necessary of such a governing system on the past-oriented countries would be met with little opposition by their citizens; as soon as the business cycle takes effect, then the processes of growth and development will begin. These countries will then shed their antiquated dogmatic ways, join the world's nations as economically productive countries, and eventually become viable trading partners. Past orientation will then be relegated to the remembrance of the past. It will perhaps be celebrated in public ceremonies, but the direction of orientation will have changed so much that these countries will be advancing along the way of economic growth and development.

NOTE

1. Karl Rodbertus, "Overproduction and Crises," from the translation by Julia Franklin of Rodbertus's second "Social Letter" to his friend Krichmann, reprinted in Karl Rodbertus, *Overproduction and Crises* (New York: Charles Scribner's Sons, 1898); quoted here from *Readings in Economics,* ed. K. William Kapp and Lore L. Kapp, (New York: Barnes and Noble, 1953), p. 249. Italics in the original text.

Chapter 12

CONCLUSION

> Social reformers and legislators will never be economists, and they
> will always work on economic theory of one kind or another. They
> will quote and apply such dicta as they can assimilate, and such
> acknowledged principles as seem to serve their turn. . . While the
> experts worked on severer methods than ever, popularizers would be
> found to drive homely illustrations and analogies into the general
> consciousness; and the roughly understood dicta bandied about in the
> name of Political Economy would at any rate stand in some relation
> to truth and to experience, instead of being, as they too often are
> at present, a mere armoury of consecrated paradoxes that cannot be
> understood because they are not true, that everyone uses as weapons
> while no one grasps them as principles.
>
> Philip H. Wicksteed,
> "The Scope and Method of Political Economy"[1]

Economics is the concern for the allocation of scarce resources among
competing ends, and political economy is this consideration on a macro
scale that includes international commerce and the political factors involved
in economic management in the governmental sector. While economics per
se involves not only professional economists, but also financiers, bankers,
businesspeople, and micro innovation and imitation, political economy
requires administrators and even popularizers who must drive the homely
illustrations and analogies of the prevailing macro theory and its system
into the general public consciousness.

The currently prevailing economic system is neo-Keynesianism, and
Keynes's theory and the contributions of its expounders are taught in our
universities and practiced in the macro sphere of political economic conduct.
In this volume, however, a serious contradiction has been pointed out in
Keynes's work, that of his argument against equilibrium as manifested in
Say's law of markets, against which he argued, but which was derived

from his argument. Moreover, the anomalies of his concept of money and its velocity and liquidity have been discussed and treated anew within the context of the theory stated here. Keynes wrote for an earlier era, one in which the Industrial Revolution had declined. The Great Depression, for which his theory was relevant, is no longer in effect, and our era has brought to the fore issues that Keynes could not address, and that Keynesian theory is inadequate to treat.

Our era of knowledge has brought awareness of the emerging and developing economies; these and the postindustrial economies are confronted with a new set of problems. The emerging and developing countries cannot undergo an industrial revolution, but within the context of their political economic procedures they can take the benefits of industrialization and adapt these contributions to suit their unique economic situations according to their abilities to allocate resources and according to the skills of their industrial and labor forces to utilize these contributions in their own markets and for their international commerce. There is still another poblem with which Keynesian theory is inadequate to deal, the paradox of industrialization. This differs from the Great Depression only because of government awareness — due, in fact, to Keynes's theory — that actions in the marketplace must be taken to stimulate economic activity when the sluggishness of recession sets in. Approaching recession in Keynesian conceptual terms, however, cannot move economies back into recovery, but can only perpetuate the paradox of industrialization. For example, when the postindustrial countries compete with each other for the same markets, consumer prices may decline, but product absorption can reach levels of market near saturation without any significant change. When market near saturation is reached, production declines, and goods and services are moved at lower rates due to the abundance of competing products. This results in unemployment and a subsequent decline in consumption. Applying Keynesian theory to this situation will do little to alleviate it. Works programs to increase aggregate employment mean that consumption liquidity is increased, but this will be used to consume the existing goods and services. Production will indeed increase, but only in proportion to increased liquidity, and employment will increase in the production sector to meet the renewed demand. International commerce will also increase, but again the markets will be fairly consistent, with little change in the available goods and services. Near saturation will set in again fairly rapidly, and unemployment will once again rise, only to be reduced again by government intervention in the form of more works projects, the utility of which is of minor consideration.

Accompanying this policy is the policy of tax reductions to stimulate consumption further. But these reductions are marginal, and indeed the income from such reductions will most likely be targeted only for consumption. The liquidity needed by industry from savings and investments, however, will not be forthcoming; because this liquidity is necessary to increase business activity, more government intervention in the form of financial backing will be required. But even if this backing is granted, it will be used to maintain the same basket of goods and services, and the paradox of industrialization will remain unresolved. Keynesian policy is effective only for a business cycle that retains the depression phase. It has been argued in this volume that the depression phase has been removed from the contemporary business cycle, and this holds for emerging and developing economies as well as the postindustrial economies. However, acting on our current recession in Keynesian terms only strengthens the paradox of industrialization, with the consequence being that as the cycle moves upward, firms that have high employment are now closing down plants and throwing more workers onto the unemployment line; the benefits of recovery are being eliminated by outmoded conceptualizations.

The key to the resolution of the paradox of industrialization and maintaining the upward momentum of the cycle lies in the market disequilibrium dynamics of innovation and imitation. Only these factors stimulate investments sufficient to support industrial activity, and only these can break existing consumption and production patterns. However, only innovation requiring high technologies is now sufficient to generate market shifts and is followed by competitive production, thereby breaking out of the paradox. Moreover, through international commerce these shifts generate the international imitation effect, resulting in imitative competition in the markets of the emerging and developing countries, improving the skills of their labor forces and making them more competitive and capable of moving up to the postindustrial stage. The paradox of industrialization and its solution through innovation and imitation have stimulated the new independence proclaimed by those countries that were once under the domination of others. Their leaders want to gain competitive competence to open their own markets and eventually to compete internationally instead of being perpetual recipients of aid and assistance. But where independence has meant exclusive nationalism, this has resulted only in chaos and geopolitical instability.

Our era holds a new promise, one that if understood and acted on accordingly can yield great wealth and accomplishments; with economic strength comes strength in the arts and sciences, and with our technologies the possibilities for humankind to acquire a better life are certainly great. We are obligated by history to try to fulfill the promise of our era, for just as we have inherited the contributions of past historical eras with their arts, sciences, wisdom, and knowledge and with their wars and other man-made tragedies, we have our era to pass on to our successors. How they live, act, think, and produce will be largely influenced by our activities and our contributions now. Despite all our great accomplishments, one consideration by which we will be viewed is whether we have brought the emerging and developing countries up to the standards of the postindustrial countries, and if not, why we have failed to realize this promise. With the opportunities available to us that we have made in our era, there is no reason why we cannot resolve our difficulties peacefully and competitively; there is no real reason why we should fail.

NOTE

1. Philip H. Wicksteed, "The Scope and Method of Political Economy," *The Economic Journal*, Vol. XXIV (1914); quoted here from *Readings in Price Theory* (London): Allen & Unwin, for the American Economic Association, 1953), p. 26.

SELECTED BIBLIOGRAPHY

Aganbegyan, Abel. *The Economic Challenge of Perestroika*. Bloomington: Indiana University Press, 1988.

Bauer, Peter T. "Background to Aid." In *Equality, the Third World, and Economic Delusion*, Peter T. Bauer, pp. 138-150. Cambridge, Mass.: Harvard University Press, 1981.

Beasley, W.G. *The Modern History of Japan*. London: Weidenfeld and Nicolson, 1967.

Bell, Daniel, and Irving Kristol, eds. *The Crisis in Economic Theory*. New York: Basic Books, 1981.

Bonner, Raymond. *Waltzing with a Dictator*. New York: Vintage Press, 1987.

Bull-Berg, Hans Jacob. *American International Oil Policy*. New York: St. Martin's Press, 1987.

Caves, Richard E. *Multinational Enterprise and Economic Analysis*. New York: Cambridge University Press, 1985.

Cockburn, Leslie. *Out of Control*. New York: Atlantic Monthly Press, 1987.

Cole, G. D. H. *Money*. London: Cassell and Co., 1945.

Deleuze, Giles, and Felix Guattari. *Anti-Oedipus: Capitalisim and Schizo phrenia*. Minniapolis: University of Minnesota Press, 1983.

Diebold, John. *The Innovators*. New York: Truman Talley Books/Plume, 1991.

Dornbusch, Rudiger, and F. Leslie Co. H. Helmers, eds. *The Open Economy*. New York: Oxford University Press, 1990.

Drucker, Peter F. *Management*. New York: Harper and Row, 1974.

Georgescu-Roegen, Nicholas. *The Entropy Law and the Economic Process*. Cambridge, Mass.: Harvard University Press, 1981.

Heilbroner, Robert L. *The Nature and Logic of Capitalism*. New York: W.W. Norton, 1985.

Heilbroner, Robert L. and Lester C. Thurow. *Five Economic Challenges*. Englewood Cliffs, N.J.: Prentice-Hall, 1981.

Johnson, E. A. J. *The Organization of Space in Developing Countries*. Cambridge, Mass.: Harvard University Press, 1970.

Kahn, Herman. *The Emerging Japanese Superstate*. Englewood Cliffs, N.J.: Prentice-Hall, 1971.

Kaldor, Nicholas. *Essays on Economic Policy*. Vol. 1. New York: Holmes and Meier, 1980.

Klitgaard, Robert. *Tropical Gangsters.* New York: Basic Books, 1990.

Krugman, Paul R. *Strategic Trade Policy and the New International Economics.* Cambridge, Mass.: M.I.T. Press, 1986.

MacDonald, Ronald. *Floating Exchange Rates.* London: Unwin Hyman, 1988.

Myrdal, Gunnar. *Asian Drama.* New York: Twentieth Century Fund, 1968.

Nora Hamilton, Jeffry A. Frieden, Linda Fuller and Manuel Pastor, Jr. ed. *Crisis in Central America.* Boulder, Colo.: Westview Press, 1988.

Olson, Mancur, *The Rise and Decline of Nations.* New Haven: Yale University Press, 1983.

Olson, Mancur, Jr. *The Logic of Collective Action.* New York: Schocken Books, 1968.

Porter, Michael E. *The Competitive Advantage of Nations.* New York: Free Press, 1990.

Powis, Robert E. *The Money Launderers.* Chicago: Probus Publishers, 1992.

Quinn, James Brian. *Intelligent Enterprise.* New York: Free Press, 1992.

Radetzki, Marian. *Aid and Development.* New York: Praeger, 1973.

Roll, Eric. *A History of Economic Thought.* New York: Prentice-Hall, 1942.

Ross, Arthur M. ed. *Unemployment and the American Economy.* New York: John Wiley and Sons, 1964.

Rostow, W.W. *Why the Poor Get Richer and the Rich Slow Down.* Austin: University of Texas Press, 1988.

Rugman, A.M. *International Diversification and the Multinational Enterprise.* Lexington, Mass.: Lexington Books, 1979.

Sampson, Anthony. *The Money Lenders.* New York: Penguin Books, 1983.

————. *The Sovereign State of ITT.* New York: Stein and Day, 1973.

Santiago, Carlos E. "The Dynamics of Minimum Wage Policy in Economic Development: A Multiple Time-Series Approach." *Economic Development and Cultural Change* 38 1989: 1-30.

Selden, Richard T. "Monetarism." In *Modern Economic Thought,* edited by Sidney Weintraub, pp. 253-274. Philadelphia: University of Pennsylvania Press, 1977.

Shackle, G. L. S. *Epistemics and Economics.* New Brunswick, N.J.: Transaction Publishers, 1992.

Simmel, Georg. *The Philosophy of Money.* edited by David Frisby. translated by Tom Bottomore and David Frisby. 2nd enl. ed. New York: Routledge, 1990.

Solomon, Robert. *The International Monetary System, 1945-1981.* New York: Harper and Row, 1982.

Solow, Robert M. *Growth Theory.* New York: Oxford University Press, 1987.

Sun Tzu. *The Art of War.* edited by James Clavell. New York: Dell, 1983.

Turner, Louis. *Multinational Companies and the Third World.* New York: Hill and Wang, 1973.

Uphoff, Norman T., and Warren F. Ilchman, eds. *The Political Economy of Development.* Berkeley: University of California Press, 1972.

Vernon, Raymond. "Foreign-owned Enterprise in the Developing Countries." In *Economics of Trade and Development,* edited by J. D. Theberge. New York: John Wiley and Sons, 1968.

————. ed. *The Oil Crisis.* New York: W. W. Norton, 1976.

Von Neumann, John, and Oskar Morgenstern. *Theory of Games and Economic Behavior.* Princeton: Princeton University Press, 1953.

Weintraub, E. Roy. *General Equilibrium Theory*. London: Macmillan, 1974.

———. "Optimization and Game Theory." In *Modern Economic Thought*. edited by Sidney Weintraub, pp. 125-136. Philadelphia: University of Pennsylvania Press, 1974.

Weintraub, Sidney. *An Approach to the Theory of Income Distribution*. Philadelphia: Chilton, 1958.

Weitz, Raanan. *New Roads to Development*. Westport, Conn.: Greenwood Press, 1986.

Worcester, Dean. "John Rawls' Justification of Unequal Income and Wealth." *University of Washington Institute of Economic Research Discussion Paper* 74-4 1975: 25-29.

INDEX

About the Author

DAVID Z. RICH is a self-employed economics consultant. He is the author of *Contemporary Economics* (Praeger, 1985), *The Dynamics of Knowledge* (Greenwood Press, 1988), *The Economics of Welfare* (Praeger, 1989), and *The Economics of International Trade* (Quorum Books, 1992).

ISBN 0-275-94687-8

HARDCOVER BAR CODE